ACTIVITIES AND GAMES FOR THE CLASSROOM

Teaching Reasoning

LAUREL HECKER

JULIA A. SIMMS

MING LEE NEWCOMB

MARZANO
Research

555 North Morton Street
Bloomington, IN 47404
888.849.0851
FAX: 866.801.1447
email: info@marzanoresearch.com
marzanoresearch.com

Visit **marzanoresearch.com/activitiesandgames** to download the reproducibles in this book.

Printed in the United States of America

Library of Congress Control Number: 2014956886

ISBN: 978-0-9903458-1-7

19 18 17 16 15   1 2 3 4 5

Text and Cover Designer: Laura Kagemann
Text Compositor: Rachel Smith

Marzano Research Development Team

Director of Publications

Julia A. Simms

Production Editor

Laurel Hecker

Editorial Assistant/Staff Writer

Ming Lee Newcomb

Marzano Research Associates

Tina Boogren

Bev Clemens

Jane Doty Fischer

Jeff Flygare

Tammy Heflebower

Mitzi Hoback

Jan K. Hoegh

Russell Jenson

Jessica Kanold-McIntyre

Sonny Magaña

Margaret McInteer

Diane E. Paynter

Kristin Poage

Salle Quackenboss

Cameron Rains

Tom Roy

Gerry Varty

Phil Warrick

Kenneth C. Williams

Visit **marzanoresearch.com/activitiesandgames**
to download reproducibles from this book.

Table of Contents

Italicized entries indicate reproducible forms.

About the Authors

Laurel Hecker is a production editor for Marzano Research in Denver, Colorado. She has written and edited across a range of topics and formats, including articles for the *Cipher* news magazine, website and social media content for local businesses, research reports, and creative pieces. She has also worked in outdoor education as a Girl Scout counselor and trip coordinator. She is a graduate of Colorado College, where she earned a bachelor of arts degree in English with a concentration in poetry writing.

Julia A. Simms is director of publications for Marzano Research in Denver, Colorado. She has worked in K–12 education as a classroom teacher, gifted education specialist, teacher leader, and coach, and her books include *Coaching Classroom Instruction*, *Using Common Core Standards to Enhance Classroom Instruction and Assessment*, *Vocabulary for the Common Core*, *Questioning Sequences in the Classroom*, *A Handbook for High Reliability Schools*, and *Teaching Argumentation: Activities and Games for the Classroom*. She received her bachelor's degree from Wheaton College in Wheaton, Illinois, and her master's degrees in educational administration and K–12 literacy from Colorado State University and the University of Northern Colorado, respectively.

Ming Lee Newcomb is an editorial assistant and staff writer at Marzano Research in Denver, Colorado. She has experience mentoring groups of students at the high school level and tutoring students at the elementary and postsecondary level. She served as an editor for *Leviathan Magazine* and has researched and written education policy briefs for the National Conference of State Legislatures and articles for the *Catalyst Newspaper*. She holds a bachelor of arts degree in English with a concentration in fiction writing from Colorado College.

About Marzano Research

Marzano Research is a joint venture between Solution Tree and Dr. Robert J. Marzano. Marzano Research combines Dr. Marzano's forty years of educational research with continuous action research in all major areas of schooling in order to provide effective and accessible instructional strategies, leadership strategies, and classroom assessment strategies that are always at the forefront of best practice. By providing such an all-inclusive research-into-practice resource center, Marzano Research provides teachers and principals with the tools they need to effect profound and immediate improvement in student achievement.

Foreword

In September 1989, President George H. W. Bush and the United States governors met in Charlottesville, Virginia, for the first Education Summit. Their goal was to improve schooling in the United States, and, to work toward that end, the leaders designed six goals for U.S. education. Of particular note was goal three: "Every school in America will ensure that all students learn to use their minds, so they may be prepared for responsible citizenship, further learning, and productive employment in our modern economy" (National Education Goals Panel, 1991, p. 4). This strong endorsement of thinking and reasoning skills was not the first of its kind. Throughout the 1980s, numerous prestigious organizations called for a stronger educational emphasis on thinking and reasoning skills, including the National Education Association (Futrell, 1987), the American Federation of Teachers (1985), the Panel on the General Professional Education of the Physician and College Preparation for Medicine (1984), the National Science Board Commission on Precollege Education in Mathematics, Science and Technology (1983), the College Board (1983), and the Commission on the Humanities (1980).

In response to these recommendations and endorsements, the next decade saw a number of programs designed to teach thinking and reasoning skills, including those by Barry Beyer (1988), Edward de Bono (1985), and Edys S. Quellmalz (1987). My colleagues and I designed several programs with the same focus, including *Tactics for Thinking* (Marzano & Arredondo, 1986), *Dimensions of Thinking* (Marzano et al., 1988), and *Dimensions of Learning* (Marzano & Pickering, 1997). Additionally, my colleague John Kendall led a team of researchers at Mid-continent Research for Education and Learning (McREL) to identify thinking and reasoning skills from numerous national standards documents. The standards highlighted specific skills, including the following (Kendall & Marzano, 2000, pp. 635–636):

Grades K–2

- Provides coherent (though not necessarily valid or convincing) answers when asked why one believes something to be true or how one knows something.

- Asks "how do you know" in appropriate situations.

Grades 3–5

- Understands that reasoning can be distorted by strong feelings.

- Seeks reasons for believing things other than the assertion that "everybody agrees."

Grades 6–8

- Questions conclusions based on very small samples of data, biased samples, or samples for which there is no central sample.

- Identifies and questions arguments in which all members of a group are implied to possess nearly identical characteristics that are considered to be different from those of another group.

Grades 9–12

- Understands that when people try to prove a point, they may at times select only the information that supports it and ignore the information that contradicts it.

- Identifies or seeks out the critical assumptions behind a line of reasoning and uses that to judge the validity of an argument.

From these auspicious beginnings, one might expect that thinking and reasoning skills would have continued to enjoy a privileged place in United States school curricula. Unfortunately, this was not the case, and enthusiasm for teaching these critical skills waned with the turn of the millennium.

Fortunately, attention to these critical skills was renewed with the release of updated standards documents a decade later, such as the Common Core State Standards. The crucial role of thinking and reasoning skills in specific content areas was again explicitly emphasized, presenting teachers with the challenge of finding practical ways to infuse these essential skills into mathematics, English language arts, science, and other subject areas.

Due to various constraints (time, money, and so on), many teachers, schools, and districts do not have the option to adopt comprehensive programs of direct instruction for thinking and reasoning skills. Therefore, I suggest an alternative approach: short, flexible lessons focused on a small set of foundational thinking and reasoning skills paired with engaging activities and games that students can use to practice and deepen their proficiency with those skills. Providing these lessons, games, and activities is the focus of each book in the *Activities and Games for the Classroom* series. These resources offer clear, accessible guidance on how to directly teach the components of specific thinking and reasoning skills, and games and activities that allow students to practice and deepen their understanding of the component skills in fun, engaging, and memorable ways.

Our goal at Marzano Research has always been to offer high-quality, research-based tools that teachers can put into immediate use. In *Teaching Reasoning*, Hecker, Simms, and Newcomb have achieved that goal. Their analysis of current standards documents to identify component skills, step-by-step guidance for teaching those skills directly, and easily understood, straightforward games with extensive item banks provide teachers with a gold mine of resources. This book gives teachers practical tools that can be used immediately in their classrooms to highlight the critical skills students need to meet the college and career readiness expectations of the twenty-first century.

—Robert J. Marzano

Introduction

Reasoning is difficult to precisely define. It encompasses a great deal and is tied to other broad terms like *argumentation* and *problem solving*. It can mean "explanation or justification" of a point in an argument or "the power of comprehending, inferring, or thinking" (*Merriam-Webster's Collegiate Dictionary*, 2012). As such, defining reasoning is often the first goal of books and articles on the subject; for examples of such definitions, see table I.1.

Table I.1: Definitions of Reasoning

Source	Definition
Johnson-Laird, 2008	"Reasoning is: A set of processes that construct and evaluate implications among sets of propositions" (p. 3).
Klenk, 2008	"The ability to reason, or infer, is simply the ability to draw appropriate conclusions from given evidence" (p. 1).
Johnson-Laird, 2008	"Reasoning is the ability to construct models from perception, description, and knowledge, to formulate novel but parsimonious conclusions from these models, and to grasp the force of counterexamples to these conclusions" (p. 249).
Brickell, Ferry, & Harper, 2002	"Reasoning is a broad term that is usually applied to a statement in justification or explanation of a thought or action that has transpired" (p. 2).

Although these definitions vary, they all establish reasoning as the link between evidence and a conclusion.

Research on Reasoning

Early research on reasoning was strongly influenced by the assumption that humans think analytically according to the rules of formal logic (for example, *all A are B and all C are A; therefore, all C are B*). However, this does not seem to be the case. When confronted with formal logic problems, people do not typically perform well (Evans, 2002; Johnson-Laird, 2008; Stanovich & West, 1999). This is not to say that humans cannot reason; rather, humans prefer to use a form of reasoning that is simpler and more intuitive than the reasoning required by formal logic problems. Philip Johnson-Laird (2008) explained:

> In life, we reason all the time, but our inferences are simple, embedded in a sensible context, invoke our knowledge, and are not a matter of chopping logic. We learn, for instance, that [a] flu vaccine will be available only for individuals who are at risk, such as infants and seniors. We know that we are not at risk, and so we realize—infer, to be precise—that we won't receive a shot. (p. 262)

In other words, humans typically prefer to reason intuitively (according to the ideas that come to us naturally) rather than analytically (according to the rules of formal logic). The dichotomy between these two forms of thinking has led to a *dual-process theory* of reasoning (Evans, 2002; Evans & Over, 1996), which states that there are two types of reasoning—here called *intuitive* and *analytical*—and that people can choose which type to use when they encounter situations requiring reasoning.

Intuitive reasoning occurs rapidly and is useful in situations where quick judgments are required or the reasoner has lots of prior experience with similar situations. When engaged in intuitive reasoning, people do not typically make the evidence they are using explicit (Mercier, 2011); instead, they rely on what feels right or seems to make sense. For example, a person trying to decide where to purchase a new refrigerator might be intuitively drawn to a store with good lighting and friendly salespeople, even though the products there may be priced higher than other stores. In unfamiliar situations, however, intuitive reasoning can be counterproductive or ineffective. As Jonathan St. B. T. Evans (2003) noted, "We cannot, for example, learn by experience to avoid disasters such as nuclear war or the effects of uncontrolled global warming" (p. 454). In other words, intuitive reasoning is not effective when addressing situations we have never encountered before.

Analytical reasoning, on the other hand, occurs at a slower pace and requires intentional thought and awareness of evidence. When people reason analytically, they explicitly think through specific evidence and use it to draw a logical conclusion. Analytical reasoning is helpful in unfamiliar situations because it allows the reasoner to compensate for their lack of experience by collecting evidence and using it to support a conclusion about what to do. Using analytical reasoning, a person shopping for a refrigerator might collect data about the relative prices, quality, size, and available warranties for fridges at different stores and compare them to determine—analytically—where to make their purchase.

Troublingly, people are not naturally very good at selecting the appropriate type of reasoning for a particular situation. Often, the effort required for analytical reasoning entices an individual to use intuitive reasoning in situations where he or she should reason analytically (for example, in unfamiliar situations). Daniel Kahneman (2011) noted that this laziness often leads to inappropriate reasoning techniques: "When people believe a conclusion is true [because it seems to make sense intuitively], they are also very likely to believe arguments that appear to support it, even when these arguments are unsound. . . . The conclusion comes first and the arguments follow" (p. 45). In essence, when people use intuitive reasoning to draw a conclusion, they tend to cling to that conclusion, often because so much energy is required to re-evaluate their conclusion using analytical reasoning. Stereotypes are a prime example of this phenomenon (Johnson-Laird, 2008). If someone has a general belief about a group of people (often the result of intuitive reasoning), that person is likely to make assumptions about specific people based on their membership in that group (rather than analytically evaluating individuals on their own character and merit). Being aware of the human tendency to substitute intuitive reasoning for analytical reasoning allows students to watch out for it in their own and others' reasoning.

Reasoning in Everyday Life

Although intuitive reasoning can be misapplied to situations that require a more analytical approach, Virginia Klenk (2008) noted that "most of our knowledge is inferential; that is, it is gained not through direct observation, but by *inferring* one thing from another" (p. 1). In other words, humans gain a great deal of valuable information using intuitive reasoning. Therefore, we do not recommend rejecting it altogether. Instead, we suggest that students use a combination of intuitive and analytical reasoning to draw inferences and conclusions in everyday life—a process we refer to as *everyday reasoning*. For example, if you are outside and see a dog walking next to a person, you might assume that the dog belongs to that person and that the person is able to control the dog. You might quickly conclude that there is no need to avoid or be afraid of the dog. This type of reasoning is predominantly intuitive. However, if you are outside and see a dog roaming around by itself, your intuitive response (running away or acting afraid) might not be the best course of action. Choosing to use a more analytical approach empowers you to consider various pieces of evidence (for example, signs that the dog is friendly or aggressive) and consider different courses of action (for example, calmly walking away from the dog, checking to see if the dog has a collar and tags, calling the local authorities, and so on). Everyday reasoning involves understanding both intuitive and analytical reasoning and knowing when it is most appropriate to use one or the other (or a combination of the two). On a grander scale, scientists use this type of everyday reasoning to arrive at scientific theories about the world we live in. No one can observe what the world looked like long ago, but fossil evidence and the layering of rock in the earth's crust allow geologists to infer an accurate description of its history. Everyday reasoning is used for many commonplace tasks, such as filling out tax forms, and in various professions, from auto repair to computer programming (Cosmides & Tooby, 1992; Evans, 2002). In these situations, a combination of analytical and intuitive reasoning allows people to arrive at reasonable conclusions.

This same combination of analytical and intuitive reasoning also allows students to evaluate others' reasoning. For instance, Johnson-Laird (2008) gave an example of a man who, when asked to argue for public subsidization of the opera, responded, "Art is good for cultural life and commerce." This man's reasoning can be examined analytically to find the premises behind his conclusion: "Art is good for cultural life and commerce. Anything that is good for cultural life and commerce should be subsidized. Opera is an art. Therefore, opera is good for cultural life and commerce. Therefore, opera should be subsidized" (Johnson-Laird, 2008, p. 171). Taking apart intuitive reasoning in this analytical way makes it much easier to evaluate; poor reasoning and questionable assumptions are often not directly stated, but concealed in the unspoken steps of an argument. As such, "the ability to identify and evaluate implicit [reasoning] in what we read or hear is one of the most powerful critical thinking skills we can develop" (Marzano, Paynter, & Doty, 2003, p. 43). Understanding intuitive and analytical reasoning and how to use them together for everyday reasoning equips students to take an evaluative attitude toward others' reasoning.

A Practical Approach to Teaching Reasoning

Traditionally, instruction in reasoning and assessment of people's reasoning abilities have been focused on the rules of strict formal logic. Unfortunately, this focus is often impractically disconnected from the real world. Johnson-Laird (2008) illustrated the tendency for abstract theories and rules to be unhelpful in the real world with an example from economics: "Would the study of economics improve our ability to manage money? Some economists have become expert investors—John Maynard Keynes, for instance—but others have been disastrous, such as the Nobel prizewinners who bankrupted a hedge fund" (p. 280). Similarly, studying formal logic does not guarantee that students will be able or motivated to improve the quality of reasoning in their everyday lives. Because of this, some educators have dismissed the idea of teaching reasoning as impractical and ineffective. On the other hand, knowledge of formal logic may serve as a foundation for effective real-life reasoning and "help children become aware that they can think in an organized way" (Lipman, Sharp, & Oscanyan, 1980, p. 138). Therefore, we believe that an understanding of the formal rules of logic can be helpful, but should not be the only goal of reasoning instruction. A practical approach to teaching everyday reasoning is easier to implement, more generally useful, and more representative of the way people actually think.

Developing Analytical Reasoning

Intuitive reasoning develops naturally in humans, but, as stated previously, is not sufficient to address the challenges of modern life. Students need to learn the skills necessary for analytical reasoning (and therefore everyday reasoning, which combines intuitive and analytical reasoning). Mila Kryjevskaia and MacKenzie R. Stetzer (2013) attributed a great deal of poor reasoning by students to "(1) a lack of relevant knowledge and skills necessary to analyze an unfamiliar situation correctly and (2) an inability to recognize *when* and *how* to apply relevant knowledge and skills acquired during formal instruction" (p. 226). A number of studies (Feuerstein, Rand, Hoffman, & Miller, 1980; Weinstein & Mayer, 1986) found that teaching reasoning skills directly to students made them more aware of situations requiring the skills and improved students' reasoning abilities, regardless of age or achievement level. There are two reasons for the efficacy of this type of reasoning instruction.

First, analytical reasoning is voluntary and can be triggered or encouraged by instruction (Evans, 2002, 2003). In experiments, "very strong instructional emphasis on logical necessity [analytical reasoning] will reduce although not eliminate belief bias [a weakness of intuitive reasoning]" (Evans, 2003, pp. 455–456). That is, people instinctually use intuitive reasoning, but if they are reminded to use analytical reasoning, they often will. A key element of helping students become better reasoners is consistently reminding them to use their analytical reasoning skills.

Second, analytical reasoning processes can be practiced to the extent that they become automatic responses (Schneider & Shiffrin, 1977; Stanovich, West, & Toplak, 2011). The idea of practicing a skill until it becomes second nature is common in many fields. Reasoning processes are no exception. For example, the first time a student encounters an unfamiliar situation—like taking a timed test—he might rely on intuitive reasoning, which tells him that he'll never finish in time so there is no point in even trying. If prompted to use analytical reasoning to think about the situation instead, the student might realize it makes more sense to get to work and complete as many items as possible, even if he can't finish. The next time he encounters a timed test, the student is more likely to use analytical reasoning again, especially if the teacher reminds him. Over time, the analytical response (completing as many problems as possible) will gradually become automatic. For this reason, extensive practice of analytical reasoning processes is a critical element to becoming a better everyday reasoner. For example, a study of students' abilities to solve logic problems at different ages showed an improvement at the tenth grade level, which the researchers suspected was related to the fact that the students had recently learned about and practiced deductive reasoning in geometry class (Roberge, 1970). Another study asked participants to solve a series of logic problems, and researchers noted that "they made fewer false moves with increasing experience. . . . They were learning the effects of various tactical moves, and deducing their consequences" (Johnson-Laird, 2008, p. 357). Essentially, analytical reasoning improves with practice.

Reasoning Collaboratively

As students acquire analytical reasoning skills and practice using them in the context of everyday reasoning, collaborative work can facilitate their learning. Collaboration improves learning outcomes across age and subject area and is fundamental to the development of reasoning abilities (Mercier, 2011; Murphy, Wilkinson, Soter, & Hennessey, 2009; Piaget, 1928). Interaction with others is so conducive to the development of good everyday reasoning that several theories, both psychological and philosophical, have suggested that reasoning is inherently tied to dialogue and discussion (Bakhtin, 1981; Mercier, 2011; Murphy et al., 2009; Sperber, 2001). That is, talking about one's reasoning with others facilitates further reasoning development. During collaboration, students present evidence and reasons to support their conclusions, which are then questioned and critiqued by other students. That leads them to refine and improve their everyday reasoning (Murphy et al., 2009). In the words of Hugo Mercier (2011), "the most natural way to force people to construct better arguments is to offer counterarguments, something that happens spontaneously in groups and explains in part their better level of reasoning performance" (p. 182). Because of this, students working in cooperative groups should be encouraged to share their thoughts, even if it means disagreeing with their classmates. (For more information on facilitating respectful and productive disagreement, see Rogers & Simms, 2015.) Robyn M. Gillies and Michele Haynes (2011) found that "students develop better capacities for problem-solving and reasoning and obtain higher learning outcomes when they are able to interact with others, share ideas, challenge perspectives, and discuss alternative propositions before reaching agreement" (p. 350). In studies of both science and English language arts, researchers found that students who were taught to engage in inquiry and discussion as a group had more knowledge, deeper understanding, and a more critical approach than students who were not (Mercer, Dawes, Wegerif, & Sams, 2004; Murphy et al., 2009). Essentially, practicing in groups can facilitate students' development of the analytical skills necessary for everyday reasoning.

Reasoning in the Common Core and Next Generation Science Standards

With recent sets of standards written for English language arts (ELA), mathematics, and science, reasoning has received a renewed emphasis in K–12 education. The Common Core State Standards (CCSS) stated that students who are college and career ready should be able to "reflexively demonstrate the cogent reasoning and use of evidence that is essential to both private deliberation and responsible citizenship in a democratic republic" (National Governors Association Center for Best Practices & Council of Chief State School Officers [NGA & CCSSO], 2010a, p. 3). An important part of this reasoning includes the ability to "distinguish correct logic or reasoning from that which is flawed, and—if there is a flaw in an argument—explain what it is" (NGA & CCSSO, 2010b, p. 7). The Next Generation Science Standards* (NGSS; NGSS Lead States, 2013) stated that "scientists and engineers rely on human qualities such as persistence, precision, reasoning, logic, imagination and creativity" (Achieve, 2013, p. 6). In sum, recent standards documents have renewed the emphasis on reasoning in U.S. education.

As with many standards statements, those in the CCSS and NGSS encompass many different elements of knowledge and skill that students are expected to master. To elucidate specific reasoning skills, we first identified those standards from the CCSS and the NGSS that relate to reasoning. Second, we examined each

---

Next Generation Science Standards is a registered trademark of Achieve. Neither Achieve nor the lead states and partners that developed the Next Generation Science Standards were involved in the production of, and do not endorse, this product.

standard to identify the components of reasoning within it. For example, students are expected to discern key points, ask questions, identify high-quality evidence, be open minded but discerning, determine the soundness of reasoning, make sense of problems, reason abstractly, construct arguments, model their thinking, ensure consistency in reasoning, plan and carry out investigations, and so on. After identifying these components, we grouped them into eight overarching reasoning skills, each of which is robust and specific enough to be the subject of direct instruction and student practice. These eight skills are described in table I.2.

Table I.2: Reasoning Skills from the CCSS and NGSS

Identifying relationships between ideas involves identifying and describing connections between items, concepts, or complex ideas.
Identifying rules and patterns involves recognizing rules and patterns or creating them through induction, as well as abstracting patterns in information to make it more useful.
Applying rules and patterns involves extrapolating patterns of information and combining general rules with observations and knowledge to arrive at deductive conclusions.
Standardizing reasoning involves breaking down reasoning that is embedded in someone's words or actions into explicit premises and conclusions.
Evaluating deductive conclusions involves determining if a conclusion is valid and true.
Explaining how evidence supports a conclusion involves describing the link between a claim or conclusion and the information offered in support of it.
Asking questions to challenge assumptions involves seeking information about beliefs or perspectives that may affect someone's line of reasoning.
Hypothetical reasoning involves playing out different scenarios in one's head or using models to identify an optimal course of action or decision.

In our analysis of the standards documents, we analyzed the reasoning skills in two types of standards. The first type is general: college and career readiness standards, mathematical practice standards, and scientific practice standards. These non-grade-specific standards refer to skills that can be applied to all content at all levels. They are shown in the left column of table I.3. The component skills from table I.2 are listed at the top of each right-hand column; Xs indicate the component skills embedded within each standard.

Table I.3: General Reasoning-Related Standards From the CCSS and NGSS

Standard	Identifying relationships between ideas	Identifying rules and patterns	Applying rules and patterns	Standardizing reasoning	Evaluating deductive conclusions	Explaining how evidence supports a conclusion	Asking questions to challenge assumptions	Hypothetical reasoning
Discern a speaker's key points, request clarification, and ask relevant questions. (NGA & CCSSO, 2010a, p. 7)	X			X			X	
Know that different disciplines call for different types of evidence (e.g., documentary evidence in history, experimental evidence in science). (NGA & CCSSO, 2010a, p. 7)	X					X		
Work diligently to understand precisely what an author or speaker is saying . . . [and] question an author's or speaker's assumptions and premises and assess the veracity of claims and the soundness of reasoning. (NGA & CCSSO, 2010a, p. 7)				X	X	X	X	
Use relevant evidence when supporting their own points in writing and speaking, making their reasoning clear to the reader or listener, and . . . constructively evaluate others' use of evidence. (NGA & CCSSO, 2010a, p. 7)					X	X		
Make sense of problems and persevere in solving them. (Practice.MP1)			X					X
Reason abstractly and quantitatively. (Practice.MP2)			X		X			X
Construct viable arguments and critique the reasoning of others. (Practice.MP3)				X	X	X		
Model with mathematics. (Practice.MP4)	X	X	X					X
Look for and express regularity in repeated reasoning. (Practice.MP8)	X	X	X					
Asking questions (for science) and defining problems (for engineering). (National Research Council [NRC], 2012, p. 42)							X	
Developing and using models. (NRC, 2012, p. 42)	X							X
Planning and carrying out investigations. (NRC, 2012, p. 42)			X			X	X	X
Constructing explanations (for science) and designing solutions (for engineering). (NRC, 2012, p. 42)			X			X		X
Engaging in argument from evidence. (NRC, 2012, p. 42)						X		

In addition to the general practice standards, we also analyzed the grade-specific content standards in the CCSS and the NGSS. Because reasoning is a fundamental skill across content areas and grade levels, many of the standards referred to reasoning. Therefore, only a sampling is listed here. Table I.4 shows two content-specific standards for each grade level as examples (the coding systems used in the CCSS and NGSS documents are also used in table I.4 to identify each standard). For a complete list of reasoning-related standards for each grade level, visit **marzanoresearch.com/activitiesandgames**.

Table I.4: Sample Reasoning-Related Content Standards From the CCSS and NGSS

Grade	Standard	Identifying relationships between ideas	Identifying rules and patterns	Applying rules and patterns	Standardizing reasoning	Evaluating deductive conclusions	Explaining how evidence supports a conclusion	Asking questions to challenge assumptions	Hypothetical reasoning
K	With prompting and support, describe the connection between two individuals, events, ideas, or pieces of information in a text. (RI.K.3)	X							
K	With prompting and support, identify the reasons an author gives to support points in a text. (RI.K.8)	X					X		
1	Identify the reasons an author gives to support points in a text. (RI.1.8)	X					X		
1	Add within 100 . . . . Relate the strategy to a written method and explain the reasoning used. (1.NBT.C.4)	X		X			X		
2	Describe the connection between a series of historical events, scientific ideas or concepts, or steps in technical procedures in a text. (RI.2.3)	X	X						
2	Write opinion pieces in which they introduce the topic or book they are writing about, state an opinion, supply reasons that support the opinion, use linking words (e.g., *because*, *and*, *also*) to connect opinion and reasons, and provide a concluding statement or section. (W.2.1)	X					X		
3	Describe the logical connection between particular sentences and paragraphs in a text (e.g., comparison, cause/effect, first/second/third in a sequence). (RI.3.8)	X	X						

Grade	Standard	Identifying relationships between ideas	Identifying rules and patterns	Applying rules and patterns	Standardizing reasoning	Evaluating deductive conclusions	Explaining how evidence supports a conclusion	Asking questions to challenge assumptions	Hypothetical reasoning
3	Use area models to represent the distributive property in mathematical reasoning. (3.MD.C.7)	X		X					X
4	Explain how an author uses reasons and evidence to support particular points in a text. (RI.4.8)						X		
4	Ask questions that can be investigated and predict reasonable outcomes based on patterns such as cause and effect relationships. (Science and Engineering Practices for 4-PS3-3)	X	X	X				X	X
5	Quote accurately from a text when explaining what the text says explicitly and when drawing inferences from the text. (RI.5.1)	X	X	X			X		
5	Add, subtract, multiply, and divide decimals to hundredths. . . . Relate the strategy to a written method and explain the reasoning used. (5.NBT.B.7)	X		X			X		
6	Trace and evaluate the argument and specific claims in a text, distinguishing claims that are supported by reasons and evidence from claims that are not. (RI.6.8)					X	X	X	X	
6	Apply and extend previous understandings of arithmetic to algebraic expressions. (6.EE.A)	X		X					
7	Delineate a speaker's argument and specific claims, evaluating the soundness of the reasoning and the relevance and sufficiency of the evidence. (SL.7.3)					X	X	X	X	
7	Draw informal comparative inferences about two populations. (7.SP.B)	X	X	X					
8	Delineate and evaluate the argument and specific claims in a text, assessing whether the reasoning is sound and the evidence is relevant and sufficient; recognize when irrelevant evidence is introduced. (RI.8.8)					X	X	X	X	
8	Use informal arguments to establish facts about the angle sum and exterior angles of triangles. (8.G.A.5)		X	X			X		

Continued on next page →

Grade	Standard	Identifying relationships between ideas	Identifying rules and patterns	Applying rules and patterns	Standardizing reasoning	Evaluating deductive conclusions	Explaining how evidence supports a conclusion	Asking questions to challenge assumptions	Hypothetical reasoning
MS	Construct and present oral and written arguments supported by empirical evidence and scientific reasoning to support or refute an explanation or a model for a phenomenon or a solution to a problem. (Science and Engineering Practices for MS-PS2-4, MS-PS3-5, MS-LS1-4, MS-LS2-4, MS-ESS3-4)			X		X	X		X
9–10	Clarify, verify, or challenge ideas and conclusions. . . . Qualify or justify their own views and understanding and make new connections in light of the evidence and reasoning presented. (SL.9–10.1.c–d)	X	X			X	X	X	
9–10	Evaluate a speaker's point of view, reasoning, and use of evidence and rhetoric, identifying any fallacious reasoning or exaggerated or distorted evidence. (SL.9–10.3)				X	X	X	X	
11–12	Evaluate a speaker's point of view, reasoning, and use of evidence and rhetoric, assessing the stance, premises, links among ideas, word choice, points of emphasis, and tone used. (SL.11–12.3)	X			X	X	X		
11–12	Present information, findings, and supporting evidence, conveying a clear and distinct perspective, such that listeners can follow the line of reasoning [and] alternative or opposing perspectives are addressed. (SL.11–12.4)				X	X	X		
HS	Understand statistics as a process for making inferences about population parameters based on a random sample from that population. (HSS.IC.A.1)	X	X	X			X		
HS	Apply scientific reasoning to link evidence to the claims to assess the extent to which the reasoning and data support the explanation or conclusion. (Science and Engineering Practices for HS-ESS1-6)	X		X	X	X	X		

While we acknowledge that the process of identifying overarching reasoning skills is not an exact science, we strove to identify those reasoning skills from the standards that could be directly taught to students and practiced through games and activities in the classroom. This book presents strategies for directly teaching each reasoning skill and includes games that teachers can use to reinforce and help students practice each skill.

Direct Instruction in Reasoning

Reasoning is an important skill to master on its own and is also "essential for the mastery of all academic disciplines" (Ricketts & Brooks, 1983, p. 385). Because students must reason *about* something, reasoning can be effectively taught in tandem with content. In turn, reasoning ability supports knowledge acquisition and allows students to extend what they learn (Cavallo, 1996; Lawson, 2001; Lawson, Alkhoury, Benford, Clark, & Falconer, 2000; Lipman et al., 1980; Marzano, 1992; Marzano & Pickering, 1997; Shayer & Adey, 1993). As with important content knowledge, direct instruction is an excellent way to introduce students to reasoning skills.

Those who question the importance of direct instruction in reasoning skills argue that everyday reasoning situations have fairly low stakes—if one makes an error, it can be corrected. However, poor everyday reasoning can also lead to disastrous consequences, such as the nuclear meltdown at Chernobyl and many of the instances described by the Darwin Awards (for example, using a lighter to see how much gasoline is left in a can; Johnson-Laird, 2008). In everyday situations, Troy Sadler (2004) noted that people

> did not frequently engage in the kind of comprehensive reflection and evaluation needed to assess the usefulness of information related to complex issues. It seems as though the participants recognized the need to evaluate the information provided, but lacked the skills and strategies to do so. (p. 528)

In light of this, the best way to ensure that students are proficient reasoners is to teach them directly.

As explained previously, each of the skills in table I.4 (pages 8–10) come directly from the CCSS and NGSS, can be the subject of direct instruction in reasoning, and can be practiced by students as they play the games in this book. Please note, however, that the games are designed to give students *practice* with reasoning skills. Before playing a game, students will need direct instruction in the skills associated with that game. Table I.5 (page 12) shows the reasoning skills associated with each game.

Table I.5: Reasoning Skills Associated With Games

Game	Grade Level	Identifying relationships between ideas	Identifying rules and patterns	Applying rules and patterns	Standardizing reasoning	Evaluating deductive conclusions	Explaining how evidence supports a conclusion	Asking questions to challenge assumptions	Hypothetical reasoning
Ready, Set, Connect!	Elementary school	X							
Relationship Bingo	Elementary and middle school	X					X		
Conditional Cards	Elementary and middle school	X			X	X			
Great Extrapolations	Upper elementary and middle school	X	X	X					
Riddle Me This	Upper elementary, middle, and high school								X
Never Tells	Middle and high school		X	X				X	
Valid or True	Middle and high school				X	X			
Proverb Pairs	Middle and high school				X	X		X	
Premises Puzzle	Middle and high school					X	X		
Reasoning Relay	Middle and high school				X	X	X	X	X
Are You Saying . . . ?	High school					X		X	
Rule Breakers	High school			X				X	X

As explained previously, teachers should use direct instruction to introduce students to the applicable skills for a game before asking students to practice the skills by playing the game. To facilitate direct instruction for these eight component skills, the following sections provide processes and strategies for teaching each one.

Although we discuss specific strategies for teaching the various component skills of reasoning, there are two important general-purpose approaches to note. First (and most simply), students exhibit better reasoning when explicitly asked to use their reasoning skills (Gillies & Haynes, 2011; Mercier, 2011; Webb et al., 2009). Basic prompts to students to explain further, justify their process, or make their reasoning explicit are necessary reminders, especially with younger and developing reasoners. Setting and enforcing consistently high expectations for the quality of reasoning also helps students reason better (Anderson, Chinn, Chang, Waggoner, & Yi, 1997; Anderson, Chinn, Waggoner, & Nguyen, 1998; Lin & Anderson, 2008; Mercier, 2011; Webb et al., 2008). Students need to know what is expected of them in terms of reasoning quality, and those expectations should be consistent so students reinforce good habits and do not fall back into bad ones. To this end, we recommend that teachers use terminology that cues specific reasoning skills when using the activities and games in this book. For example, once students have learned to standardize reasoning by breaking it down into premises and a conclusion, teachers should routinely use the term *standardize* to prompt students to use that skill.

The second general-purpose approach is the use of both abstract rules and concrete examples. The exclusive use of either abstract or content-specific examples has been found to be ineffective in teaching reasoning (Nisbett, Fong, Lehman, & Cheng, 1987). Asking students to memorize abstract rules is too theoretical; students have difficulty conceptualizing the abstractions and applying them to real-life situations (Lipman et al., 1980). Concrete examples, on the other hand, can be too specific; students are often unable to generalize from the example to form more widely applicable rules. In short, students need real-life, concrete examples to help them understand the abstract rules involved in reasoning, but they also need to learn the abstract rules themselves so they can reason in a wide range of situations. To achieve this goal, discuss with students how the reasoning skills underlying the activities and games might relate to their everyday lives. For example, after playing Great Extrapolations (see chapter 4), a teacher could have a short discussion with the class about how the skills used in that game—identifying rules and patterns and applying rules and patterns—could be used in real life. She might point out that if a person was getting a pet or buying a car, that person could identify the features of a particular pet or car he or she liked and extrapolate those features to other pets or cars to broaden his or her list of acceptable options.

As noted previously, there are eight component skills that can be the subject of direct instruction:

1. Identifying relationships between ideas

2. Identifying rules and patterns

3. Applying rules and patterns

4. Standardizing reasoning

5. Evaluating deductive conclusions

6. Explaining how evidence supports a conclusion

7. Asking questions to challenge assumptions

8. Hypothetical reasoning

In this book, we provide specific direction and guidance for teaching each component skill.

Identifying Relationships Between Ideas

Identifying relationships between ideas or concepts is a foundational skill that underlies all reasoning activities. To introduce and teach this skill in the classroom, teachers can follow these three steps.

1. Introduce students to specific types of basic relationships.

2. Ask students to diagram basic relationships between ideas.

3. Ask students to find basic relationships between objects and ideas in real life.

Here we provide specific guidance and examples for each step.

Introduce Basic Relationships

Language, thought, and reasoning are founded on relationships. In language, words are connected to form clauses, clauses are connected to form sentences, sentences are connected to form paragraphs, and so on. In thought, various mental representations are linked together to form complex ideas or structures. In reasoning, support and evidence are linked together and connected back to conclusions. All these connections represent different relationships. As more concepts are linked, the web of relationships expands and ideas become more complex.

Robert J. Marzano and Janice A. Dole (1985) identified four basic types of relationships that can be directly taught to students:

1. **Addition**—Two ideas go together in some way (for example, *He is kind, **and** he is intelligent*).

2. **Contrast**—Two ideas oppose each other in some way (for example, *He is fast **but** he isn't a good basketball player*).

3. **Time**—One event happens before, during, or after another event (for example, *He went home **before** he went to the party*).

4. **Cause**—One event causes another (for example, *He went home **because** the girl he liked wasn't at the party*).

Each relationship has a number of subtypes, as shown in table I.6 (page 15). Additionally, table I.6 lists linguistic cues called *signal words and phrases* that students can look for to identify the presence of particular relationships. As students encounter information, they can be taught to look for individual ideas and identify relationships between those ideas using signal words and phrases as clues.

Table I.6: Basic Relationship Types, Subtypes, and Signal Words and Phrases

Type	Subtype	Signal Words and Phrases
Addition	1. Equality: He is tall *and* he is handsome.	*and, as well, at the same time, besides, equally, furthermore, in addition, likewise, moreover, similarly, too, what is more*
	2. Restatement: I am tired. *In fact,* I am exhausted.	*actually, another way of saying this, in actuality, indeed, in fact, namely, that is, that is to say*
	3. Example: He does many things well. *For example*, he is excellent at cards.	*another example would be; first, second, third . . .; for a start; for example; for another thing; for one thing; last but not least; next, then, finally . . .; one, two, three . . .; such as; to begin with*
	4. Summation: He cooks. He sews. He fixes appliances. *In all*, he is an excellent homemaker.	*all in all, altogether, briefly, in all, in a word, in brief, in conclusion, in short, in sum, overall, then, therefore, thus, to summarize, to sum up*
Contrast	1. Antithesis: I will be there, *but* I won't be happy.	*but, contrariwise, conversely, else, not, on the contrary, on the other hand, oppositely, or rather, otherwise, what is better, what is worse, yet*
	2. Alternative: *Either* it will rain *or* it will snow.	*alternatively, either . . . or, neither . . . nor, or, rather than, sooner than*
	3. Comparison: Bill is tall. *In comparison*, his brother is short.	*but, compared to, in comparison, in contrast, like, whereas*
	4. Concession: I don't like rock music. *Nonetheless*, I'll meet you at the concert.	*all the same, anyhow, anyway, at any rate, besides, else, for all that, however, in any case, in any event, in spite of that, nevertheless, nonetheless, only, regardless of this, still, though*
Cause	1. Direct cause: He won the race *by* maintaining his concentration.	*by, due to, owing to, through*
	2. Result: Bill went home. *Consequently*, the party ended.	*accordingly, as a consequence, as a result, consequently, for all that, hence, now, so, therefore, the result was, thus, whereupon*
	3. Reason: He went to the store *because* he needed food.	*because, because of, for the fact that, in that, on account of, since, so, so that, this is the reason*
	4. Inference: Mary is going on a long trip. *In that case*, she should plan well.	*in that case, or else, otherwise, so, then*
	5. Condition: *Unless* you stop, I will leave.	*admitting that, as long as, assuming that, considering that, granted that, if, if . . . then, in so far as, no sooner, now that, presuming that, seeing that, providing that, supposing that, unless, when . . . then, where . . . there*
Time	1. Subsequent action: They went to the game. *Afterward*, they went to the dance.	*after, after that, afterward, as yet, before, finally, in the end, later, next, shortly, since, so far, subsequently, then, until*
	2. Prior action: Math class is *before* lunch.	*at first, before, beforehand, before now, before that, by now, by then, earlier, formerly, initially, in the beginning, originally, previously, until, until then, up to now*
	3. Concurrent action: Mary and Bill watched television *during* dinner.	*at the same time, at this point, during, meantime, meanwhile, simultaneously, when, while*

Source: Adapted from Marzano & Dole, 1985.

Diagram Basic Relationships

When relationships are interwoven or nested inside each other (for example, *The kind and pretty* [addition] *woman was tired. Nevertheless* [contrast], *she delighted the children by* [cause] *taking them on a picnic*), diagramming the structure of the ideas and their relationships can help students break down complex ideas into simpler pieces. To that end, Marzano and Dole (1985) suggested using the symbols in table I.7 for each of the major types of relationships.

Table I.7: Symbols for Basic Relationships

Relationship	Symbol
Addition	=
Contrast	≠
Time	→
Cause	⇒

Source: Marzano & Dole, 1985.

As shown in table I.7, *addition* is represented by an equals sign, *contrast* by a not-equal sign, *time* by an arrow with a single line, and *cause* by an arrow with a double line. Students can circle ideas and connect them with a line, drawing the appropriate symbol next to the line and signal word or phrase to indicate the appropriate relationship. The relationships in the previous example sentence and in a content-related sentence such as the one in figure I.1 could be diagrammed as shown.

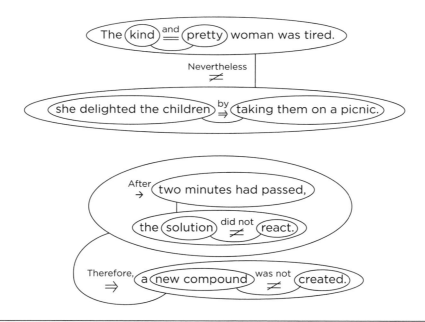

Figure I.1: Sample relationship diagram.

As shown in figure I.1, individual ideas have been enclosed in circles, and the symbols from table I.7 have been used to show how the circles relate to one another. Sometimes, one relationship is nested inside others. Students can perform this type of analysis and diagramming with any type of text (oral or written) in any content area to help them better understand the relationships found therein. This type of diagramming is also particularly useful when evaluating deductive reasoning (see pages 20–21).

Find Basic Relationships in Real Life

Finally, ask students to look for basic relationships between objects and ideas in real life. The simplest version of this is to practice identifying similarities (addition) and differences (contrast). You might point out two objects in the classroom, ask students to identify whether they are similar or different, and have them explain why. You could also read a passage or book as a class and ask students to point out similarities and differences between characters, as well as other addition and contrast relationships in the text.

Time and cause relationships can be more difficult to identify in real life, as they are often not physically visible. For time relationships, begin by asking *when* questions, such as "In relation to going to school, when do you eat breakfast?" Point out that the relationship between these two events is a time relationship. It may also be helpful for students to realize that time relationships usually exist between events, rather than objects. If students can put the words *before*, *after*, or *during* between two events, there is likely a time relationship. Once students are comfortable identifying time relationships between two given events, ask them to point out or come up with pairs of time-related events on their own.

For cause relationships, begin by asking *why* questions, such as "Why did everyone wear big heavy coats to school today?" The answer is probably something along the lines of "Because it's cold out." Point out to students that the cold weather *causes* everyone to wear coats. Generally speaking, cause relationships exist when one event or condition (the cause) leads directly to another event or condition (the effect). You can also help students grasp the idea of cause relationships by presenting a cause event and asking them to suggest the effect, or vice versa. This works particularly well with cause and effect in stories and other texts. Once students are comfortable noticing cause relationships, ask them to find or come up with them on their own.

Identifying Rules and Patterns

As students approach tasks involving reasoning, they will often need to identify rules and patterns. To help students develop this skill, teachers can break it into two parts:

1. Ask students to create rules and patterns using induction.
2. Ask students to abstract rules and patterns that they find.

The following sections provide detail about each step.

Induction

Creating rules and patterns commonly takes the form of *induction*—the process of looking at a number of instances and coming up with a rule or pattern that governs all of them. For example: Imagine a person sitting in the lobby of a European hotel. Again and again, she sees people come out of the elevator and give their room keys to the front desk. But they don't seem to be checking out; some of them are wearing coats, but none have luggage with them. Similarly, people come in off the street, quickly pick up a key from the desk, and head to the elevator, without luggage or the paperwork that usually comes with checking into a hotel. After a while, she sees a person who left earlier come back, pick up a key, and go back upstairs. From these instances, she creates a rule: when you leave the hotel, you leave your room key at the front desk. At first, people's entrances and exits seemed peculiar, but after seeing enough instances, she was able to inductively create a rule that governs them. In this example, the observer had to generate an original rule, but creating rules and patterns can also consist of identifying existing patterns in information, such as a sequence of events in a text.

Students should be aware that induction can sometimes lead a person to identify a rule that is not always true. For example, if someone has seen many swans and they have all been white, he or she will probably reach the inductive conclusion that all swans are white. However, black swans do, in fact, exist in Australia. This is one of the pitfalls of inductive reasoning: it can lead to conclusions that are probably—but not necessarily—true.

To formalize the process of induction for students, you might present them with the following process (Marzano & Pickering, 1997):

1. Identify specific and objective information or observations.

2. Examine your pieces of information for patterns, similarities, or connections.

3. Write a rule or general statement that describes the pattern.

4. Test your rule against further observations and modify the rule if it does not apply.

For the first step, students will need a set of facts or observations. For a more structured approach, you might compile this list. For a less structured approach, you might simply present students with a topic or a situation and ask them to compile a list of their own observations. Based on their lists, students move to the second step and look for patterns or connections within the information. The basic relationships from table I.7 (page 16) can be particularly helpful during this step. The third step is the heart of the inductive process: using the similarities or connections between individual observations to come up with a general statement or rule to describe the whole set. Fortunately, human beings are hardwired to look for patterns in this manner, so inductions often come quite naturally. Once students have done this, they should test their rule by trying to find instances or observations that do not fit the established pattern. This final step is a critical aspect of the process: students use their analytical reasoning to examine the quality of their inductions.

Emphasize to students the probabilistic aspect of inductive conclusions: they are likely but not certain, since they are based on only the available information. Since it is always possible that information exists that is simply unavailable to the person making the inductive conclusion, inductive conclusions can never be treated as completely true. For example, stereotypes are examples of inductive rules usually based on too few observations or too little information. Students should understand that, when making inductions, they should seek to validate them by collecting as much supporting information as possible. They can ask themselves the following questions to assess the level of certainty—and the consequences of that level of certainty—of their inductive rules (Marzano & Heflebower, 2012):

◆ Is it important that I am right about this?

◆ If so, how sure am I about my prediction?

  ✧ Very sure

  ✧ Somewhat sure

  ✧ Could go either way

  ✧ Somewhat unsure

  ✧ Very unsure

◆ If I'm not very sure, what should I do about it?

Once students have created or discovered a pattern or rule from a set of observations, they can be asked to abstract it to make it more generally useful.

Abstracting

Abstracting a rule or pattern involves stating it more generally so that it can be applied to a wider variety of situations. This allows students to see similarities between situations or information that initially seem quite disparate. For example, students who have read a number of books in which characters change their minds about something (such as *Green Eggs and Ham* [Dr. Seuss, 1960]) might discover a pattern of characters changing their minds about something after experiencing it themselves. To abstract this rule, they might say, "The only way to really know whether or not you like something is to try it."

To help students abstract patterns they have identified, we recommend using the following process, adapted from Robert Marzano and Debra Pickering (1997):

1. Determine which parts of the pattern are most essential.

2. Rewrite the essential information using more general, widely applicable language.

    ◆   Use general words (especially nouns) instead of specific words.

    ◆   Shorten or sum up information instead of including lots of details.

Because abstracting is a fairly complex skill, you might introduce it to students using familiar content that has an easily recognizable pattern. For example, you might present the fable of *The Ant and the Grasshopper* to students. Students might summarize it using the following series of statements:

◆   A grasshopper didn't work all summer long.

◆   An ant worked all summer long.

◆   When winter came, the grasshopper didn't have any food, but the ant did.

◆   Being prepared is worth the work it takes.

The students might write the information in a more general form by making the following statements:

◆   Someone didn't work for a period of time.

◆   A different person did work during the same period of time.

◆   At the end of the period of time, the person who worked was better off than the person who didn't.

◆   This shows that working is better than not working.

Once students have abstracted a pattern by stating it generally, as shown here, they can apply it to a novel situation or new set of information, which is the next component skill.

Applying Rules and Patterns

Application is a useful extension of identifying rules and patterns, and can also be used on its own during deductive reasoning. Essentially, students use a rule or pattern to gain insight into unfamiliar information or to predict what will happen in an unfamiliar situation. There are two aspects to teaching students to apply rules and patterns:

1. Ask students to extrapolate rules and patterns onto new sets of information.

2. Guide students to reason deductively.

Here we provide more detail about each one.

Extrapolation

The process of extending an abstracted (or generalized) pattern to new situations or information is called *extrapolation*. Once students have identified and abstracted a rule or pattern, they can extrapolate that pattern onto another set of information. To introduce the idea of extrapolating, you could use well-known similar sets of information, such as Shakespeare's *Romeo and Juliet* and its modern musical retelling, *West Side Story*. First, lead students through identifying and abstracting the sequence of events in *Romeo and Juliet* using the processes described in the previous component skill (identifying rules and patterns, pages 17–19). Then, to set them up to apply that pattern, introduce the setting, context, and characters of *West Side Story* and ask students to make connections between the two—which characters correspond, which plot points are parallel, and so on. Finally, ask students to extrapolate their knowledge of *Romeo and Juliet* by making predictions about what will happen in *West Side Story*.

Essentially, when extrapolating patterns, students are looking for a different set of information that fits the same general pattern as the original set of information. In the previous example of *The Ant and the Grasshopper* fable, students might decide that the generalized pattern they identified during the abstracting phase applies to a different story, wherein an industrious farmer tricks a lazy nobleman out of the products of his fields three years in a row.

One of the benefits of extrapolations is that applying generalized patterns to new situations may highlight elements of information that students have not considered before. In the previous example, students might come across sets of information that *do not* fit their abstracted pattern. For example, they might discover the fable of *The Fisherman and the Businessman*, wherein a businessman confronts a fisherman lounging on the shore, exhorting him to work harder so he will catch more fish and be able to build a fleet of fishing boats manned by his own employees. In response, the fisherman asks the businessman why he would build such a fleet. "So you will have time to relax and do the things you want to do," replies the businessman. The fisherman replies, "You mean the things I'm doing right now?" The abstracted pattern from this story is very different from the other abstracted pattern. By recognizing this difference, students can deepen their understanding of both stories.

Deduction

A useful way to think of deduction is as the application of general rules and patterns to specific situations. These rules often take the form of broad statements or principles. For example, if students know that addition involves combining two or more quantities, they can apply that rule or principle to specific situations that involve the combination of two quantities to conclude that addition might be helpful in those situations. As with induction, you can present students with a process for deductive reasoning (Marzano & Pickering, 1997):

1. Identify the specific topic, situation, or thing in question.

2. Identify general rules or principles that are relevant to the situation at hand.

3. Check to make sure that the general rule actually applies to the specific situation; ensure that there is nothing about the specific situation that would make it an exception to the rule or otherwise make the general rule inapplicable.

4. If the general rule is applicable, use it to draw conclusions, make predictions, or identify new information about the specific situation.

To help students apply this process to various content and in their lives, overtly point out general rules or principles that apply to new content being introduced. For example, when studying the French Revolution, you might point out the principle that war often occurs when one group of people feels oppressed or unfairly treated. You might ask students to keep a log or journal of important principles. Then, when students learn about new events or situations, you might ask them to revisit their lists to see if any of the principles apply.

The power of deductive reasoning lies in the fact that certain principles can be counted on to be true. Obvious examples are the postulates and theories of mathematics, though deductive reasoning is also used in other content areas and disciplines. Any time general statements are used to come to conclusions about specific information or situations, deductive reasoning has occurred. For example, a student who understands the principle that war often occurs when one group of people feels oppressed or unfairly treated could look for examples of oppression when asked to identify causes of a particular war. She might identify the Treaty of Versailles as unfair treatment of Germany by other world powers and conclude that the Treaty of Versailles was one of the causes of World War II. Similarly, she might identify King George's unfair treatment of the American colonies as one of the causes of the American Revolution. This is deductive reasoning.

To prompt students to generate deductive conclusions, you can ask them any (or all) of the following questions:

- Based on the following generalization (or rule or principle), what predictions can you make or what conclusions can you draw that must be true?

- If _____, then what can you conclude must happen?

- What are the conditions that make this conclusion inevitable? (Marzano, 1992, pp. 71–72)

Essentially, deductive reasoning allows students to apply principles they have learned to many different situations. Marzano and Pickering (1997) pointed out that although some teachers might object to directly presenting important principles to students and then asking them to apply them to various situations, this is actually a critical skill for students to develop:

> Some educators would assert that it is not as effective to present important generalizations and principles to students as it is to ask them to discover this knowledge. However, directly teaching important knowledge, and then asking students to apply that knowledge, can be just as effective as discovery methods. Using deductive reasoning to apply knowledge requires students to develop an understanding of both the concepts within a principle and the conditions that make it applicable. It also requires that this understanding be sufficient to help them determine if the general statement applies to the new situation. If students are required to apply their understanding to increasingly complex and diverse situations, they may develop a level of understanding that equals—or even exceeds—what could be attained with inductive instructional approaches. (pp. 150–151)

As explained previously, we acquire a great deal of our knowledge not through direct observation, but through inferences and deductions. Teaching important principles and rules directly to students allows them to draw conclusions in a wide variety of situations.

Standardizing Reasoning

Standardizing refers to restating information in the form of several premises and a conclusion. This format is called a *standardized argument*. One of the most important rationales for teaching students to standardize reasoning is that students are surrounded by hidden reasoning every day. Discerning whether or not someone's reasoning is valid may be insignificant in some situations (such as two friends discussing where they should go for lunch), but can be critically important in other situations (such as a financial salesperson explaining why investing in his mutual fund is better than investing in another fund). To be able to evaluate reasoning, students must first make it explicit through standardization. For example, a student might say that he is not going to eat cookies at lunch because cookies are not healthy. Instead, he eats Cheetos® and drinks a Coke®. This student and his friends may or may not be aware that he has used reasoning to arrive at his lunch choices. Standardizing his reasoning, however, makes his thinking explicit and allows students to identify invalid or untrue assumptions. To standardize reasoning, students should know how to do the following:

◆ Make embedded or hidden information and reasoning explicit.

◆ Standardize reasoning into syllogisms (two premises and a conclusion).

◆ Standardize reasoning that is based on more than two premises.

Here we provide detail about each aspect of this skill.

Making Embedded Information and Reasoning Explicit

The first aspect of standardization is simply to make information or reasoning that is implicit in a person's words or actions explicit. The student who has chosen to eat Cheetos and drink Coke for lunch—reasoning that since they aren't cookies, they are healthy—has embedded his reasoning in his actions. To make the information in this situation explicit, one of his friends might say, "You said you wanted to eat healthy food, but I notice that you're eating Cheetos and drinking Coke for lunch." Here, the friend has made explicit the information that was embedded in the situation: what the student said about his eating habits and what the student is eating. An easy way to make reasoning explicit is to ask questions. Matthew Lipman, Ann M. Sharp, and Frederick S. Oscanyan suggested the following:

- What is your reason for saying that . . . ?

- What makes you think that . . . ?

- On what grounds do you believe that . . . ?

- Can you offer an argument in support of your claim that . . . ?

- Why do you say that . . . ?

- Why do you believe your view is correct?

- What can you say in defense of your view?

- Is there anything you'd like to say in order to prove your view correct?

- Would you like to tell us why you think that's so? (1980, p. 121)

Once students have surfaced the embedded reasoning within a statement or action, they can standardize that reasoning.

Standardizing Reasoning Into Syllogisms

Once embedded information has been made explicit, students can begin to form a standardized argument by identifying which parts of that information represent premises and which information represents a conclusion. Standardized arguments expressed in exactly two premises (a foundational premise and a minor premise) and a conclusion are called *syllogisms*. To standardize reasoning into a syllogism, students must identify each of these three elements: (1) foundational premise, (2) minor premise, and (3) conclusion. It is important to realize that identifying the three parts of a syllogism does not always happen in a particular order. Students might first identify a premise, or they might begin by identifying a conclusion, depending on what information is available.

In a syllogism, the two premises are traditionally called the *foundational premise* and the *minor premise*. The foundational premise (such as premise 1 in the following example) is a general belief, principle, or assumption—it makes a broad statement. It typically appears first when writing out a standardized argument. A foundational premise is often a starting point for standardizing reasoning because people hold many general beliefs about the world. If a student has already identified a conclusion and minor premise and is seeking a foundational premise, it can be helpful to ask, "What assumptions underlie this conclusion?" or "What general principles govern this situation?" Foundational premises, since they are general rules, can also be generated through induction, as described previously (see pages 17–18).

The minor premise (such as premise 2 in the following example) usually refers to one instance, example, or situation—it makes a specific statement. The minor premise of a syllogism identifies a specific situation to which the foundational premise is being applied. If a student has already identified a foundational premise, he or she can look for specific situations that fit that general principle. If a student has already identified a conclusion, he or she can identify the minor premise by asking questions, such as "What specific evidence leads to this conclusion?" or (to a person who has just stated a conclusion) "What makes you think that?"

The conclusion of a syllogism usually makes a statement about a situation, makes a prediction, or states what must be true if the premises are true. If one has already identified the premises, one can use them to generate a conclusion. A conclusion, however, is often the starting point for standardization because people often state conclusions in daily life (without stating the corresponding premises). For example, while watching a news broadcast about the Israeli-Palestinian conflict, someone might say, "I think the U.S. should attack Israel." Clearly, this is a conclusion that he has come to through unstated premises, which should be identified, standardized, and evaluated (which is a separate component skill).

To return to the student who chose Cheetos and Coke for lunch (because cookies were unhealthy) and his friends who have made his reasoning explicit, the student or his friends might standardize his reasoning as follows.

> Premise 1: Cookies are unhealthy.
>
> Premise 2: I'm not eating cookies.
>
> Conclusion: What I'm eating is healthy.

Alternatively, the following standardization might be used:

> Premise 1: I only eat healthy things.
>
> Premise 2: I'm eating Cheetos and drinking a Coke.
>
> Conclusion: Cheetos and Coke are healthy.

The fact that there are multiple ways to standardize the student's thinking is completely acceptable. It is typical to be able to standardize an argument in multiple ways, depending on what information students choose to focus on. This approach to standardizing is designed to help students recognize, understand, and explicitly state the reasoning they encounter in everyday conversations. Standardizing an argument is also a prerequisite to evaluating it.

Standardizing Arguments With More Than Two Premises

Syllogisms are a special kind of standardized argument that is limited to two premises (foundational and minor) and a conclusion. When students are learning to standardize reasoning, syllogisms are a helpful structure because students know exactly what elements they are looking for. However, as students gain experience and skill with standardizing reasoning, extended standardized arguments can be created that incorporate as many premises as are necessary to explain the information that was used to draw a conclusion. Some of these premises may take the form of general principles (like a foundational premise) while others will be more specific (like a minor premise). For example, a student who has observed that her school is decorated using the primary colors of red, blue, and yellow (making embedded information explicit) might conclude that her school is designed to stimulate students' attention and standardize her reasoning as follows:

Premise 1: Certain colors stimulate attention, such as yellow, orange, and red.

Premise 2: My school is designed to highlight the primary colors.

Premise 3: Two of the primary colors are yellow and red.

Conclusion: The colors used in my school are designed to stimulate attention.

These chains of evidence are fairly common, as many instances of everyday reasoning cannot be sufficiently explained with only two premises.

Overall, this less formal approach to standardizing reasoning—a concept that is typically the purview of formal courses in logic—highlights one of the key messages of this book: reasoning surrounds us every day in many different areas, and it is often messier and more organic than formal logic suggests. Lipman and his colleagues (1980) explained that

> the contributions of formal logic to developing organized thinking lie less in application of its rules and far more in encouraging special traits such as a sensitivity to inconsistency, a concern for logical consequence, and an awareness of whether or not one's thoughts really hold together. . . . These traits do apply in situations far beyond the scope of formal logic. (p. 138)

Because this is the case, we opt for strategies that will help students interact with reasoning on a daily basis. Once students have standardized reasoning, they can evaluate it.

Evaluating Deductive Conclusions

Evaluating deductive conclusions (that is, conclusions based on premises) is a crucial skill for students to learn. It is often the missing piece in everyday reasoning—people draw conclusions but fail to analyze whether the conclusions are logical or based on true premises. When evaluating reasoning in real life, students may need to be prompted to evaluate deductive conclusions and their underlying premises. Teachers can use the following questions for this purpose:

- Who is making this claim and in what context? Is he trustworthy? Does he have something to gain by convincing others of this?

- Is this conclusion supportable? Is it specific or vague? Is it precisely worded or intentionally confusing? Is it actually meaningful?

- Does this conclusion overgeneralize? Does it use words like *all, none, always,* or *never*? Does it go beyond the premises or evidence supporting it?

- ◆ Does this conclusion oversimplify? Does it ignore nuances or conflicting evidence?

- ◆ What is the source of the premises or evidence? Is it reliable? Is it biased?

- ◆ How is this person trying to convince me? Is she using facts and good evidence? Is she using anecdotes or stories and appealing to emotion?

When asking students to evaluate reasoning, teachers can give each student a copy of these (or similar) questions as a reference or starting point. These informal questions help cue a critical mindset; however, there is also a more formal process for evaluating deductive conclusions. It has two steps:

1. Evaluate conclusions for validity.

2. Evaluate conclusions for truth.

Here we provide detail about each step.

Evaluating for Validity

As explained previously, students standardize reasoning by identifying a series of premises—often a foundational premise and a minor premise—and a conclusion. Once reasoning has been standardized, it should be evaluated for *validity*. A conclusion is valid if it follows logically from its premises. For example, consider the following standardization of the student's lunch choices from the previous example:

Premise 1: Cookies are unhealthy.

Premise 2: I'm not eating cookies.

Conclusion: What I'm eating is healthy.

This argument is not valid. Cookies are unhealthy, but so are lots of other things. It is illogical to conclude that because one thing is unhealthy, it is the *only* thing that is unhealthy. If the student standardized his reasoning this way, his error would be one of validity. Because he isn't reasoning logically, his conclusion is invalid.

One of the best ways to evaluate the validity of a standardized argument is to use Euler (pronounced "oiler") diagrams, which have traditionally been used to evaluate syllogisms (sets of two premises and a conclusion) but can also be used to evaluate standardized arguments with more than two premises. We recommend that students use an informal version of the Euler diagram. In our version, students simply use circles to represent groups or categories and points to represent individual people or objects as expressed by a standardized set of premises and conclusions. To illustrate, figure I.2 shows an Euler diagram for the preceding standardized argument about cookies.

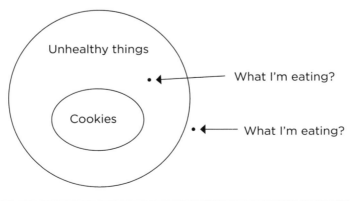

Figure I.2: Sample Euler diagram.

In this Euler diagram, the category "Cookies" is completely contained within the category "Unhealthy things" to reflect the premise "Cookies are unhealthy." However, one cannot be sure where to represent "What I'm eating." Premise 2 states that "What I'm eating" is not cookies, but "What I'm eating" could exist either inside or outside the category "Unhealthy things." As in this example, if there is more than one way to diagram the premises (that is, it is not completely certain how the categories and individual items in the premises relate to each other), no conclusion can be logically drawn from them. The argument is invalid.

As another example, consider the following set of premises and conclusion:

Premise 1: All students have logins for the school network.

Premise 2: Haley has a login for the school network.

Premise 3: Greer does not have a login for the school network.

Conclusion: Haley is a student but Greer is not.

To evaluate for validity, students ask whether the conclusion follows logically from the premises. On the surface, this conclusion seems to follow logically from the premises, but when diagrammed using an Euler diagram like the one in figure I.3, it becomes clear that only part of the conclusion is valid.

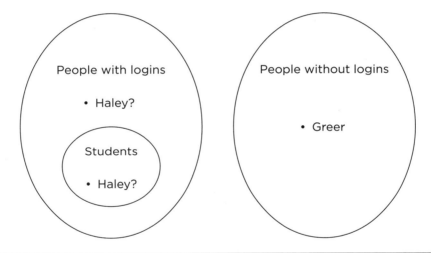

Figure I.3: Sample Euler diagram.

As shown in figure I.3, it is valid to conclude that Greer is not a student, but it is not valid to conclude that Haley *is* a student. She might be a teacher or someone else who happens to have a login to the school network. From the information given in the premises, there is no way to logically and definitively conclude that Haley is a student.

The power of informal Euler diagrams is that they work for more complex sets of premises as well as simpler ones. Additionally, students sometimes need to figure out what logical conclusions are possible given a specific set of information. Consider the following set of premises without a conclusion:

Premise 1: All foods that are healthy to eat do not taste good.

Premise 2: Tofu is healthy to eat.

Premise 3: You only eat what tastes good.

Premise 4: Cheeseburgers are not healthy to eat.

Figure I.4 shows an informal Euler diagram for this set of premises.

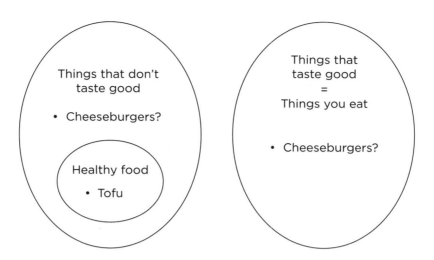

Figure I.4: Sample Euler diagram.

Note in figure I.4 that the student has used one of the symbols for basic relationships (see table I.7 on page 16) to indicate an addition relationship between "Things that taste good" and "Things you eat." This is an extremely useful application of the relationship symbols to indicate that two labels ("Things that taste good" and "Things you eat") apply to the same category.

As seen in figure I.4, students could draw several logical conclusions from the premises given:

◆ You do not eat healthy food.

◆ You do not eat tofu.

◆ All things that taste good are not healthy.

◆ Tofu does not taste good.

However, they could *not* make any conclusions about cheeseburgers, since cheeseburgers could be in at least two different categories, as shown in figure I.4.

Evaluating for Truth

If an argument is valid, students will next need to evaluate it for truth. Note that an argument's validity takes precedence over the truth of its premises: if an argument is found to be invalid, there is no need to evaluate the premises for truth. However, if an argument is valid, the premises should always be evaluated for truth. Students do this by examining each premise. If all premises are true (and the argument is valid), the conclusion can be considered true. If one or more premises are false (even if the logic of the argument is valid), the conclusion is false. Some premises may take the form of opinions, in which case some people may think the argument is true and some may not. In this case, it may be necessary to investigate support for the opinion.

To illustrate, this standardization of the reasoning about lunch choices is valid, as shown by the Euler diagram in figure I.5 (page 28).

Premise 1: I only eat healthy things.

Premise 2: I'm eating Cheetos and drinking a Coke.

Conclusion: Cheetos and Coke are healthy.

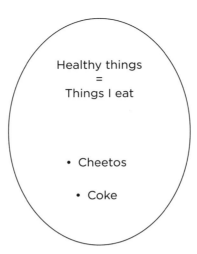

Figure I.5: Euler diagram showing validity.

Because the syllogism is valid, it needs to be evaluated for truth. Only one of the premises is true ("I'm eating Cheetos and drinking a Coke"); the other ("I only eat healthy things") is false, since Cheetos and Coke are both generally acknowledged to be unhealthy and the student is eating them anyway. Because the student is using an untrue statement as one of his premises, his conclusion is false.

When evaluating for truth, it can be helpful for students to establish criteria to judge the truth of premises leading to a conclusion. Marzano and his colleagues (1988) called this process *verification*:

> Verification involves confirming or proving the truth of an idea, using specific standards or criteria of evaluation. Verification may be as formal as a scientific experiment or as casual as noticing that something does not make sense and checking the accuracy of facts. (p. 111)

One criterion students can use to determine whether or not a premise is true is to ask themselves if it is a good reason. Lipman, Sharp, and Oscanyan (1979) presented the following four qualities of good reasons:

1. **Reasons that are factual** are better than opinions or false statements. Facts provide support for a conclusion or argument. For example, a fact like "Prairie dogs live in underground burrows," is better support for a conclusion than an opinion like "Prairie dogs are annoying."

2. **Reasons that are relevant** have a legitimate connection to the conclusion that they support, whereas irrelevant reasons do not. For example, "Barack Obama passed the Affordable Care Act" is more relevant to a conclusion about the quality of Obama as president than a statement like "George W. Bush was a good president."

3. **Reasons that provide understanding** offer explanation or clarity to the reader or listener. For example, saying "I like dogs because they can come with you on camping trips" provides more understanding than saying "I like dogs because they're cool."

4. **Reasons that are known** (or familiar) to the reader or listener are better than obscure or unfamiliar reasons. For example, saying "This is a better photograph because the black and white areas really stand out" is likely more familiar to most people than saying "This is a better photograph because it was shot with a narrow aperture and rapid shutter speed."

If a premise seems to be false or is not a good reason, students should investigate further or should reject the conclusion based on the untrue premise.

Explaining How Evidence Supports a Conclusion

One of the most important uses of reasoning is to explain how evidence supports a conclusion. While it is important to provide evidence for a conclusion, that evidence is not effective support unless one can explain *why* the evidence supports the conclusion. For example, a student might conclude that air is matter. As evidence, he might offer research results from an experiment he conducted himself:

> First I weighed a completely deflated rubber ball. Then I pumped some air into the ball and weighed it again—it weighed more. I pumped more air into the ball and reweighed it. Its weight had increased again.

So far, the student has offered a conclusion and evidence to support it. However, a critical element of his argument is missing; he has not explained exactly how the evidence supports his conclusion that air is matter. To explain his reasoning, he might say:

> The results of my experiment show that air has weight, and weight is one of the characteristics of matter.

Essentially, the student's explanation of his reasoning connects his evidence to his conclusion. You can help students develop this skill using the following three steps:

1. Ask students to state a conclusion.

2. Ask students to provide evidence for their conclusion.

3. Ask students to explain the reasoning that connects their evidence to their conclusion.

Here we provide guidance for each step.

State a Conclusion

The easiest way to help students state a conclusion is to ask them to collect evidence on a particular topic. For example, for the topic of energy drinks, a student might find the following evidence:

◆ Energy drinks can improve a person's physical and mental performance (Scholey & Kennedy, 2004).

◆ Energy drinks can improve a tired person's driving ability (Reyner & Horne, 2002).

◆ Energy drinks can decrease the amount of mental fatigue a person experiences when he or she has to concentrate for an extended period of time (Kennedy & Scholey, 2004).

◆ Energy drinks contain high levels of caffeine—as high as 294 mg per bottle (Heneman & Zidenberg-Cherr, 2007).

◆ Consuming more than 400 mg of caffeine can lead to nervousness, irritability, sleeplessness, abnormal heart rhythms, decreased bone mass, and upset stomach (Nawrot et al., 2003).

◆ Teenagers who consumed high levels of caffeine had elevated blood pressure (Savoca, Evans, Wilson, Harshfield, & Ludwig, 2004).

◆ Most energy drinks contain a lot of sugar, which should be limited in a normal daily diet (U.S. Department of Agriculture, 2010).

Once students have compiled a list of evidence related to a topic, they can use that evidence to generate a conclusion. In this example, the student might conclude, based on her evidence, that energy drinks are bad for one's health.

Provide Evidence

Once students have stated a conclusion, they should be asked to provide evidence to support it. In the previous example, the student examines her evidence and realizes that only some of her evidence supports her conclusion.

- Energy drinks contain high levels of caffeine—as high as 294 mg per bottle (Heneman & Zidenberg-Cherr, 2007).

- Consuming more than 400 mg of caffeine can lead to nervousness, irritability, sleeplessness, abnormal heart rhythms, decreased bone mass, and upset stomach (Nawrot et al., 2003).

- Teenagers who consumed high levels of caffeine had elevated blood pressure (Savoca et al., 2004).

- Most energy drinks contain a lot of sugar, which should be limited in a normal daily diet (U.S. Department of Agriculture, 2010).

Since the first three items of evidence are all related to caffeine, the student combines them, resulting in the following two pieces of evidence to support her conclusion.

- The high levels of caffeine in energy drinks—as high as 294 mg per bottle—are associated with a number of adverse health effects, including nervousness, irritability, sleeplessness, abnormal heart rhythms, decreased bone mass, upset stomach, and high blood pressure (Heneman & Zidenberg-Cherr, 2007; Nawrot et al., 2003; Savoca et al., 2004).

- Most energy drinks contain a lot of sugar, which should be limited in a normal daily diet (U.S. Department of Agriculture, 2010).

Once students have stated their conclusions and identified the pieces of evidence that support them, they can move on to explaining the reasoning that connects their evidence to their conclusion.

Explain Reasoning

As explained previously, reasoning is used to connect evidence to claims or conclusions. In the previous example, the student stated the conclusion that energy drinks are bad for one's health and provided two items of evidence in support of her conclusion. To explain her reasoning, the student might say:

> Energy drinks contain a lot of sugar and caffeine, which can lead to conditions such as nervousness, irritability, sleeplessness, abnormal heart rhythms, decreased bone mass, upset stomach, and high blood pressure. These conditions are all associated with poor health. Therefore, energy drinks are not good for one's health.

To deepen students' explanations, they can be asked to add qualifiers to their reasoning. *Qualifiers* are statements that acknowledge exceptions to a conclusion or situations in which a conclusion might not be true. An effective way to prompt students to generate qualifiers is to ask them to return to the original evidence they collected to see if they found any information that did not support their conclusion. In this student's case, she found three pieces of evidence that highlighted benefits of energy drinks:

1. Energy drinks can improve a person's physical and mental performance (Scholey & Kennedy, 2004).

2. Energy drinks can improve a tired person's driving ability (Reyner & Horne, 2002).

3. Energy drinks can decrease the amount of mental fatigue a person experiences when he or she has to concentrate for an extended period of time (Kennedy & Scholey, 2004).

Acknowledging evidence that does not support a conclusion strengthens students' explanations of their reasoning. The student explaining the reasoning behind her conclusion that energy drinks are bad for one's health might add qualifiers to her reasoning, as follows:

> While energy drinks have been found to increase physical and mental performance, improve driving ability when tired, and reduce mental fatigue during periods of sustained concentration, these drinks contain a lot of sugar and caffeine. Sugar and caffeine can lead to conditions such as nervousness, irritability, sleeplessness, abnormal heart rhythms, decreased bone mass, upset stomach, and high blood pressure. These conditions are all associated with poor health. Therefore, energy drinks are not good for one's health.

The process of gathering evidence, stating conclusions, sorting evidence into supporting and nonsupporting information, and then explaining their reasoning (with qualifiers, if applicable) gives students practice explaining exactly how reasoning supports a conclusion.

Asking Questions to Challenge Assumptions

As students formulate conclusions based on premises and explain how evidence supports those conclusions, they will inevitably encounter reasoning based on assumptions. For example, consider the puzzle in figure I.6.

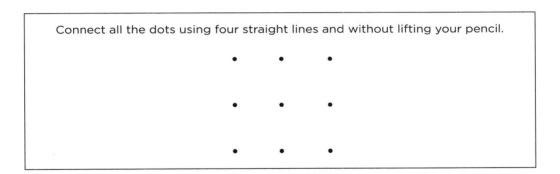

Figure I.6: Reasoning puzzle.

When faced with a puzzle of this nature, students often assume that they must solve it while staying within the "box" formed by the dots on the outer corners, as shown in figure I.7.

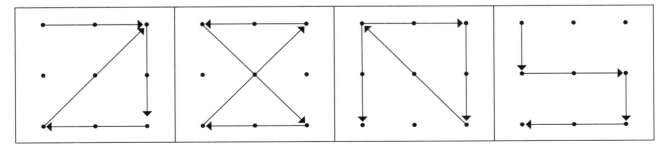

Figure I.7: Attempted solutions based on faulty assumptions.

In fact, the solution can only be found by challenging that assumption and going outside the box, as shown in figure I.8 (page 32).

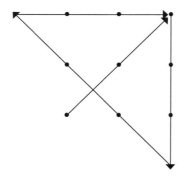

Figure I.8: A correct solution.

Reasoning is not necessarily invalid or untrue simply because it is based on assumptions. However, it is important for students to understand that challenging assumptions is both acceptable and recommended. One of the most effective ways to challenge assumptions is by asking questions.

As students ask questions to challenge assumptions, they must be aware of a fundamental human tendency called *confirmation bias*. Confirmation bias is the human propensity to seek out information that confirms our assumptions. As Thomas Gilovich (1991) put it:

> When trying to assess whether a belief is valid, people tend to seek out information that would confirm the belief over information that might disconfirm it. In other words, people ask questions or seek information for which the equivalent of a "yes" response would lend credence to their hypothesis. (p. 33)

For example, consider the following series of numbers: 2, 4, 6, 8, 10. When asked to figure out the rule being used to generate the sequence and predict what the next number in the series should be, most people assume that the rule for the series is "add two," and say that 12 should come next. In this case, 12 is an example that confirms what most people suspect—that the series of numbers is growing by two each time. However, it would be more productive to guess a number that has a good chance of *disproving* the hypothesis that the series is growing by two each time, such as 11. Guessing 11 and finding out that it is *not* the next number in the series provides more information than a confirmatory example like 12, as guessing 11 and finding it incorrect would rule out several alternative hypotheses (such as "a series of numbers in ascending order" or "growth through addition"). At the same time, guessing 11 and finding out that it *is* the next number in the series would quickly disprove the initial hypothesis that the series is growing by two. In this example, 11 is called a *counterexample*: an example that, if correct, disproves the hypothesis. Testing counterexamples to try to disprove one's hypothesis gives a person more information than testing examples that confirm one's hypothesis. In other words, resisting the natural inclination to seek confirmation and testing counterexamples instead is a more efficient course to determine the truth of a hypothesis.

To help make students aware of their own and others' assumptions and their tendency to seek confirmation when asking questions, you can use several strategies:

◆ Equip students with questions they can use to examine their own and others' reasoning.

◆ Directly teach students a process for analyzing perspectives, which they can use to become more aware of their own and others' assumptions.

◆ Acquaint students with a process for examining their values, which often underlie assumptions.

Here we provide more detail about each of these strategies.

Questions to Examine Reasoning

As students examine the reasoning behind their own and others' perspectives, assumptions, and conclusions, there are a number of specific questions they can use to elicit that reasoning. As mentioned previously, Lipman and his colleagues (1980, p. 121) offered the following list of helpful questions:

- What is your reason for saying that . . . ?
- What makes you think that . . . ?
- On what grounds do you believe that . . . ?
- Can you offer an argument in support of your claim that . . . ?
- Why do you say that . . . ?
- Why do you believe your view is correct?
- What can you say in defense of your view?
- Is there anything you'd like to say in order to prove your view correct?
- Would you like to tell us why you think that's so?

Once students have surfaced the reasoning for a conclusion or perspective (either their own or another's), they can think about that reasoning from their own and others' perspectives.

Analyzing Perspectives

In the complex society of the 21st century, students must be able to identify and acknowledge how alternative systems of reasoning yield different perspectives or values (and vice versa). Marzano (1992) noted that this is "one of the most important intellectual skills a person can develop" (p. 98). Following Marzano and Pickering (1997), we call the process of identifying multiple perspectives on an issue and examining the reasons or logic behind them *perspective analysis*; the basic process for analyzing perspectives is as follows:

1. Identify and describe one point of view about a controversial topic.
2. Figure out the reasons and logic that support that point of view.
3. Identify and describe an opposing point of view.
4. Figure out the reasons and logic behind the opposing point of view.

As students analyze perspectives, they generate reasoning to support positions they may not personally agree with. This is an excellent way for them to practice seeking counterexamples and avoiding confirmation bias. For example, a student who believes that any kind of animal testing is wrong might support his position by explaining that animals have the right to be protected from pain while in human care and that using them as test subjects violates that right. Then, the student identifies an opposing point of view: it is justifiable to test potentially life-saving medicines on animals. To support this view, he might state that when one has to choose between a human life and an animal life, the human life takes precedence. To extend the analysis of perspectives, students can also examine the underlying values for a particular point of view or assumption.

Examination of Values

The reasons that support a position are typically related to an underlying value that a person holds. This can make the perspective analysis process somewhat emotionally charged. Marzano and Arredondo (1986) observed that the value a person places on something can normally be measured by the emotional reaction it elicits. Humans often mentally attach *value weights* to various concepts. For ease of understanding, we might consider those value weights to be positive, negative, or neutral; an individual's set of assumptions or beliefs determines the value weight he or she attaches to a concept. Because these value weights are based on ideas and values closely related to a person's identity, students must practice reacting in healthy, objective ways to emotionally charged issues. Marzano and Pickering (1997) observed:

> It takes discipline and skill to stop during an argument . . . and take enough of a step back to gain an understanding of your own or another's perspective. This is why it is important for students to develop this ability in the classroom through the examination of academic issues that are not emotionally charged. (p. 178)

By examining academic issues that are not emotionally charged, students can develop the understanding that many of their value weights are determined by a set of subjective assumptions. Under a different set of assumptions, the associated value weight could be very different.

To examine academic issues in terms of values, we recommend the following process designed by Marzano and Arredondo (1986, p. 83):

1. Identify whether you consider a concept or a statement to be *positive*, *negative*, or *neutral*. Usually your emotional response to the concept or statement will help identify your value evaluation.

2. Identify the assumptions or knowledge base from which you assigned the value rating.

3. Consider the accuracy of the knowledge base for your assumptions.

4. Identify a set of assumptions that might give you a different value weight for the statement or concept.

To illustrate, imagine a high school student who realizes he has a negative value weight attached to the concept of fiscally liberal political views. He investigates this value by identifying a few of the reasons he feels this way: his parents told him that people should not give the government more tax money because it already wastes so much, and that if you make businesses pay less in taxes, they will have more money to hire more employees. To consider the accuracy of his knowledge, he does some research about how the government spends its money and how tax breaks for businesses affect national employment rates. He also tries to consider a set of assumptions that would give him a positive value weight toward fiscally liberal political views, such as "The government provides many necessary services that are funded through taxes," and "The government should directly help middle and working class citizens instead of relying on businesses to do it."

As stated previously, students will likely recognize that their value systems are somewhat subjective as a result of appraising their values. This is a useful realization for students to make:

> [Children] can learn to consider it natural that people differ in their beliefs and points of view. And they can learn to grasp this not as a quaint peculiarity of people but as a tool for learning. They can learn how to learn from others, even from their objections, contrary perceptions, and differing ways of thinking. (Paul, 1984, p. 12)

Recognizing the information base from which one's judgments are created is a central aspect of reasoning and cognition. However, it is important to recognize and remember that the goal of analyzing perspectives and examining values is not solely to prompt students to accept, appreciate, or agree with perspectives and values opposite to their own. Rather, students' original positions are often solidified once they better understand the reasons underlying them; if they change their minds, it should be because they have discovered errors or inconsistencies in their original thinking.

Hypothetical Reasoning

The final component skill involves figuring out various pathways one might take in a situation. Quite simply, in situations where there is uncertainty about what to do, students need to be able to pause, figure out what they know for certain, and then look ahead and anticipate what will happen if certain steps are taken. We call this *hypothetical reasoning*. Johnson-Laird (2008) characterized hypothetical reasoning as "reasoning from *if*" and stated that it is "commonplace, because so much of our knowledge is conditional in form. If we get caught speeding then we pay a fine. If we have an operation then we need time to recuperate" (p. 296). Keith E. Stanovich, Richard F. West, and Maggie E. Toplak (2011) added, "When we reason hypothetically, we create temporary models of the world and test out actions (or alternative causes) in that simulated world" (p. 106). Learning to reason hypothetically empowers students to systematically solve problems and deal with unfamiliar situations in everyday life. Essentially, reasoning hypothetically involves the following four-step process:

1. Figure out what you know for certain.

2. Identify your goal.

3. Create an imaginary or simulated world based on information that is certain.

4. Try out different actions or choices in that imaginary or simulated world to see if they will help you achieve your goal.

For example, if a student is faced with a choice of whether she should go to a movie or to a party on Saturday night, she could start by figuring out what she knows for certain about each situation and herself, as shown in table I.8.

Table I.8: Examples of Known Information

Movie	Party	Me
It will cost $10.	It will not cost anything.	I feel pretty tired tonight.
My parents said they could drive me there and pick me up afterwards.	Sera can give me a ride there, but she can't bring me back home afterwards.	I don't like having to ask for rides.
My friend Julie will meet me there.	My friends Josh, Kali, Athena, and Garek will be there.	Athena has not been very nice to me lately.
The theater is at the mall.	It is at Raina's house.	I don't know Raina very well.
It is a romantic comedy.	It is a dance party.	I hate dancing in front of other people.

Once the student has figured out what she knows for certain, she might identify her goal as "having the most fun." Then, she might create two imaginary scenarios in her head: one of going to the movie and one of going to the party. Finally, she imagines what will happen in each scenario and compares her predictions with her goal (having the most fun). Based on her hypothetical reasoning, she might conclude that if she goes to the party, she will be anxious about getting a ride home, might have a negative interaction with Athena, and might feel awkward standing around while others dance. Therefore, she chooses the movie. Once students are familiar with this basic process, they can be asked to apply it to various real-world situations.

Hypothetical reasoning is cognitively difficult. Often, there is too much information or too many possibilities to hold in one's mind at once. As such, we suggest teaching students to use models when they have more information than they can mentally hold onto or manipulate at once. Models may simply be diagrams, but students can also use tangible models to help them reason. For example, Riddle Me This (see chapter 5) helps students practice hypothetical reasoning by using physical models. One riddle in particular presents the following problem:

> A man needs to cross a river in a canoe. He also needs to transport a bag of grain, a chicken, and a fox across the river. He can only carry one of the three with him in the canoe at a time. If he leaves the grain and the chicken alone together anywhere, the chicken will eat the grain. If he leaves the chicken and the fox alone together anywhere, the fox will eat the chicken. How can he transport himself, the grain, the chicken, and the fox across the river without anything being left behind or eaten?

Solving this riddle requires hypothetical reasoning. The known information and the goal are given in the riddle, and one must think through or imagine the consequences of various possibilities to find one that will achieve the goal. However, problems such as this one with many possibilities and limitations are intimidating. It's difficult to know where to start and—after making the first move (for example, deciding to take the chicken across the river first)—it can be overwhelming to keep track of which things are where. Creating a model using props or other people to represent each element of the riddle can help students keep track of information and possibilities, as well as visualize what to do next.

Physical models are especially useful when reasoning about a real-world problem with a number of possible solutions because they allow students to manipulate the pieces of the model to show a choice and its consequences. These pieces often take the form of tokens or other small objects that represent larger objects, people, or ideas. To illustrate, imagine a group of students that is in charge of organizing the school carnival. They have recruited student volunteers who will staff the different booths and now need to assign each volunteer to a booth that fits his or her skills. The group could use a physical model to help them with this task. First, they make a list of the volunteers and their skills. Then, they draw a diagram of the carnival and use tokens labeled with names to represent each volunteer. They place the tokens on the booths in the diagram to show possible booth assignments. Figure I.9 shows the group's model.

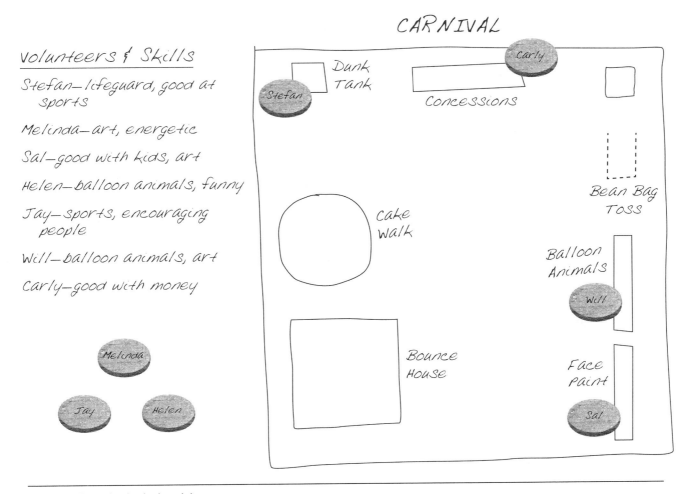

CARNIVAL

Volunteers & Skills

Stefan—lifeguard, good at
    sports

Melinda—art, energetic

Sal—good with kids, art

Helen—balloon animals, funny

Jay—sports, encouraging
    people

Will—balloon animals, art

Carly—good with money

Figure I.9: Example physical model.

This flexible model helps the group keep track of various combinations as they try different possibilities to make sure every booth is staffed by an appropriately skilled volunteer.

Hypothetical reasoning is essential to problem solving, decision making, and any situation in which a person must reason about the consequences of different possibilities. As such, it is an important skill for students to practice in the classroom. Due to the difficulty associated with hypothetical reasoning, it is critical that students have strategies (such as modeling) to help them through the process.

How to Use This Book

The activities and games in this book fuse two key elements of effective engagement—academic games and friendly controversy—to help students practice reasoning skills outlined in the CCSS and the NGSS. According to over sixty studies conducted by Marzano Research, the use of academic games in the classroom is associated with an average gain of 20 percentile points in student achievement (Haystead & Marzano, 2009). Additionally, Nancy Lowry and David W. Johnson (1981) demonstrated that infusing lessons with a sense of friendly controversy enhances students' curiosity, achievement, and attitudes regarding the subject matter.

A word of caution: while supporting friendly controversy in the classroom, take care to avoid placing inordinate pressure on winning. Mild pressure can increase students' focus (Cahill, Gorski, & Le, 2003; Shors, Weiss, & Thompson, 1992; Van Honk et al., 2003), but too much pressure can have negative consequences (Ito, Larsen, Smith, & Cacioppo, 2002; Roozendaal, 2003). Students who feel compelled to win a game can be embarrassed if they lose (Epstein & Harackiewicz, 1992; Moriarty, Douglas, Punch, & Hattie, 1995; Reeve & Deci, 1996).

Fortunately, students do not need to be motivated by external pressures, prizes, or rewards to enjoy academic games. As Thomas L. Good and Jere E. Brophy (2003) observed:

> The opportunity to compete can add excitement to classroom activities, whether the competition is for prizes or merely for the satisfaction of winning. Competition may be either individual (students compete against everyone else) or group (students are divided into teams that compete with one another). (p. 227)

Marzano (2007) calls this type of fun, low-stakes interaction *inconsequential competition* because it has no bearing on a student's grade or status in the class.

This book contains twelve reasoning activities and games for classroom use:

1. Ready, Set, Connect!
2. Relationship Bingo
3. Conditional Cards
4. Great Extrapolations
5. Riddle Me This
6. Never Tells
7. Valid or True
8. Proverb Pairs
9. Premises Puzzle
10. Reasoning Relay
11. Are You Saying . . . ?
12. Rule Breakers

Activities and games are ordered by grade level, with those for younger students in earlier chapters and those for older students in later chapters. Each one involves a different combination of standards-based reasoning skills. The activities and games at the beginning of the book require more basic skills (such as identifying basic relationships and identifying rules and patterns) than those at the end. For easy reference, the first page of each game or activity lists the suggested age group, the reasoning skills involved, and materials needed for the game or activity. You can also identify activities and games that align with specific reasoning standards. For non-grade-specific practice standards, simply refer to table I.3 (page 7). For grade-specific content standards, refer to the table at **marzanoresearch.com/activitiesandgames**. Locate the standards you would like to focus on, take note of the skills associated with the standards, directly teach those skills to students, and then choose activities and games from table I.5 (page 12) that allow students to practice those skills.

 Throughout the book, you will also notice teacher tips for executing each game. These tips are indicated by the light bulb icon. Refer to these tips for useful hints regarding variations in gameplay and setup, solutions to potential pitfalls, and differentiation strategies to meet the needs of all students.

Remember that the activities and games are meant not to replace direct instruction in reasoning, but to provide different ways to practice and develop reasoning skills. Feel free to adapt or supplement to suit the requirements of your school, curriculum, and students. Finally—and most importantly—have fun!

Ready, Set, Connect!

For elementary school students

This activity is a scavenger hunt intended for younger students. It helps them begin to notice relationships between items and concepts, which is the most basic skill associated with reasoning.

As described previously (see pages 14–15 in the introduction), there are four types of basic relationships, and each of those types can be further divided into subtypes. To review, the categorization of types and subtypes (with signal words and phrases for each) is shown in table 1.1 (page 40).

 As this game is designed for elementary school students, we suggest you focus on the four basic types of relationships. You might also choose to use age-appropriate terms to discuss these relationships with your students: "alike" or "things that go together" for addition, "different" or "opposite" for contrast, and so on.

Setup

Ready, Set, Connect! requires very little preparation. The youngest students can play it orally as a whole class. Slightly older students can work individually or in pairs and only need simple cards or worksheets (see pages 44–48), depending on the version of the activity.

Reasoning Skills

- Identifying relationships between ideas

Materials

- Ready, Set, Connect! cards (for version 2; see reproducible, pages 44–46)
- Ready, Set, Connect! relationship log (for version 3; see reproducible, pages 47–48)

Table 1.1: Basic Relationship Types, Subtypes, and Signal Words and Phrases

Type	Subtype	Signal Words and Phrases
Addition	1. Equality: He is tall *and* he is handsome.	*and, as well, at the same time, besides, equally, furthermore, in addition, likewise, moreover, similarly, too, what is more*
	2. Restatement: I am tired. *In fact,* I am exhausted.	*actually, another way of saying this, in actuality, indeed, in fact, namely, that is, that is to say*
	3. Example: He does many things well. *For example,* he is excellent at cards.	*another example would be; first, second, third . . .; for a start; for example; for another thing; for one thing; last but not least; next, then, finally . . .; one, two, three . . .; such as; to begin with*
	4. Summation: He cooks. He sews. He fixes appliances. *In all,* he is an excellent homemaker.	*all in all, altogether, briefly, in all, in a word, in brief, in conclusion, in short, in sum, overall, then, therefore, thus, to summarize, to sum up*
Contrast	1. Antithesis: I will be there, *but* I won't be happy.	*but, contrariwise, conversely, else, not, on the contrary, on the other hand, oppositely, or rather, otherwise, what is better, what is worse, yet*
	2. Alternative: *Either* it will rain *or* it will snow.	*alternatively, either . . . or, neither . . . nor, or, rather than, sooner than*
	3. Comparison: Bill is tall. *In comparison,* his brother is short.	*but, compared to, in comparison, in contrast, like, whereas*
	4. Concession: I don't like rock music. *Nonetheless,* I'll meet you at the concert.	*all the same, anyhow, anyway, at any rate, besides, else, for all that, however, in any case, in any event, in spite of that, nevertheless, nonetheless, only, regardless of this, still, though*
Cause	1. Direct cause: He won the race *by* maintaining his concentration.	*by, due to, owing to, through*
	2. Result: Bill went home. *Consequently,* the party ended.	*accordingly, as a consequence, as a result, consequently, for all that, hence, now, so, therefore, the result was, thus, whereupon*
	3. Reason: He went to the store *because* he needed food.	*because, because of, for the fact that, in that, on account of, since, so, so that, this is the reason*
	4. Inference: Mary is going on a long trip. *In that case,* she should plan well.	*in that case, or else, otherwise, so, then*
	5. Condition: *Unless* you stop, I will leave.	*admitting that, as long as, assuming that, considering that, granted that, if, if . . . then, in so far as, no sooner, now that, presuming that, seeing that, providing that, supposing that, unless, when . . . then, where . . . there*
Time	1. Subsequent action: They went to the game. *Afterward,* they went to the dance.	*after, after that, afterward, as yet, before, finally, in the end, later, next, shortly, since, so far, subsequently, then, until*
	2. Prior action: Math class is *before* lunch.	*at first, before, beforehand, before now, before that, by now, by then, earlier, formerly, initially, in the beginning, originally, previously, until, until then, up to now*
	3. Concurrent action: Mary and Bill watched television *during* dinner.	*at the same time, at this point, during, meantime, meanwhile, simultaneously, when, while*

Source: Adapted from Marzano & Dole, 1985.

Play

Under your supervision, students look for examples of basic relationships in the classroom, around the school, or on the playground. There are three ways to go about this; the version you choose will depend on the age and ability of your students.

The first version is for very young students (that is, K–1 students). In this version, the whole class plays together. Prompt students to look for one relationship at a time, help them find examples if needed, and then immediately discuss the relationship. For example, you could take students to the sink area of your classroom and ask them to find a contrast or "difference" relationship. Students might reply that the sink and the water fountain are different because one is for washing your hands and the other one is for drinking. Alternatively, you could draw the class's attention to an addition relationship between two specific objects by asking, for instance, "How are the calendar and the number line alike?"

The second, intermediate version (grades 1–2), involves handing out cards that prompt students to look for specific relationships. This book includes reproducible cards for this purpose (see pages 44–46), or you can write relationship words on index cards (one relationship word per card, either a relationship type or a signal word or phrase) to give to students. See table 1.1 (page 40) for a complete list of signal words and phrases associated with each basic relationship. Depending on how comfortable your students are with this activity, you could have them work in pairs or individually. Each student or pair of students finds the relationship on their card somewhere in the room and stands next to it. For example, if Kris and Maria receive a card that says "and," they would look around the classroom for an addition relationship. They notice the reading area has pillows *and* a carpet, so they go stand by their newly discovered example. When everyone is standing still, quickly go around the room and have students share with the class what they found.

The third, more independent version for older elementary school students (grades 2 and up) involves a longer scavenger hunt. Distribute a relationship log (see the reproducible on pages 47–48) to every student or pair of students. The log lists several options for each of the basic relationships and provides space for students to write down examples they find. Figure 1.1 (page 42) shows an example of the contrast section of a Ready, Set, Connect! relationship log that a student has filled out.

Name: Hakim

Find two things that are opposites or different in some way.

my desk _____ **and** the teacher desk _____

How they are different: one is big and one is little _____

Find a situation where you can choose between one option or another.

Situation: lunch menu _____

Choices: _____ pizza _____ **or** _____ PB&J _____

Compare two things.

_____ calendar _____ **and** _____ number line _____

Alike because: they both have numbers in order _____

Different because: one is dates and one is for _____

_____ counting _____

Figure 1.1: Example contrast section of Ready, Set, Connect! relationship log.

Be sure to set time and area limits before sending students to look for relationships.

Wrap-Up

With the two more independent options, it is important to discuss the examples that students find. In the second option (using cards), quickly discuss students' examples at the end of each round. With the third option (using worksheets), bring the class back together once time is up to share an example or two of each type of relationship. This step allows you to clarify, correct, and make sure that students understand the relationships. For example, if a student points out the addition relationship between a black and white picture *and* a color picture on the wall, you could clarify by saying, "You might notice that these pictures are different because one is in color and the other is in black and white. However, Hakim was right to say that this is an addition relationship because they are both pictures hanging on the wall." You may also choose to collect students' worksheets to use as an unobtrusive assessment.

 You can easily transform this activity into a game by adding a simple scoring element: give students or pairs a point for each relationship that they find and identify successfully. We recommend, however, that you use this modification with caution. Young students can quickly become distracted or frustrated by competition, especially if they perceive it to be unfair. Introduce scoring only if your students are able to stay focused on the task at hand.

Example Relationships

There are many relationships to be found in classrooms and schools. Encourage students to be creative—not all relationships need to be between two physical objects. For example, looking for relationships in the gym might inspire a student to think of the similarities between volleyball and tennis. Here, we provide a few examples for each type of basic relationship that students might find around their schools.

Addition

- ◆ "There is a poster and a calendar on the wall."
- ◆ "This is the cafeteria. This is where we eat."
- ◆ "There are lots of things on Ms. Xavier's desk. For example, there is a pencil."
- ◆ "Mickey does baseball, soccer, and swimming. He is very athletic."

Contrast

- ◆ "I like science but not math."
- ◆ "My classmates either buy lunch or bring it from home."
- ◆ "During quiet time, I like to read but Ally likes to draw."
- ◆ "This is my favorite water fountain, even though the water is warm."

Cause and Effect

- ◆ "Our class will win a pizza party when we all read five books."
- ◆ "Zac has a scrape on his leg because he tripped on the playground."
- ◆ "There are coats in our cubbies because it's cold out."
- ◆ "The lunch menu says it's pizza day, so a lot of kids will buy lunch."
- ◆ "If I run in the hallway, I have to go back and walk."

Time

- ◆ "Some kids go to extended day after school ends."
- ◆ "The third graders eat lunch before the fourth graders."
- ◆ "The janitor is mowing the lawn while no one is outside for recess."

Cards for Ready, Set, Connect!

Here we provide cards that can be copied, cut apart, and given to students to assign them a specific relationship to hunt for. These cards are sorted by the grade levels for which they are likely to be appropriate.

Grades 1–2

And	Alike	But
Different	Before	After
Because		

Grades 2+

Addition

Addition	And	Equal
Also	Alike	

Contrast

Contrast	Opposite	Differences
But	Either . . . Or	

Cause

Because	The reason for this is . . .

Time

Before	After	During

Teaching Reasoning: Activities and Games for the Classroom © 2015 Marzano Research • marzanoresearch.com
Visit **marzanoresearch.com/activitiesandgames** to download this page.

Relationship Log for Ready, Set, Connect!

Addition

Find two things that are equal or the same in some way.	_____ and _____ How they are the same: _____ _____
Find a group of things and list two examples from that group.	Group: _____ Example: _____ _____ Example: _____ _____
Find three related objects and make a category for them.	_____, _____ and _____ Category: _____

Contrast

Find two things that are opposites or different in some way.	_____ and _____ How they are different: _____ _____
Find a situation where you can choose between one option or another.	Situation: _____ _____ Choices: _____ or _____
Compare two things.	_____ and _____ Alike because: _____ _____ _____ Different because: _____ _____

Teaching Reasoning: Activities and Games for the Classroom © 2015 Marzano Research • marzanoresearch.com
Visit **marzanoresearch.com/activitiesandgames** to download this page.

Cause and Effect

Find something that happens because of something else.	_____ _____ because _____ _____
Find a situation and write down the reason ("why") for it.	Situation: _____ _____ Reason: _____ _____
Find something that only happens if something else happens first.	If _____ _____ _____ then _____ _____ _____

Time

Find something that happens after something else.	_____ _____ after _____ _____
Find something that happens before something else.	_____ _____ before _____ _____
Find something that happens at the same time as something else.	_____ _____ while _____ _____

Teaching Reasoning: Activities and Games for the Classroom © 2015 Marzano Research • marzanoresearch.com
Visit **marzanoresearch.com/activitiesandgames** to download this page.

Relationship Bingo

For elementary school and middle school students

Relationship Bingo helps elementary and middle school students extend their ability to identify relationships between ideas. While Ready, Set, Connect! (see chapter 1) asks students to look for concrete examples in real life, Relationship Bingo helps them to start listening for relationships in what people say. This game is also easily adapted to various skill levels.

Setup

Distribute a bingo board (see the reproducible on page 64) to each student and ask students to write a relationship type in each space, excluding the center free space. Allowing students to fill in their own boards adds a sense of control to a typically luck-based game and ensures that each student will have a different arrangement of relationship types. Either display a list of relationship types on the board or give a list to each student (see the reproducible on page 65). You can easily adapt the game for the age and ability of students by giving them different sets of relationship types to write in the spaces on their bingo boards. Younger students can focus on the four basic relationships using simpler words (such as *alike* instead of addition, *opposite* instead of contrast, and *because* for cause) to talk about them. Older elementary school students can use the standard terms (*addition*, *contrast*, *cause*, and *time*) for the different relationships, and middle school students can further differentiate between the subtypes of the basic relationships. Table 2.1 (page 50) shows the relationship terms we recommend you give to students of different ages to use to fill in their bingo boards.

Reasoning Skills

- Identifying relationships between ideas
- Explaining how evidence supports a conclusion

Materials

- Twenty-five tokens for each student (plastic chips, tiddlywinks, foam pieces, pretzels, and so on)
- Blank bingo board for each student (see reproducible on page 64)
- List of relationship types and signal words (see reproducible on page 66) for each student or displayed where all students can see it
- Teacher clues—pairs of objects or ideas (see pages 54–63)
- Note-taking materials for each student

Table 2.1: Grade-Appropriate Relationship Terms for Bingo Boards

Grades 1–2	Grades 3–5	Middle School
alike	addition	equality
opposite	contrast	restatement
because	cause	example
time	time	summation
		antithesis
		alternative
		comparison
		concession
		direct cause
		result
		reason
		inference
		condition
		subsequent action
		prior action
		concurrent action

 To speed up the process of filling out bingo boards, you can have students use the symbols for the different types of relationships (=, ≠, →, ⇒; see table 1.7 on page 16) instead of writing out the words.

Distribute twenty-five tokens to each student. Students can begin by placing a token on the free space. For older students (grades 3–5 and middle school students), also distribute a copy of the handout showing the relationship types, subtypes, and signal words (see the reproducible on page 66) to each student or display it where all students can refer to it.

Because there are twenty-four spaces to fill in and either four or sixteen words (depending on the age and ability of students), each word will be used multiple times on each student's board. To illustrate, figure 2.1 shows a second grader's Relationship Bingo board after it has been filled in.

 Although each type of relationship appears multiple times on the board, remind students that they may only place one token per clue! Once they have placed a token on a space, they cannot move it later in the game.

B	I	N	G	O
alike	opposite	time	opposite	because
time	because	alike	because	alike
because	opposite	**FREE SPACE**	time	opposite
time	opposite	alike	alike	because
because	time	opposite	because	time

Figure 2.1: Example Relationship Bingo board.

Play

To play Relationship Bingo, the teacher reads out a clue (see items on pages 54–63) and the students listen to the clue and decide what kind of relationship best describes the connection between the two items or sentences in the clue. Then, they search their bingo board for the term that describes that relationship. When they find the word for that relationship in one of their spaces, they place a token on it. If they do not have a space with the appropriate relationship (or if they have already covered all the spaces with that relationship), they do not place a token for that clue. Finally, they use their notepaper to write down why they marked that relationship type for that particular clue so that they can explain their answers at the end of the game.

Along with the terms that students write on their boards, the clues that the teacher reads vary the difficulty level of the game. This chapter includes three types of clues (see pages 54–63). The easiest are word pairs—two words or short phrases. For example, the teacher calls out, "Big . . . little." Students recognize that these words are opposites and mark an appropriate square (*opposite* for younger students, *contrast* for older students) on their boards. They then write "big—little—opposite" or "big—little—contrast" on their notepaper. We recommend these types of clues for students in grades 1–5.

A slightly more difficult type of clue is fill-in-the-blank—a sentence that has a blank where a signal word or phrase would go. Students must think of a signal word or phrase that would fit in the blank and then mark the relationship type associated with that signal word on their bingo board. For example, the teacher says, "I have two pets, a cat _____ a dog." Students realize that the word *and* makes sense in the blank, so they mark an addition square on their boards and write, for example, "cat and dog—addition" on their notepaper. We recommend these types of clues for grades 3 and up.

 The three lists of relationship terms and the three levels of clues can be combined in many ways to help your students progress in their ability to identify relationships. For example, you might have your sixth graders play with sentence pairs and the four main types of relationships before they advance to sentence pairs and the sixteen subtypes. The one combination we do not recommend is using word pair clues with subtype bingo boards, since subtype answers are not provided for word pair clues.

The third and most challenging type of clue is sentence pairs. The teacher reads two short sentences, and students identify and mark the relationship between the ideas expressed in each. For example, consider "The grass is wet. It rained last night." Students would mark the word *cause* (or *direct cause*, if subtypes have been included) on their boards. Last, they record their answers on their papers. Here, a student might write "wet grass—rain—cause (or direct cause)." We recommend these types of clues for middle school students.

Continue to read clues and give students time to identify relationships, place tokens, and record notes about their answers. Traditionally, a winning bingo board consists of five tokens in a row (horizontally, vertically, or diagonally). If a student has placed five tokens (or four and the free space) in a row, he or she calls out "Bingo!" to signal a win.

To add further interest to the game, you can introduce winning bingo patterns other than the traditional five-in-a-row, as shown in table 2.2.

Table 2.2: Bingo Pattern Variations

Variation	Description	Example
Traditional	Five spaces are marked on the board in a horizontal, vertical, or diagonal line. The free space in the center of the board may count toward a bingo.	
Six Pack	The board is marked with a pattern of six connected spaces (three spaces from two rows arranged horizontally or vertically). The free space in the center of the board may count toward a bingo.	
Bullseye	The free space in the center of the board is surrounded by marked spaces.	

Postage Stamps	Four spaces are marked to create a square in a corner of the board. To make the game last longer, mark a total of eight spaces to create two squares in separate corners of the board.	
Flying Kite	Four spaces are marked to create a square in a corner of the board. From here, three spaces are marked diagonally from the corner space to an opposite corner of the board, resembling a kite. The free space counts toward a bingo.	
Sandwich	The entire top and bottom rows of the board are marked.	
Railroad	The entire left and right columns of the board are marked.	
Inverted Bingo	In this twist, any player that gets a bingo is knocked out of the game. The player that marks the most spaces on his or her board without getting a bingo is the winner. A fun way to play this game is to have everyone stand at their seats at first, then sit when they are eliminated. The free space counts toward a bingo.	
Blackout	All spaces on the board are marked. This variation can take a lot of time and works best at the end of a bingo session.	

Source: Adapted from Rogers & Simms, 2015.

Wrap-Up

Once a student has a winning board, he must then explain each token that led to the bingo. For each space involved in the bingo, the student must explain which clue he used to cover that space. Using the notes taken at each move, the student reads the two ideas and the relationship between them. For example, if the first space of the bingo says *cause*, the student would need to explain that he used a clue involving, for example, bug bites and no insect repellent. If necessary, ask the student to explain his thinking. In some cases, the relationship between two things or ideas might be interpreted in different ways. For example, if you read the word pair "cats . . . dogs," some students might identify that as an *alike* relationship because they are both pet animals, while others could view them as *opposites*. Similarly, the sentence pair "The grass is wet. It rained last night" could be appropriately classified as a *direct cause* relationship or an *inference* relationship.

If a student calls out "Bingo!" but has incorrectly marked a relationship on his or her board, that student must remove that token, and the game continues. Therefore, remind other students not to clear their boards when someone says "Bingo!" For example, if a student heard the clue, "I have two pets, a cat _____ a dog" and marked "contrast" on her board, thinking that the missing word was *or* (which does not make sense, given the phrase "I have two pets"), she would not have a complete bingo.

Teacher Clues for Relationship Bingo

These sets of clues are for teachers to read out during a game of Relationship Bingo. They are divided into three sets and ordered by difficulty:

1. **Word Pairs**—Simplest version. The teacher reads out two words or short phrases, and students mark the basic relationship that describes how the two words relate to each other.

2. **Fill-in-the-Blank**—Intermediate version. The teacher reads a sentence that has a word or phrase missing. Students listen, decide what signal word or phrase best fits in the blank, and mark the relationship type or subtype that corresponds to the missing word or phrase.

3. **Sentence Pairs**—Most challenging version. The teacher reads two sentences. Students decide what relationship type or subtype connects the ideas expressed in each sentence and mark a corresponding space on their boards.

Each teacher clue also lists at least one correct relationship that students might mark on their board. Where more than one correct relationship is listed, they are separated by a semicolon (for example, *addition; contrast*). For the word pairs, we list the simpler term for the relationship in parentheses after the traditional term—for example, *cause (because)*. For fill-in-the-blank and sentence pair clues, we list the basic relationship type and the subtype, separated by a dash (for example, *addition—restatement*). Keep in mind, however, that these answers are not exhaustive and there may be further interpretations of the clue. For example, the word pair *stay home from school; you are sick* has a cause relationship listed with it. Students could, however, think, "Well, you stay home from school *while* you are sick," and mark it as a time relationship. When students who get a bingo are explaining their answers, it is okay to accept answers other than those listed here, as long as the student's reasoning makes sense.

Word Pairs

Word 1	Word 2	Relationship(s)
winter	summer	addition (alike); contrast (opposite); time
sit on the couch	watch television	cause (because); time
bug bites	no insect repellent	cause (because)
dog's tail wagging	dog treats	cause (because)
movie	play (in a theater)	addition (alike); contrast (opposite)
wind	rain	addition (alike); contrast (opposite)
over	under	contrast (opposite)
today	tomorrow	time
solid	liquid	contrast (opposite)

Word 1	Word 2	Relationship(s)
eat breakfast	eat lunch	time
sunrise	sunset	contrast (opposite); time
hat	gloves	addition (alike); contrast (opposite)
stop the car	red light	cause (because)
bird	butterfly	addition (alike); contrast (opposite)
the dog is panting	it is hot out	cause (because)
tongue	teeth	addition (alike); contrast (opposite)
now	then	contrast (opposite); time
tuna	turkey	addition (alike); contrast (opposite)
eat lunch	eat dinner	time
October	November	addition (alike); time
rain	storm	addition (alike)
cup	mug	addition (alike)
baseball	football	addition (alike); contrast (opposite)
drop-off	pick-up	contrast (opposite); time
school	home	contrast (opposite)
cats	dogs	addition (alike); contrast (opposite)
funny	hilarious	addition (alike)
turn on air conditioning	hot outside	cause (because)
close	near	addition (alike)
wide	narrow	contrast (opposite)
first grade	second grade	addition (alike); time
happy	recess	cause (because)
snow	snow day	cause (because)
scarves	winter clothes	addition (alike)
fish	dolphins	addition (alike); contrast (opposite)
book	movie	addition (alike); contrast (opposite)
young	old	contrast (opposite)
smooth	rough	contrast (opposite)
yell	whisper	contrast (opposite)
trip	fall down	cause (because)
doll	toy	addition (alike)
sleepy	tired	addition (alike)
blocks	marbles	addition (alike); contrast (opposite)
pencils	paper	addition (alike); contrast (opposite)
see lightning	hear thunder	time
it is light out	daytime	addition (alike); cause (because)
pencils	markers	addition (alike)
use lots of tissues	nose is runny	cause (because)

Continued on next page →

Word 1	Word 2	Relationship(s)
leaves are red	colder temperatures	cause (because)
delicious	disgusting	contrast (opposite)
lions	tigers	addition (alike); contrast (opposite)
fun	boring	contrast (opposite)
bus	car	addition (alike); contrast (opposite)
hungry	forgot to eat breakfast	cause (because)
cry	see something sad	cause (because)
basketball	baseball	addition (alike); contrast (opposite)
window	door	addition (alike); contrast (opposite)
sister	brother	addition (alike); contrast (opposite)
morning	evening	contrast (opposite); time
uncle	grandfather	addition (alike); contrast (opposite)
tired	stayed up late	cause (because)
kindergarten	first grade	addition (alike); time
6 a.m.	11 a.m.	time
tight	loose	contrast (opposite)
skiing	snowboarding	addition (alike); contrast (opposite)
brush your teeth	go to bed	time
curvy	straight	contrast (opposite)
teacher	principal	addition (alike); contrast (opposite)
back	front	contrast (opposite)
dogs	wolves	addition (alike); contrast (opposite)
inside	outside	contrast (opposite)
air	earth	addition (alike); contrast (opposite)
morning	night	contrast (opposite); time
sunny	cloudy	contrast (opposite)
eat dinner	eat dessert	time
car	truck	addition (alike); contrast (opposite)
short	tall	contrast (opposite)
thirsty	drink water	cause (because); time
ocean	lake	addition (alike); contrast (opposite)
mix cake batter	bake the cake	time
become smart	go to school	cause (because)
mom	dad	addition (alike); contrast (opposite)
cartoons	news	addition (alike); contrast (opposite)
owls	hawks	addition (alike); contrast (opposite)
glass of orange juice	breakfast	addition (alike); time
see	hear	addition (alike); contrast (opposite)
stay home from school	you are sick	cause (because)
big	little	contrast (opposite)

Word 1	Word 2	Relationship(s)
cut	scab	addition (alike); contrast (opposite); cause (because)
before	after	contrast (opposite); time
wise	foolish	contrast (opposite)
cut	bruise	addition (alike)
angry	calm	contrast (opposite)
blue	orange	addition (alike); contrast (opposite)
bedtime story	go to sleep	time
the grass is wet	it rained	cause (because)
January	September	time
clean	dirty	contrast (opposite)
pants	shirts	addition (alike); contrast (opposite)
lots of energy	good night's sleep	cause (because)

Fill-in-the-Blank

Sentence	Relationship Type & Subtype
The Rocky Mountains are tall, _____ the Himalayas are taller.	contrast—comparison
We let the dog outside on a hot day. _____ she was panting when she came inside.	time—subsequent action; cause—result
The cat is scared _____ Julian threw a baseball at it.	cause—reason
Yvette slept through her alarm clock, _____ she missed the bus.	cause—result
Keely writes in her diary daily; _____ she must be a good writer with all that practice.	cause—inference, result
April doesn't like mosquitoes _____ they bite her.	cause—reason
Our dog is ferocious. _____ her dog is friendly.	contrast—comparison
Betty waited in the car _____ her mom went into the store.	time—concurrent action
Pedro earns his allowance _____ helping his mom in the garden.	cause—direct cause
We could watch a scary movie _____ a funny movie.	contrast—alternative
_____ we forget to pick her up, _____ she will be angry with us.	cause—condition
She went for a run _____ she took a long, cold shower.	time—subsequent action; cause—result
Jamal felt sick _____ eating twelve hot dogs.	time—subsequent action
I have two pets, a cat _____ a dog.	addition—equality
Trina likes to eat southern food, _____ collard greens.	addition—example
The state bird of Massachusetts is the chickadee, _____ it is not the robin.	contrast—antithesis
I would like to either go to the beach _____ go hiking.	contrast—alternative

Continued on next page →

Sentence	Relationship Type & Subtype
I went jogging, did jumping jacks, and lifted weights. _____, I am tired.	addition—summation; cause—result
There are many ways to get around, _____ on a bike, on foot, or by car.	addition—example
Ants are insects; _____ they have six legs and three body segments.	addition—restatement
It rained the whole time; _____ we had a fun camping trip.	contrast—concession
If it's raining, bring an umbrella _____ wear a raincoat.	contrast—alternative
I love unicorns. _____, they are my favorite animal.	addition—restatement
We'll be able to sneak some cookies from the cookie jar _____ you stay really quiet when we're downstairs.	cause—condition
We could play four square. _____, we could play soccer and everyone could play.	contrast—alternative
Cara must be a good singer, _____ she would not be in a band.	cause—inference
Mpesh bumped into the table, _____ she has a bruise.	cause—result
_____, you, the rest of the class, and I are doing a great job.	addition—summation
I like school _____ I get to see my friends.	cause—reason
Bekah eats pretzels every day, _____ she will probably get sick of them.	cause—inference
Restaurants usually serve desserts that many people like. _____, tiramisu is one type of dessert that is popular.	addition—example
Kyle and Tim are both fast runners. _____ Kyle is definitely the fastest.	contrast—concession
Brian has to _____ vacuum the floor _____ put away the dishes.	contrast—alternative
The United States became a country _____ the Revolutionary War.	time—subsequent action; cause—result
We forgot our mittens; _____ we should keep our hands in our pockets.	cause—inference
Billy was acting inappropriately. _____, he is in time-out.	cause—result
Sarai likes pizza _____ not breadsticks.	contrast—antithesis
Her hair is red _____ her brother's hair is black.	contrast—comparison
Vivi's favorite animal is a badger _____ it is fierce.	cause—reason
My brother is annoying; _____ I love him.	contrast—concession
Breakfast _____ lunch are my favorite meals.	addition—equality
I burned the roof of my mouth _____ the pizza was too hot.	cause—reason
Recess is my favorite time of day _____ I like going outside to play.	cause—reason
It is summer in the southern hemisphere _____ it is winter in the northern hemisphere.	time—concurrent action
I like books. _____, reading is my favorite hobby.	addition—restatement
We eat lunch _____ we are at school.	time—concurrent action
We all went on a long hike, _____ we need to take a nap.	cause—result

Sentence	Relationship Type & Subtype
The moon _____ the sun are in the sky.	addition—equality
Matt writes great poems, _____ sings horribly.	contrast—antithesis
Dinosaurs lived _____ humans.	time—prior action
Many animals come out at night, _____ owls.	addition—example
We are going to the mall; _____ my sister will buy another pair of shoes!	cause—inference
She loves to read _____ watch movies.	addition—equality
Sure, Kate runs fast, _____ she does not run as fast as someone in the Olympics.	contrast—comparison, concession
Sven didn't study for the test, _____ he failed.	cause—result
Eli and Martha arrived late to the concert; _____ they had a good time.	contrast—concession
Lisa is blonde, _____ she dyes her hair brown.	contrast—antithesis
_____ the traffic is clear, then we can drive faster.	cause—condition; time—subsequent action
There was a crack in the window _____ the hail.	cause—reason, direct cause
I got a fine from the library _____ I lost my book on the bus.	cause—reason; time—subsequent action
Write your essay either on the computer _____ by hand.	contrast—alternative
We waited an hour _____ Mr. Jones showed up.	time—prior action
During recess, Haley jumped rope _____ Megan did the monkey bars.	time—concurrent action
This restaurant serves Indian food _____ curry.	addition—example
You can prevent sickness _____ eating a balanced diet.	cause—direct cause
Chris got a lot of votes, _____ not as many votes as Diane.	contrast—comparison
Justin loves to skateboard, _____ Elle just likes to watch.	contrast—comparison
Jessica takes ballet and tap classes; _____ she is a dancer.	addition—summation
_____ the weather, school is going to be closed today.	cause—reason
She is wearing a blue skirt _____ blue shoes.	addition—equality
Peanut butter _____ jelly are a match made in sandwich heaven.	addition—equality
The road was closed _____ we had to go the other way.	cause—result
She plays soccer, softball, and basketball. _____, she is very athletic.	addition—summation
Marcus is tall, _____ his brother is short.	contrast—comparison
Baseball has many different positions; _____, there are nine people on the field.	addition—summation
Candy is the snack I eat the most. _____, it's my favorite snack.	addition—restatement
_____ it is August, it will be hot outside.	cause—condition, result; time—concurrent action
We are talking about famous baseball players, _____ Babe Ruth.	addition—example
He likes to read fantasy books: _____, the *Harry Potter* series.	addition—example

Continued on next page →

Sentence	Relationship Type & Subtype
Before class, I was confused; _____ class, I understood.	time—subsequent action
_____ I was hungry, but then I ate dinner.	time—prior action
I brush my teeth, _____ I use mouthwash.	time—subsequent action
I want to join the swim team; _____ my schedule is already pretty full.	contrast—concession
The nail goes into the board _____ you hammer it.	cause—direct cause; time—concurrent action
He is my dad's brother; _____ he is my uncle.	addition—restatement
_____, Jerome, Mikey, Sebastian, Will, and Niall make up the boys' basketball team.	addition—summation
You turn off the water _____ I go get some towels!	time—concurrent action
We should leave now, _____ we will be late.	cause—inference
We danced _____ dawn.	time—subsequent action, prior action
_____ we study, _____ we will do well on our test.	cause—condition
There is a poster _____ a calendar hanging on the wall.	addition—equality
_____ we stick together, then everything will be okay.	cause—condition
Caitlyn's hair was shorter on one side _____ an accident with the scissors.	cause—reason, direct cause
The hamster is cute, _____ he is not that fun to play with.	contrast—concession
For dinner I had pasta. _____ I had green beans.	addition—equality
Wolves are big _____ coyotes.	contrast—comparison
_____ there were three kids on the swings, but after a few minutes there were five.	time—prior action
He is mean. _____ he is cruel.	addition—restatement
I like grapes, _____ I like oranges more.	contrast—antithesis
The answer is A, _____ C.	contrast—antithesis

Sentence Pairs

Sentence Pair	Relationship Type & Subtype
She went by Catherine in high school. She went by Tinkerbell in middle school.	time—prior action
Toby picked up the toys off the floor. He vacuumed.	time—subsequent action
Please turn in your homework. If you didn't do it, you must stay inside for recess.	cause—condition
I like art class the most. I love drawing.	cause—reason; addition—restatement
Derek aced that test. Marie answered all the questions correctly.	addition—equality
We should buy streamers, pick up the cake, and clean the house. We have a lot of work to do before the party.	addition—summation
She likes to alpine ski. She doesn't like to waterski.	contrast—antithesis

Sentence Pair	Relationship Type & Subtype
The United States, Spain, Ghana, and Costa Rica all qualified for the World Cup. They all have good soccer teams.	addition—restatement
Addis is great at trivia. He knows the capitals of all the countries in the world.	addition—example
Superman, Batman, Wonder Woman, Flash, Green Lantern, and Aquaman are all superheroes. When they are together, they form the Justice League.	addition—summation
Morning is my favorite time of day. My brother stays up all night.	contrast—comparison
Nanette ate a slug. Nanette got sick.	cause—result
We will not leave the classroom during the test. We will leave the classroom if the fire alarm goes off.	cause—condition
The carnival workers give out ribbons, stuffed animals, and stickers. The carnival workers give out prizes.	addition—summation
There was turbulence on the plane. The wind was stronger than expected.	cause—reason, direct cause
We will go swimming. We must wait twenty minutes from when we've last eaten.	cause—condition; time—subsequent action
Breton drinks green tea. Breton's throat hurts.	cause—reason
I just saw lightning and heard thunder. The weather is not good.	addition—restatement
We have to pay the water bill and the electric bill. That's over one hundred dollars.	addition—summation
You can drive. You must be sixteen to drive.	cause—condition
Cathy is afraid of flying. She will fly in an airplane to her sister's wedding.	contrast—concession
My dad drinks his juice during breakfast. My mom eats her eggs during breakfast.	time—concurrent action
There are many great sleuths in literature. Sherlock Holmes is a sleuth.	addition—example
Naya might go swimming. She might go on a hike with her mom.	contrast—alternative
The grass is wet. It rained last night.	cause—direct result, inference
The phone rang. Marianne was calling.	cause—reason
There is a crack in the windshield. There was hail last night.	cause—inference, reason
I thought I didn't like pomegranates. I tried pomegranates, and they were yummy.	contrast—concession; time—subsequent action
We could drive to the movie theater. We could ride our bikes there.	contrast—alternative
Bertha loves roller coasters. The Cyclone is a rollercoaster.	addition—example
Earth orbits the sun. Venus orbits the sun.	addition—equality
Math is hard. Vocabulary is harder.	contrast—comparison
Julia will answer the phone. Julia will let it go to voicemail.	contrast—alternative
There are many chores to do. You could sweep the kitchen.	addition—example
The Prime Minister is the head of the government of Canada. The President is the head of the government of the United States.	contrast—comparison
Lacey likes to paint. Lacey does not like to clean.	contrast—antithesis
Jasmina gets straight As. Jasmina is one of the best students in the class.	addition—restatement
We are going to several European countries. We are going to England.	addition—example

Continued on next page →

Sentence Pair	Relationship Type & Subtype
My cat is brown. My dog is brown.	addition—equality
Bethany stayed motivated. She gave herself small rewards.	cause—direct cause
The North won the American Civil War. Slaves were freed.	cause—result
Lia gave her teacher a present. Lia went on summer vacation.	time—prior action
Martin Luther King Jr. won the Nobel Peace Prize. He did great things for this world.	cause—reason
France used to be an empire. Britain used to be an empire.	addition—equality
War and Peace is a very long book. "The Lottery" is a short story.	contrast—comparison
She likes to cook. She likes to run after dinner.	addition—equality; time—subsequent action
Dillon is tall. Michael Jordan is taller.	contrast—comparison
Let's play rock-paper-scissors to figure out who goes first. We could flip a coin to figure out who goes first.	contrast—alternative
Raquel took off her shoes. She came into the house.	time—prior action
The new carpet in the living room is shaggy and soft. Our dog is shaggy and soft.	addition—equality
Missy doesn't seem happy. She must have lost her favorite necklace.	cause—inference
Ming Lee is very hungry. She won't eat her vegetables.	contrast—concession
The painting sold for a million dollars. I still didn't think it was very good.	contrast—concession
We ate spaghetti and meatballs. We ate a dessert of chocolate cake.	time—prior action, subsequent action
In the morning, it was cloudy. It cleared up to be a nice day.	time—subsequent action
Albert Einstein is a famous scientist. Isaac Newton is a famous scientist.	addition—equality
Eliza will eat Thai food. She does not eat food with peanuts in it.	contrast—concession
Mrs. Norris found a wallet on the ground. She turned it in to the police station.	time—prior action, subsequent action
An iris is a type of flower. A sunflower is a type of flower.	addition—equality
We ate dinner. Our puppy begged at the table.	time—concurrent action
She thinks kangaroos are cute. She thinks koala bears are ugly and weird.	contrast—antithesis
Kaitlyn eats oranges. They are delicious.	cause—reason
Roberta tore a hole in the knee of her jeans. She fell on concrete.	cause—direct cause
The jury thought he was not guilty. The judge thought he was guilty.	time—concurrent action; contrast—antithesis
There are many women who are scientists. Marie Curie was a female scientist.	addition—example
Hillary has bad eyesight. She has to wear glasses.	cause—result
Horace was texting while driving. Horace ran into a telephone pole.	time—subsequent action; cause—result
I'm going to read *The Bridge to Terabithia*. Noel is going to read *The Giver.*	contrast—comparison; time—concurrent action
We could go to Japan! We could go to Kenya!	contrast—alternative
The dog is panting. She just went on a long run.	cause—reason

Sentence Pair	Relationship Type & Subtype
The house smells good. Bread is baking.	time—concurrent action; cause—reason
Laurel has red hair. Neither of her parents has red hair.	contrast—comparison, concession
I'm grateful. I have a great family and great friends.	cause—reason
Xander fell off his bike. He has a cast on his arm.	cause—result
An American invented the lightning rod. Benjamin Franklin invented the lightning rod.	addition—restatement
We saw alligators, lions, and polar bears. There are many different animals at the zoo.	addition—summation
Usain Bolt set a world record for sprinting at the Olympics. He is the fastest man in the world.	addition—restatement
The pharaohs built the pyramids. They used thousands of workers to build the pyramids.	cause—direct cause
George Washington was a president. Abraham Lincoln was a president.	addition—equality
The cat will let me pet her. The cat tries to scratch my mom.	contrast—antithesis
The seeds Nora planted grew. The seeds Jaime planted did not grow.	contrast—comparison, antithesis
Henry put his shoes on the wrong feet. He knocked out his two front teeth when he tripped.	cause—result
Someone is knocking at the door. Someone must be there.	cause—inference
I'll eat the spoonful of mustard. You will give me twenty dollars.	cause—condition
Colorado has the highest average elevation of any U.S. state. Delaware has the lowest.	contrast—comparison
In the story you meet a girl. The girl moves away.	time—subsequent action
I am tired. I want to go to bed.	addition—restatement; cause—result
We washed our hands. We cooked dinner.	time—subsequent action
You can make a diorama for your book report. You can write a short essay.	contrast—alternative
Greta usually gets to class early. Today she was late.	contrast—antithesis
She smells bad. She should take a shower.	cause—inference
Our dog ate from the trash can. Our dog threw up on the steps.	cause—result
Frances did not win. It is still good that she tried.	contrast—concession
There are many breeds of dogs. The dog we have is a Great Dane.	addition—example
Be nice to your younger sister. She will probably yell at you if you are not nice.	cause—inference
They repaved the road. The road had many potholes.	cause—reason
We could have pancakes for dinner. We could have waffles for dinner.	contrast—alternative
The rollerblades are twenty dollars. That is still a pretty good price.	contrast—concession
The recipe needs eggs, butter, spinach, tortillas, and chocolate. The recipe calls for a lot of things we don't have.	addition—summation
The United States colonies fought for independence from Britain during the Revolutionary War. The United States became its own country.	cause—result; time—subsequent action
Jojo is good at violin. She must have practiced a lot.	cause—inference

Student Bingo Board for Relationship Bingo

B	I	N	G	O
		FREE SPACE		

Relationship Types (for Filling in Bingo Boards)

Grades 1–2

alike

opposite

because

time

Grades 3–5

addition

contrast

cause

time

Middle School

equality

restatement

example

summation

antithesis

alternative

comparison

concession

direct cause

result

reason

inference

condition

subsequent action

prior action

concurrent action

Relationship Types, Subtypes, and Signal Words and Phrases Chart for Relationship Bingo

Type	Subtype	Signal Words and Phrases
Addition	1. Equality: He is tall *and* he is handsome.	*and, as well, at the same time, besides, equally, furthermore, in addition, likewise, moreover, similarly, too, what is more*
	2. Restatement: I am tired. *In fact*, I am exhausted.	*actually, another way of saying this, in actuality, indeed, in fact, namely, that is, that is to say*
	3. Example: He does many things well. *For example*, he is excellent at cards.	*another example would be; first, second, third . . .; for a start; for example; for another thing; for one thing; last but not least; next, then, finally . . .; one, two, three . . .; such as; to begin with*
	4. Summation: He cooks. He sews. He fixes appliances. *In all*, he is an excellent homemaker.	*all in all, altogether, briefly, in all, in a word, in brief, in conclusion, in short, in sum, overall, then, therefore, thus, to summarize, to sum up*
Contrast	1. Antithesis: I will be there, *but* I won't be happy.	*but, contrariwise, conversely, else, not, on the contrary, on the other hand, oppositely, or rather, otherwise, what is better, what is worse, yet*
	2. Alternative: *Either* it will rain *or* it will snow.	*alternatively, either . . . or, neither . . . nor, or, rather than, sooner than*
	3. Comparison: Bill is tall. *In comparison*, his brother is short.	*but, compared to, in comparison, in contrast, like, whereas*
	4. Concession: I don't like rock music. *Nonetheless*, I'll meet you at the concert.	*all the same, anyhow, anyway, at any rate, besides, else, for all that, however, in any case, in any event, in spite of that, nevertheless, nonetheless, only, regardless of this, still, though*
Cause	1. Direct cause: He won the race *by* maintaining his concentration.	*by, due to, owing to, through*
	2. Result: Bill went home. *Consequently*, the party ended.	*accordingly, as a consequence, as a result, consequently, for all that, hence, now, so, therefore, the result was, thus, whereupon*
	3. Reason: He went to the store *because* he needed food.	*because, because of, for the fact that, in that, on account of, since, so, so that, this is the reason*
	4. Inference: Mary is going on a long trip. *In that case*, she should plan well.	*in that case, or else, otherwise, so, then*
	5. Condition: *Unless* you stop, I will leave.	*admitting that, as long as, assuming that, considering that, granted that, if, if . . . then, in so far as, no sooner, now that, presuming that, seeing that, providing that, supposing that, unless, when . . . then, where . . . there*
Time	1. Subsequent action: They went to the game. *Afterward*, they went to the dance.	*after, after that, afterward, as yet, before, finally, in the end, later, next, shortly, since, so far, subsequently, then, until*
	2. Prior action: Math class is *before* lunch.	*at first, before, beforehand, before now, before that, by now, by then, earlier, formerly, initially, in the beginning, originally, previously, until, until then, up to now*
	3. Concurrent action: Mary and Bill watched television *during* dinner.	*at the same time, at this point, during, meantime, meanwhile, simultaneously, when, while*

3 Conditional Cards

For elementary school and middle school students

Conditional Cards allows students to practice identifying and creating conditional (if–then) statements that logically correspond to declarative statements. People often make declarative statements that have hidden reasoning in them; Conditional Cards gives students the opportunity to analyze declarative statements and transform them into conditional statements that logically follow from the original. This skill allows them to better understand the reasoning in statements they hear and to detect errors that may be present in those statements. Students will also practice identifying relationships between phrases (such as cause and effect or evidence and conclusion) that only make logical sense in a specific order. This game is based on an activity from Khan Academy's online tutorial on logical reasoning (see www.khanacademy.org). Here, we give an overview of the game, followed by four variations on how to play: (1) as a collaborative class activity, (2) as an individual activity, (3) as a competitive team game, and (4) as a competitive individual game. Setup, play, and wrap-up are described for each variation.

Each variation of this game involves presenting students with a declarative prompt statement, which they then transform into a conditional statement by ordering the elements of the statement logically. The component words and phrases that make up the conditional statement are printed on a number of separate cards which students arrange like puzzle pieces to create the solution.

Reasoning Skills

- Identifying relationships between ideas
- Standardizing reasoning
- Evaluating deductive conclusions

Materials

- Larger printouts of Conditional Cards (for variation 1)
- Sets of Conditional Cards (see reproducibles, pages 75–90)
- Answer sheets for Conditional Cards (for variation 2; see reproducible on page 74)
- Glue sticks (for variation 2)
- Timer (for variations 3 and 4)

For example, the teacher presents this declarative statement:

Kangaroos cannot walk backward.

Students receive a set of cards like the one shown in figure 3.1, cut apart and shuffled into random order.

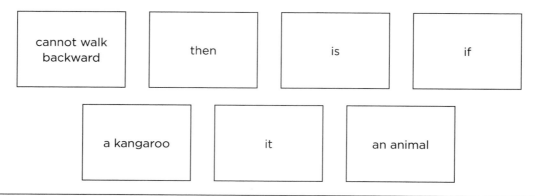

Figure 3.1: Conditional Cards for "Kangaroos cannot walk backward" in random order.

Students must rearrange the cards into a correct conditional statement, like "If an animal is a kangaroo then it cannot walk backward," as shown in figure 3.2.

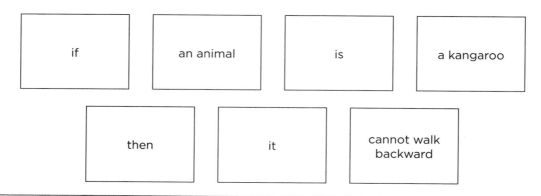

Figure 3.2: Correct arrangement of Conditional Cards.

As students work, they may mistakenly create a sentence like "If an animal cannot walk backward, then it is a kangaroo." If this happens, you should discuss with students why the statement is not logically valid: there could be other animals that cannot walk backward. Being a kangaroo guarantees that the animal cannot walk backward, but lacking the ability to walk backward does not guarantee that an animal is a kangaroo—it could be an emu, which also cannot walk backward. In this relationship, *kangaroo* is an item inside the larger category of *animals that cannot walk backward*; reversing the reasoning is not valid. You might illustrate this using an Euler diagram (see page 69) as in figure 3.3.

Figure 3.3: Euler diagram of "Kangaroos cannot walk backward."

Some statements, however, may be translated into conditionals that *do* work both backward and forward. For example, the statement "Water boils at 212 degrees Fahrenheit" can be expressed conditionally as either "If water is boiling, then it is at 212 degrees Fahrenheit" or "If water is at 212 degrees Fahrenheit, then it is boiling," as shown by the Euler diagram in figure 3.4.

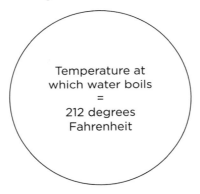

Figure 3.4: Euler diagram for "Water boils at 212 degrees Fahrenheit."

As a general rule, statements that describe categories (for example, "Pandas are a type of bear that does not hibernate") or cause and effect relationships (for example, "Washing your hands helps you not get sick") will only work in one direction, whereas statements that define something or relate two equivalent concepts (for example, "A leap year has 366 days") will work either way.

This chapter includes premade sets of Conditional Cards (see pages 75–90); each one has a declarative statement and a related conditional sentence broken up onto reproducible cards. The cards in the reproducibles appear in the correct order so that teachers can use those pages as an answer key to check students' work during the activities. Declarative statements that can be arranged in multiple ways (such as "Water boils at 212 degrees Fahrenheit") are indicated with an asterisk. We suggest that teachers white out or cut off the asterisks before presenting the statements and cards to students.

Variation 1: Collaborative Class Activity

In this variation, selected students hold large-print versions of Conditional Cards and arrange themselves in front of the class to form a logical conditional statement. The rest of the class checks the conditional statement and offers suggestions for improvement or correction, if necessary.

Setup

The only advance preparation required for this version of the game is to create sets of large-print Conditional Cards. The cards must be fairly large—4" × 6" index cards at minimum—with large print so all students can read them from a distance.

Play

Choose students to hold the Conditional Cards at the front of the class. You will need the same number of students as there are cards in a particular conditional statement (typically four to eight). Give one card to each student. Read the related declarative statement, and then give the selected students a few moments to arrange themselves into a conditional statement that logically follows from the original. It is also helpful to display or write the prompt on the board so students can reference it as needed. Once the students holding the cards think they have the answer, ask the rest of the class to evaluate the statement. If the class agrees with the students at the front, ask a seated student to explain the reasoning. If the class does not agree, seated students can politely direct the students at the front into a different order and explain why they think the new statement is correct.

 This version of the game focuses the whole class's attention on a small group of students. As such, you will likely want to set guidelines for behavior to make sure it stays fun for everyone. Before starting the activity, establish rules such as "Class members must raise their hands to change the order of the cards" and "Class members should use polite words and tone of voice when evaluating the statement."

Wrap-Up

Once the correct answer has been achieved, briefly discuss it or diagram it on the board (using an Euler diagram), as it may not be immediately obvious to all students why, for example, "If an animal is a dog, then it has four legs" is the correct interpretation of "Dogs have four legs," but "If an animal has four legs, then it is a dog" is not.

If there is conflict about the correctness of the conditional statement (that is, some students think it is right and some think it is wrong), give students from both sides the chance to explain their reasoning. Encourage them to draw Euler diagrams to explain and support their positions. In the course of this discussion, students may naturally come to agreement about the correct answer; however, if the conversation becomes stalled or unproductive, you may need to end it and explain which conditional statement is correct.

Variation 2: Individual Activity

In this variation, students arrange their cards, glue them onto an answer sheet (see reproducible, page 74), and explain their reasoning.

Setup

For each declarative statement, you will need as many answer sheets and sets of cards as there are students in the class. Each student will also need a glue stick. We recommend writing the appropriate declarative statement for each round at the top of the answer sheet before making copies for students. To familiarize students with declarative and conditional statements, you might play a few rounds of variation 1 before asking students to play this variation. Be sure to establish ground rules for this variation, such as whether students should work individually or are allowed to confer with neighbors. Explain to students that they should arrange their cards to match the statement written at the top of their answer sheet, and then explain their reasoning using words or pictures (Euler diagrams are an excellent option). This low-pressure activity is ideal for use with younger students; we recommend that you distribute answer sheets and cards for one statement at a time, and let students finish arranging and gluing before passing out the next set, so as to prevent confusion.

Play

Once all students have their cards and answer sheets, ask them to arrange the cards into a conditional statement that follows logically from the declarative statement on their papers. You might read the statement aloud or write it on the board before students start working. Encourage students to arrange their cards and explain their reasoning before they glue the cards down. To explain their reasoning, they might use words (for example, "Lots of animals have four legs, so 'dogs' has to come first") or Euler diagrams. This activity can be easily scaffolded at various levels depending on the ability and experience of the students. You might talk through the first few examples before letting students try the rest on their own. Diagramming statements on the board and asking leading questions are also effective ways to prompt students toward the correct solution. For example, you might ask, "Which category is bigger? Dogs, or animals with four legs?" or "Are dogs the only animals with four legs?"

Wrap-Up

After this activity is complete, you can collect the answer sheets and use them as an unobtrusive assessment to gauge student progress.

Variation 3: Competitive Team Game

In this variation, students work in teams to arrange the cards into a conditional statement in competition with other groups.

Setup

For each declarative statement, you will need as many sets of cards as there are groups in the class (if the class is split into five groups, you will need five copies of the same set of cards). Students will need to be able to work together, so make sure each group has enough space to do so. If you are using this as a brief sponge activity to "soak up" a few minutes at the beginning or end of class, students may be able to simply gather around one desk. If you plan to play numerous rounds, consider arranging the desks into groups to create more comfortable spaces for students to work.

Divide the class into groups of four to six students. Pass out a face-down set of cards to each group, but instruct them not to look at the cards yet. With the cards still face down, have students divide the cards up between the members of the group. Because the number of cards in each set will vary slightly and groups might not all be the same size, a student might be responsible for one card or two. Explain that each student can only touch his or her own card(s)—this is to ensure that all students participate and that a group does not become dominated by one member. Set a time limit for each round of the game. Rounds will be fairly short—perhaps only thirty seconds or one minute.

Play

Once the cards have been distributed, write or display the corresponding declarative statement on the board and read it aloud. When you say "Go" and start the timer, students can then flip over their cards. Working as a group and touching only their own cards, students race to form a conditional statement that follows logically from the original. When time is up, all groups must stop working. You can then quickly check each team's conditional statement.

Wrap-Up

If a team has created a valid conditional statement, award them a point. If the team has created an incorrect conditional statement or failed to create a complete statement, they do not receive a point for that round. You might keep score on chart paper or a whiteboard at the front of the room.

This game is versatile because you can play numerous rounds in a row, play a single round as a sponge activity, or use it as the basis for a long-term competition.

 If students become very comfortable with this activity and consistently arrange the statements correctly, you can up the ante for an additional challenge. Give each team multiple sets of cards—perhaps ten or twenty—and a time limit. Each set will need to include a slip of paper or additional card with the appropriate declarative statement for that set of cards written on it. The time limit will depend on how many sets each team has, as well as the proficiency level of the students, but we suggest starting with two to three minutes for every ten sets of cards. When you start the timer, the teams start solving the sets. Whichever team correctly arranges the most conditional statements before time runs out wins!

Variation 4: Competitive Individual Game

In this variation, individual students compete against each other.

Setup

For this game, you will need as many sets of Conditional Cards as there are students in the class. Each set need not be the same as long as the difficulty level is fairly consistent—try to use sets that consist of approximately the same number of cards. In fact, using a different set for each student means you can play multiple rounds in a row simply by asking students to trade sets with someone else (we recommend keeping each set in its own plastic sandwich bag or paper clip to avoid mixing sets). For this variation, each set of cards must also come with a slip of paper or card that shows its declarative statement. Set a brief time limit and distribute a set of cards to each student.

Play

When you say "Go" and start the timer, students read their declarative statement and use the cards to form a valid conditional statement based on the statement.

Wrap-Up

When time is up, quickly check each student's answer. If the student is correct, he or she gets a point. Students who are familiar with the game can pair up and check each other's answers. Once everyone's answer has been checked and points recorded, each student passes his or her set of cards to another student and the next round begins.

This variation can also be played as a relay. Divide the class into two teams, and give each student a set of cards, face down. When you say "Go," the first student on each team flips over the cards and solves the statement. The next student cannot flip over his or her cards and start working until the first has finished and you have checked the answer. Do not spend time explaining why a conditional statement is right or wrong; a simple *yes* or *no* is most appropriate for this relay race. If the answer is incorrect, you say "No" and that student keeps trying. If the answer is correct, you say "Yes" and the next student in the relay flips over his or her cards and begins working. The first team on which every student has created a valid conditional statement wins.

Answer Sheet for Conditional Cards (Variation 2)

Declarative Statement: _____

PASTE YOUR CONDITIONAL CARDS HERE

Explain your reasoning in words or pictures:

Sets of Conditional Cards

These sets of Conditional Cards are organized into age-appropriate sets for lower elementary, upper elementary, and middle school students. If you are a teacher of older students, you may decide to start off with lower-level sets to help familiarize students with the game before moving to more challenging items. Each set consists of a declarative statement and its conditional translation, which can be copied and cut apart for student use. The order in which the cards appear here is the correct order of the cards. As mentioned previously, some statements make sense in more than one conditional arrangement. These are marked with an asterisk (we suggest cutting off or otherwise removing the asterisks before presenting students with the statements and card sets).

Lower Elementary

Dogs shed all over the house.

if	you have a dog	then	there is hair all over your house

Marker stains don't come out of your clothes.

if	you wrote on your clothes	with marker	then	the stains will not come out

Cats are quiet pets.

if	you have a cat	then	you have a quiet pet

Carrots are great snacks.

if	you have a carrot	then	you have a great snack

Teaching Reasoning: Activities and Games for the Classroom © 2015 Marzano Research • marzanoresearch.com
Visit **marzanoresearch.com/activitiesandgames** to download this page.

Dogs can hear very high-pitched sounds that we can't hear.

if	you have a dog	then	your pet can hear better than you

Reading Dr. Seuss is fun.

if	you read Dr. Seuss	then	you have fun

She always asks to have food she likes for dinner. *

if	she likes Brussels sprouts	then	she asks for them for dinner

Poison ivy makes your skin itchy and red.

if	it is poison ivy	then	it makes your skin itchy and red

Too much ice cream makes you sick.

if	you ate too much ice cream	then	you are sick

One of Harry's jobs is to answer the phone.

if	the phone is ringing	then	Harry should answer it

Fish need to stay in water to survive.

if	it is a fish	then	it needs water to survive

Ants and bees live in big groups.

if	an insect	is	an ant or a bee	then	it	lives in big groups

Birds have bones that are very light.

if	an animal	is	a bird	then	it	has very light bones

Benjamin Franklin was never president.

if	a person	is Benjamin Franklin	then	he	was never president

Pandas do not hibernate, even though they are bears.

if	a bear	is a panda	then	it	does not hibernate

Snakes swallow their prey whole.

if	a snake	is swallowing	prey	then	it	is whole

Lobsters have ten legs.

if	an animal	is a lobster	then	it	has ten legs

The book *Bud, Not Buddy* was written by Christopher Paul Curtis.

if	a book	is	*Bud, Not Buddy*	then	it	was written by Christopher Paul Curtis

Leopards hunt their food at night.

if	an animal	is	a leopard	then	it	hunts at night

Fish can breathe underwater.

if	an animal	is a fish	then	it	can breathe underwater

Giraffes have four stomachs to help with digesting food.

if	an animal	is a giraffe	then	it	has four stomachs

Whooping cranes are an endangered species.

if	an animal	is a whooping crane	then	it	is endangered

Condors have very large wingspans.

if	an animal	is	a condor	then	it	has a very large wingspan

Prairie dogs live in underground burrows.

if	an animal	is	a prairie dog	then	it	lives in an underground burrow

Dogs pant when they are tired or hot. *

if	a dog is	panting	then	it is	tired or hot

Owls are birds that come out at night.

if	a bird	is	an owl	then	it	comes out at night

A raisin is a dried grape. *

if	a fruit	is	a dried grape	then	it	is a raisin

I do not go to see scary movies.

if	a movie	is	scary	then	I don't go see it

Teaching Reasoning: Activities and Games for the Classroom © 2015 Marzano Research • marzanoresearch.com
Visit **marzanoresearch.com/activitiesandgames** to download this page.

Fruits and vegetables are always part of a healthy diet.

if	you eat a healthy diet	then	you eat fruits and vegetables

Washing your hands gets germs off them.

if	you just washed your hands	then	you don't have germs on your hands

Upper Elementary

Humans first flew using hot air balloons.

if	a human	was the first to fly	then	he or she	used	a hot air balloon

The Eiffel Tower is in Paris, France.

if	you are at	the Eiffel Tower	then	you are in	Paris, France

Plants need light and water to grow.

if	a living thing	is a plant	then	it	needs	light and water

When cranberries are ripe, they bounce. *

if	a cranberry	is bouncy	then	it	is ripe

A coyote can run up to forty miles per hour.

if	an animal	is	a coyote	then	it	can run up to forty miles per hour

Skunks attack beehives because they want to eat bees. *

if	a skunk	attacks a beehive	then	it	wants to eat bees

A worm will die if you cut it in half.

if	an animal	is a worm	then	it	will die when cut in half

A group of cats is called a clowder. *

if	it is	a group of cats	then	the group	is called	a clowder

The longest river in the U.S. is the Missouri River. *

if	the river	is the longest	in the U.S.	then	it	is the Missouri River

A leap year is a year with 366 days instead of 365. *

if	a year	has	366 days	then	it	is a leap year

Bamboo can grow more than three feet a day.

if	a plant	is	bamboo	then	it	can grow more than three feet a day

Mercury is a metal that is liquid at room temperature.

if	a metal	is	mercury	then it is	liquid	at room temperature

Polar bears can live in the Arctic.

if	you are in	the Arctic	then	you could see	polar bears

Wolves have two layers of fur.

if	an animal	is	a wolf	then	it	has two layers of fur

Olympic gold medals are made mostly of silver.

if	a medal	is	an Olympic gold medal	then	it is	mostly silver

The capital of Kenya is Nairobi. *

if	a country	has a capital	called	Nairobi	then	it	is Kenya

Amphibians, like frogs, can live on land or in water.

if	an animal	is	a frog	then	it	can live on land or in water

Diamonds are the hardest substance known to man. *

if	a substance	is	a diamond	then	it	is	the hardest substance known to man

Teaching Reasoning: Activities and Games for the Classroom © 2015 Marzano Research • marzanoresearch.com
Visit **marzanoresearch.com/activitiesandgames** to download this page.

Gorillas can live for forty to fifty years.

if	an animal	is	a gorilla	then	it	can live for forty to fifty years

Australia's Great Barrier Reef is the largest living thing on Earth. *

if	a reef	is	the largest living thing on Earth	then	it	is the Great Barrier Reef

In order to burn, a fire needs oxygen, heat, and fuel. *

if	a fire	has	oxygen, heat, and fuel	then	it	can burn

Magnets are used at recycling plants to sort through different metals.

if	a magnet	is in	a recycling plant	then	it	is used to sort through metals

Every baseball used in Major League Baseball is wiped with special mud before the game.

if	a baseball	has been used in	a Major League Baseball game	then	it	has been wiped with mud

A blizzard is a snowstorm with high winds. *

if	there is	a snow-storm	with	high winds	then	it is	a blizzard

Snapping turtles bite things to defend themselves.

if	it is	a snapping turtle	then	it	will bite to defend itself

Smoking causes many health problems.

if	you	smoke	then	you	have health problems

Butterflies develop from caterpillars.

if	it will turn into a butterfly	then	it is a caterpillar

Adult humans have thirty-two teeth.

if	you are an adult human	then	you have thirty-two teeth

A hippopotamus can run faster than a human.

if	an animal	is a hippo	then	it	can run faster than	a human

Comets orbit the sun.

if	an object	is	a comet	then	it	orbits the sun

Middle School

Sunscreen with a high SPF helps prevent sunburns.

if	you	are wearing	sunscreen with a high SPF	then	you are less likely to get a sunburn

The cafeteria at school is serving nachos today.

if	you	ate	at the cafeteria today	then	you	ate	nachos

A scientist who studies dinosaurs is a type of paleontologist.

if	a scientist	studies	dinosaurs	then	he or she	is a pale-ontologist

Water boils at 212 degrees Fahrenheit. *

if	water	is boiling	then	it	is 212 degrees Fahrenheit

A marine biologist is a type of scientist who studies things underwater.

if	a scientist	is a marine biologist	then	he or she	studies things underwater

Hair is made of a protein called keratin.

if	he	has	hair	then	it	is made of	keratin

Teaching Reasoning: Activities and Games for the Classroom © 2015 Marzano Research • marzanoresearch.com
Visit **marzanoresearch.com/activitiesandgames** to download this page.

Refraction is when light rays bend as they pass through a substance. *

if	the light	was not bent	then	it	was not refracted

Antibiotics can fight bacteria but not viruses. *

if	an infection	can be cured	by antibiotics	then	it	is bacterial

Koalas are native to Australia.

if	an animal	is	a koala	then	it	is native to Australia

In a half-inch square of human skin, there are one hundred sweat glands.

if	it is	a half-inch square	of human skin	then	it	has one hundred sweat glands

Bicycles are healthier for the environment than cars.

if	you are	riding a bike	then	it is better for the environment	than	driving a car

Five-cent coins minted from 1942 to 1945 aren't made of nickel.

if	you	have	a nickel from 1943	then	it	is	not made of nickel

Teaching Reasoning: Activities and Games for the Classroom © 2015 Marzano Research • marzanoresearch.com
Visit **marzanoresearch.com/activitiesandgames** to download this page.

Lightning is caused by the small bits of ice rubbing together and creating an electrical charge.

if	there	is	lightning	then	there are	small bits of ice	in the sky

People who are afraid of clowns don't go to the circus.

if	a person	is afraid of clowns	then	he or she	will not	go	to the circus

The iris responds to low light by making the pupil larger.

if	it is dark	then	the iris	makes the pupil	larger

He had to buy new tires after driving over a box of spilled nails.

if	he	drove over	nails	then	he	had to buy	new tires

At cold temperatures, water turns into ice. *

if	it is cold	then	the state of matter of water	is more likely to be	ice	than	steam

Credit card companies allow you to buy something and pay for it later.

if	you	bought something with a credit card	then	you	pay for the purchase	later

Teaching Reasoning: Activities and Games for the Classroom © 2015 Marzano Research • marzanoresearch.com
Visit **marzanoresearch.com/activitiesandgames** to download this page.

F. Scott Fitzgerald wrote *The Great Gatsby.* *

if	an author	wrote	*The Great Gatsby*	then	he	is	F. Scott Fitzgerald

The chemical DDT causes harm to the environment.

if	a chemical	is	DDT	then	it	causes harm to the environment

The femur—the strongest bone in the human body—is hollow.

if	a bone	is	the femur	then	it	is hollow

Tension in your neck muscles gives you a headache.

if	you	have tension in your neck muscles	then	you	have a headache

President Barack Obama is the forty-fourth president of the United States. *

if	a person	is	Barack Obama	then	he is	the forty-fourth president of the U.S.

Pluto stopped being considered a planet on August 24, 2006.

if	you	studied the solar system in the 1990s	then	you learned	that Pluto	is a planet

Teaching Reasoning: Activities and Games for the Classroom © 2015 Marzano Research • marzanoresearch.com
Visit **marzanoresearch.com/activitiesandgames** to download this page.

Rabbits and parrots have very wide fields of vision.

if	an animal	is a rabbit or a parrot	then	it	has a very wide field of vision

The position of the moon affects high and low tides.

if	the moon	is directly overhead	then	the tide	is high

Approximately 10 percent of the world's known species live in the Amazon rainforest.

if	the Amazon rainforest	is destroyed	then	10 percent of the world's species	are destroyed

Niagara Falls is right on the border between the United States and Canada.

if	you are at	Niagara Falls	then	you can	see	Canada

The coast of North Carolina is a dangerous place to sail because of strong ocean currents, low-lying islands, and severe weather.

if	you	are sailing	near North Carolina	then	you	are	in a dangerous place to sail

Many people like dolphins because of their human-like characteristics.

if	an animal	is	a dolphin	then	it	seems	similar to humans

4 Great Extrapolations

For upper elementary and middle school students

Great Extrapolations helps students recognize characteristics and patterns in a situation and apply them to new situations. Upper elementary students practice generalizing characteristics from descriptions of objects, while middle school students identify and extrapolate patterns from sequences of events. Great Extrapolations is based on an activity outlined in *Tactics for Thinking* by Robert J. Marzano and Daisy Arredondo (1986).

Setup

To play Great Extrapolations you will need a number of short, content-specific paragraphs, such as those at the end of this chapter (see pages 94–113). You may also elect to create your own. For younger students or students who do not have much experience with extrapolation, use paragraphs that describe characteristics of items or objects (such as those on pages 95–103). From these paragraphs, students must identify and extrapolate individual characteristics. With older and more experienced students, use paragraphs that involve sequence patterns or cause-and-effect patterns (such as those on pages 103–113). Students must then identify and extrapolate the patterns from these sequences.

 The best way to play this game is with paragraphs specific to content you've covered in class—this improves gameplay because students will have the background knowledge to come up with examples. It also allows students to make connections within the content, thereby expanding their content knowledge as well as their reasoning skills.

Reasoning Skills

- Identifying relationships between ideas
- Identifying rules and patterns
- Applying rules and patterns

Materials

- Short, content-specific paragraphs (see pages 94–113)
- Note-taking materials for each team
- Projector to display paragraphs (optional)

Divide the class into teams of about five or six students and distribute note-taking materials to each team. Teams will need to write down their ideas, so you should decide if each team will designate a scribe or if all students will write down ideas.

Play

Display a paragraph on a projector or give each team a printed copy. If students are working on identifying and extrapolating characteristics, the paragraph might say:

> The U.S.S. *Constitution* was built in 1794 and is the oldest commissioned ship in the world. It is 304 feet long and weighs over fifteen hundred tons. Along with crew-members and weapons, it also carries a number of smaller boats that can be used for going ashore. The ship is no longer actively used in wars, but it is docked near Boston, Massachusetts, and is a historical site that people can go and visit.

If students are working on identifying and extrapolating patterns, the paragraph might say:

> The Chernobyl disaster was a meltdown at a nuclear power plant in Ukraine that occurred on April 26, 1986 when workers ignored warning signs and continued with a test of the reactor under dangerous conditions. The meltdown released massive amounts of radiation into the atmosphere, which spread to many of the surrounding countries. The disaster was made worse by the fact that the Soviet Union did not tell anyone about it until two days later.

Read the paragraph aloud and then say "Go!" First, the class must identify and abstract information from the paragraph to come up with either generalized characteristics or a generalized pattern of ideas or events. They read the paragraph and look for general characteristics or an underlying pattern of ideas. For the example paragraphs about the U.S.S. *Constitution* and the Chernobyl disaster, the class might come up with lists or patterns such as the following.

Generalized Characteristics (based on U.S.S. *Constitution* paragraph): built long ago; long; heavy; carries people; used in war; has smaller boats inside; historical object/site

Generalized Pattern (based on Chernobyl disaster paragraph): people ignore warning signs; a disaster occurs; environmentally damaging material spreads over a large area; the people in charge don't want to admit the mistake

There are three ways to structure the process of students coming up with generalized characteristics or patterns.

Option 1: Students brainstorm within their teams for a minute or two. The teacher calls everyone back together, and teams share their ideas so the class can collaboratively establish a list of generalized characteristics or a generalized pattern—depending on which version is being played—that will be used by all teams in the next stage of the game. Other teams can weigh in on the validity of an idea, and the teacher can clarify and correct. No points are awarded at this stage. This option is recommended for younger students and novice extrapolators.

Option 2: All teams brainstorm in competition with each other. Students may offer ideas as they think of them. Characteristics or elements of a pattern that the teacher deems appropriate are added to the class's list, and the team that thought of them receives a point. Note that generalized characteristics and patterns are provided for all sample paragraphs on pages 96–103. Sample extrapolations are also provided. Teachers can use the examples to provide guidance to students.

Option 3: Students brainstorm within their teams to create a list of characteristics or a pattern. They then move on to the next stage of the game without sharing their ideas with the rest of the class. This option is recommended only for students who have extensively practiced identifying and abstracting characteristics and patterns, as it requires them to work independently and does not give the teacher the opportunity to catch and correct mistakes or misconceptions during the first stage of the game.

Regardless of which option you choose, the generalized characteristics or pattern that students come up with should accurately reflect the original paragraph, and be stated broadly enough to apply to other items and situations.

In the second stage of the game, teams compete to come up with another item or situation that best fits the generalized characteristics or pattern. Each team only has to come up with one answer, but their response will be judged by how many of the characteristics it fits. For example, if the class (using options 1 or 2) listed seven characteristics, and one team's answer fits five of those while another team's answer fits only three, the first team has a better answer. If option 3 is used, each team's answer is evaluated against that team's list of characteristics. If one team generated six characteristics and their example fits five of them, it is a better answer than one of a team who generated only three characteristics, even if that team's answer fits all three of their characteristics. This incentivizes teams to generate more characteristics and to find examples that fit as many of them as possible. Students may also think of additional generalized characteristics or elements of the pattern during this stage of the game; however, we suggest that characteristics thought of in the second stage *not* be added to the list from the first stage (though they may be discussed at the end of the round).

Examples of good extrapolations from the characteristics of the U.S.S. *Constitution* or the sequence of events at Chernobyl are as follows.

Extrapolation of Characteristics (based on U.S.S. *Constitution* paragraph): The Titanic is another boat that was built long ago (built in 1912) and was extremely large and heavy (882 feet long and 46,000 tons). It also carried people and lifeboats (smaller boats).

Extrapolation of Pattern (based on Chernobyl disaster paragraph): The Exxon Valdez oil spill was a major oil spill off the coast of Alaska in 1989. The ship's radar was broken and the crew was overtired; the ship crashed into a reef. Ten million gallons of oil spilled out and covered thousands of miles of coastline and ocean. In the aftermath, Exxon apologized but did not take responsibility for the spill.

Give the teams between two and five minutes for this phase, depending on their skill level and the difficulty of the characteristics or pattern. Once you announce that time is up, the class comes back together to share their answers. Again, you can use the sample characteristics, patterns, and extrapolations at the end of this chapter to guide your interaction with students.

Wrap-Up

Assess each team's answer, and give points to each team based on how many characteristics or elements of the pattern their answer fits. If they've only accounted for one characteristic or element of the pattern, they get one point; two characteristics or elements earns them two points, and so on. The previous example of the *Titanic* would earn five points, as it fits five of the generalized characteristics from the U.S.S. *Constitution* paragraph (built long ago, long, heavy, carried people, and had smaller boats inside). The previous example of the Exxon Valdez oil spill would earn four points because it matches all four elements of the generalized pattern from the paragraph about the Chernobyl disaster. After reviewing each team's response, record the points for that round. Then display or hand out another paragraph and begin a new round.

If students are new to extrapolation, you may want to model an example for the whole class before dividing up teams and beginning the game. Display a paragraph as you would during gameplay, and then walk the class through the steps of identifying, abstracting, and applying characteristics or patterns.

Variation

A simpler version of this game asks students (or small groups of students) to recognize the similar characteristics or patterns between two things, rather than create them. The materials for this game can easily be created using the paragraphs provided at the end of this chapter (since each paragraph includes an extrapolated example, teachers will not need to come up with these on their own). From each paragraph, create an index card for the source paragraph and an index card for the extrapolated example. Each card should list the name of the item or event and several of its key characteristics or elements, as pictured (with a pattern example) in figure 4.1.

Chernobyl Disaster	*Exxon Valdez Oil Spill*
nuclear test under dangerous conditions led to meltdown	ship's crew and instruments were in poor condition and the ship crashed
massive amounts of radiation released	ten million gallons of oil spilled
the Soviet Union tried to cover it up	Exxon shirked their responsibility

Figure 4.1: Example cards for matching variation of Great Extrapolations.

Create at least ten pairs of cards for each student or team that will be playing (that is, if there are four groups doing the activity, you will need four sets of ten pairs of cards; the sets can be identical). Shuffle the cards and spread them out on a table or desk. Students must then match each card to its partner by identifying those with similar characteristics or patterns (similar to the classic game of Memory™).

Source Paragraphs for Great Extrapolations

This section includes paragraphs from which students can identify generalizable characteristics or patterns that they then extrapolate to other items or events. The paragraphs are divided into two categories: (1) characteristics paragraphs, which are easier and ask students to generalize characteristics of an item or object; and (2) pattern paragraphs, which are more challenging and require students to extrapolate patterns or sequences of events. To guide evaluation of students' answers, we also provide examples of generalized characteristics or patterns for each paragraph, as well as an example extrapolation. Note that not every generalized characteristic or pattern element corresponds to a feature of the example extrapolation—the idea is to match up as many of the features as possible, which may not always be all of them. To download reproducible versions of the source paragraphs only (without example generalizations or extrapolations) that can be copied and handed out or displayed during the game, visit **marzanoresearch.com/activitiesandgames**.

Characteristics (Easier)

The U.S.S. *Constitution* was built in 1794 and is the oldest commissioned ship in the world. It is 304 feet long and weighs over fifteen hundred tons. Along with crewmembers and weapons, it also carries a number of smaller boats that can be used for going ashore. The ship is no longer actively used in wars, but it is docked near Boston, Massachusetts, and is a historical site that people can go and visit.

Example generalized characteristics: built long ago; long; heavy; carries people; used in war; has smaller boats inside; historical object/site

Example extrapolation: The *Titanic* is another boat that was built long ago (in 1912) and was extremely large and heavy (882 feet long and 46,000 tons). It also carried people and lifeboats (smaller boats).

Colorado's state animal is the Rocky Mountain bighorn sheep. Bighorn sheep horns can weigh up to thirty pounds! Male bighorn sheep are called rams, and the females are called ewes. They eat grass and other small plants and are hunted by mountain predators like coyotes, mountain lions, and bears.

Example generalized characteristics: state animal; large horns; rams; ewes; herbivorous; eaten by mountain predators

Example extrapolation: The white-tailed deer is the state animal of Nebraska. It has horns, eats plants, and is hunted by mountain lions and bears.

The National Aquarium opened on August 8, 1981 and is located in Baltimore, Maryland, which is very close to Washington, DC. The angular concrete and glass structure holds seventeen thousand specimens representing seven hundred and fifty species. These specimens are divided between the different exhibits, which are supposed to represent different geographical locations. The aquarium contains so many different types of fish, reptiles, and amphibians because it has made a goal to conserve aquatic life that is threatened.

Example generalized characteristics: recently opened; located in Baltimore; close to Washington, DC; lots of specimens inside; separated into exhibits; separated by geography; goal for conservation

Example extrapolation: The National Zoo is located in Washington, DC. It contains over two thousand animals from four hundred species. These animals are separated into exhibits that are modeled after different parts of the world. The zoo also tries to conserve endangered animals.

Woodpeckers are found throughout the world from the United States to Africa to Australia. They are a family of birds that use their beaks to carve holes into wood. Oftentimes, the holes they make become their homes. However, they have to be careful because other birds will often try to steal the newly carved holes as soon as they're habitable. Because of how competitive other birds are, the woodpecker will often start over, even if it takes a long time, to find the perfect spot that is protected from other birds.

Example generalized characteristics: all over the world; carve wood; take a long time to do their work; use wood to make homes; selective about location

Example extrapolation: Carpenters are like human woodpeckers. They are found all over the world, work with wood, and use wood to make houses. Sometimes they take a long time to do their work.

Acorn squash has a sweet, yellow-orange meat inside. The outside is often dark green in color with a splotch of orange somewhere on its main body. It also has ridges that run from its base to its stem. Squash can be baked, sautéed, or steamed, and its seeds are traditionally toasted and eaten as a snack.

Example generalized characteristics: sweet yellow-orange meat inside; dark green with some orange; ridges; can be cooked in different ways; seeds are edible

Example extrapolation: A pumpkin is another plant with sweet yellow-orange meat inside. The outside has ridges. Pumpkins can be baked or cooked into pies, and the seeds can also be toasted.

The English Channel is part of the Atlantic Ocean that separates England from the main continent of Europe (or more specifically, from France). Though it varies in width, its narrowest point is the Strait of Dover, which is just over twenty miles across, and its widest point is one hundred fifty miles across. The Channel Tunnel is an underwater tunnel that runs across the Strait of Dover and connects Great Britain with France via train.

Example generalized characteristics: body of water; divides two land masses; varies in width; two sides are connected by a man-made structure

Example extrapolation: The Chesapeake Bay is a body of water that divides eastern Maryland from western Maryland. It varies in width, with the narrowest point being 2.8 miles across and the widest thirty miles across. It has a bridge that connects the two sides.

Yellowstone National Park is a national park located in Wyoming, though parts of the park extend into Montana and Idaho. It was established in 1872 by Ulysses S. Grant, the president at the time. It was one of the first national parks in the world and attracts many tourists throughout the seasons. The park is made up of a little less than 3,500 square miles and encompasses lakes, canyons, rivers, geysers, and mountains.

Example generalized characteristics: national park; crosses borders; established by a president; source of tourism; many square miles; diverse landscape

Example extrapolation: Grand Canyon National Park was established by Theodore Roosevelt. It covers over 1,900 square miles of land around the Grand Canyon and stretches across two counties. Many people visit it every year.

Mia Hamm is a retired American soccer player who played for the national women's soccer team and was named FIFA World Player of the Year in 2001 and 2002. She has played in many international games and is a founding member of the Washington Freedom soccer team. Before she retired, she was often considered one of the best female soccer players in the world. She started the Mia Hamm Foundation, a nonprofit dedicated to raising funds for families in need of bone marrow or blood transplants.

Example generalized characteristics: female athlete; former world player of the year; participated in many international games; founding member of a sports team; considered one of the best female athletes; started a nonprofit; retired

Example extrapolation: Serena Williams is a female tennis player who has played in many tournaments all over the world. She has been ranked number one in the world six times. She also does charity work and founded the Serena Williams Secondary School in Matooni, Kenya.

Construction takes many steps including planning, designing, financing, and working until the structure is complete and ready for use. A supervisor called a *project manager* oversees the various steps and coordinates with different teams to successfully build a building. The most successful projects have a doable plan, so they start off on the right foot from the beginning. From there, the project manager ensures that teams stick with the plan in a timely fashion.

Example generalized characteristics: has many different steps; needs a good plan from the beginning; has a project manager; requires coordination of different teams; needs to be finished on time; worked on until done

Example extrapolation: When you do a project in school, you are the project manager. School projects have many different steps, need a good plan from the beginning, and sometimes require cooperation from a group of students. They also need to be finished on time and worked on until done.

A hailstorm is when balls of ice—ranging in size from a BB gun pellet to bigger than a tennis ball—fall from the sky. Although it is made of ice, larger hail occurs in warmer weather. In fact, hailstone growth is slowed by cold temperatures. Hail also generally occurs toward the interior of continents or at high altitudes because it requires specific wind movement that infrequently occurs on the coast.

Example generalized characteristics: ice falls from the sky; weather pattern; occurs in warmer weather; occurs toward the interior of continents; likely to occur at high altitudes; differs in size; requires wind; type of storm

Example extrapolation: A blizzard is a stormy weather pattern in which large amounts of frozen water fall as snow from the sky. To be considered a blizzard, a snowstorm must have sustained winds of over thirty-five miles per hour. They frequently occur at high altitudes.

Cacti are plants with spines covering their body. The spines help the cactus by defending against predators and reducing water loss. Cacti are native to the Americas and have been found from the tip of South America to northwest Canada. They have also been found in parts of Africa and Sri Lanka. Most of the time, cacti live in very dry environments like the desert.

Example generalized characteristics: covered in spines; spines defend against predators; spines help with water loss; found on several continents; live in dry environments

Example extrapolation: Porcupines are medium-sized rodents that are covered in spines. These spines defend them from predators. There are many varieties of porcupines, and they live in North America, South America, Europe, Africa, and Asia.

Ball pythons are a popular pet reptile because of their easygoing temperament. They are covered in smooth scales that are typically black or dark brown with a light-colored belly. They are called ball pythons because of their tendency to curl into a ball when stressed or frightened. Adults rarely grow past six feet, with the females being slightly larger than the males. Often when a ball python starts to get too big, careless owners release it into the wild, which causes disturbances in the local ecosystem.

Example generalized characteristics: reptile; has no legs; curls into a ball when frightened; easygoing; good pet; can grow to be very long; covered in scales; females are larger than males; owners release into wild when too big; can cause disturbances to ecosystems

Example extrapolation: An alligator is a reptile that is covered in scales. They can grow to be well over ten feet long. Some people take baby alligators as pets, but they quickly become unmanageable due to their size, and the owners sometimes release them into the wild. This is a major problem for both the alligator and the local environment.

Harley-Davidson is an American motorcycle company that has been around since 1903. Their motorcycles are generally very heavy models that are designed for highway cruising, rather than smaller standard bikes or dirt bikes. One way that Harley-Davidson keeps ahead of the competition is through a close-knit community explicitly affiliated with the brand. In fact, the brand is so famous that it made $40 million dollars in profit from other people using their logo in 2010.

Example generalized characteristics: has been around for a long time; builds motorcycles for the highway; American company; close-knit community; makes money from people using their logo

Example extrapolation: The Green Bay Packers is an American football team that has existed since 1919. Its many die-hard fans form a close-knit community, and the team is actually owned by its supporters through stocks. The team receives millions of dollars each year from sales of merchandise bearing its logo.

Andy Warhol was a contemporary American artist who led the pop art movement that flourished in the 1960s. His art was considered a commentary on the relationship between art, Hollywood, and advertising. He used many different mediums like drawing, painting, photography, sculpture, and film to explore these areas. Perhaps his most famous work of art is the painting *Campbell's Soup Cans*, which features portraits of thirty-two soup cans (one of each variety offered by Campbell's in 1962).

Example generalized characteristics: artist; contemporary; American; led a movement; popular in the 1960s; art was social commentary; used different media

Example extrapolation: Salvador Dalí was a Spanish artist who lived and worked during the 20th century. He was a prominent painter of the surrealist movement and used art to comment on time and human life. He is most famous for his paintings, but he also sculpted, wrote, and designed fashion and architecture.

A chef is a professional cook who is very good at all aspects of making food. Chefs often design the menus of restaurants, which involves a lot of experimentation to create the perfect dishes. Working with food requires both the creativity of art and the precision of science. Often you can tell who the chefs are by their long white coats and their floppy white hats that help keep their hair out of the food.

Example generalized characteristics: professional; good at what they do; creative; precise; wear long white coats; wear floppy white hats; experiment; create menus

Example extrapolation: A scientist is another type of professional with expert knowledge of his or her field. A good scientist is both creative and precise in designing and carrying out experiments. Typically, scientists wear white lab coats while working.

A croissant is a pastry that gets its name from its crescent-moon shape. In particular, the French are famous for making perfectly flaky and buttery croissants. Sometimes bakers will fill their croissants with chocolate, ham, cheese, or spinach to add their own touch into the baking process. However, making these breakfast treats is not easy. It can take hours to roll out the dough and butter into the right consistency. However, it's worth it! Even if you're not baking them from scratch, they're a great grab-and-go option for breakfast when you're in a rush.

Example generalized characteristics: pastry; interesting shape; eaten for breakfast; comes from Europe; people put butter on them; can have fillings inside; takes a long time to make; easy to eat in the morning

Example extrapolation: A bagel is a round bread product with a hole in the middle. It is commonly eaten as a quick breakfast, and many people put butter or other toppings on it. When bagels are made, they are first boiled and then baked. Although bagels are very popular in the U.S., they actually originated in Poland.

The Prime Minister of the United Kingdom is the head of the king or queen's government in a parliamentary system. He or she takes responsibility for the political decisions made during his or her time in office. In the United Kingdom, citizens do not vote for the prime minister; rather the king or queen will ask someone to serve as prime minister depending on which parties have the majority after a parliamentary election.

Example generalized characteristics: leader of a country; takes responsibility for political decisions; not voted in; king or queen appoints; associated with a party

Example extrapolation: The president is the leader of government in the United States. He or she is generally perceived to be responsible for any and all decisions made by all branches of government while in office. Before the citizens vote in the presidential election, each of the major political parties nominates a representative to run for election.

Jupiter is the largest planet in our solar system and the fifth planet from the sun. It is called a gas giant because of its large mass and its gaseous composition. It has at least sixty-seven moons, though it is possible that more exist and we haven't discovered them yet. Jupiter itself was discovered in ancient times and was named after the Roman king of the gods.

Example generalized characteristics: planet orbiting our sun; largest planet; gas giant; many moons; discovered in ancient times; named from Roman mythology

Example extrapolation: Saturn is the sixth planet from the sun. It is very large and gaseous. It has sixty-two moons. Humans have observed Saturn since ancient times. Our current name for it comes from the Roman god of agriculture.

Irises are a type of plant with uniquely shaped and recognizable flowers. The iris is the state flower of Tennessee. Its name reflects the flower's diversity of colors because it stems from the Greek word for rainbow. It is popular as a garden flower and also as the subject of many paintings. One of the most famous paintings of irises is by Vincent van Gogh.

Example generalized characteristics: type of flower; recognizable; state flower; comes in diverse colors; garden flower; subject of famous paintings

Example extrapolation: The sunflower is a very well-known and recognizable type of flower due to its bright yellow petals and large size. In fact, sunflowers can be over ten feet tall! The sunflower is the state flower of

Kansas and is frequently found in home gardens, as well as in art. Vincent van Gogh painted a famous still-life of sunflowers.

Rutherford Birchard Hayes was the president of the United States from 1877 to 1881. Following Ulysses S. Grant, he was responsible for the end of the Reconstruction period after the Civil War. This was not an easy job, as it was his responsibility to find areas of compromise between the North and the South. His election was highly debated, as he lost the popular vote and barely won the Electoral College vote. He held office for one term before retiring to work as an education and social reform advocate.

Example generalized characteristics: president of the United States; president during 1800s; tried to find areas of compromise between the North and South; election highly debated; tried to make life better for other people

Example extrapolation: Abraham Lincoln was president of the United States during the Civil War, from 1861 to 1865. He was president during a very challenging time for the country and had to try to reconcile the differences between the North and South to keep the country together. One of his most important acts as president was the Emancipation Proclamation, which declared all slaves to be free.

The Iditarod Trail Sled Dog Race is a long-distance dog sled race that takes place in Alaska every March. Each participant and his or her team of sixteen dogs typically run the race over the course of nine to fifteen days. The race began in 1973 in honor of mushers (sled dog drivers) and dogs who brought emergency medicine to Nome, Alaska in the winter of 1925, and it has become a popular competitive sporting event. The teams race through very difficult conditions, including below-zero temperatures, high winds, and blizzards.

Example generalized characteristics: competitive sporting race; based on history; uses animals; long distance; difficult conditions; in Alaska; happens annually; takes many days to finish

Example extrapolation: The Western States Trail Ride is an annual endurance horse race in which horses and riders try to complete a hundred-mile trek in twenty-four hours. Endurance rides like this one are reminders that people used to travel long distances by horse before trains, cars, and planes existed. The Western States Trail Ride is considered the most difficult of all endurance horse races because it takes place in the tough, high-altitude terrain and extreme heat of the Sierra Nevada mountains in the summer.

Martin Luther King Jr. was an American pastor, activist, and leader in the civil rights movement. He advanced the civil rights of African Americans by practicing nonviolent civil disobedience. He received the Nobel Peace Prize in 1964. He also worked to combat poverty and protested the Vietnam War. Sadly, he was assassinated on April 4, 1968. The United States honored him by establishing a national holiday that occurs every year in January.

Example generalized characteristics: leader in a civil rights movement; practiced nonviolent civil disobedience; received Nobel Peace Prize; fought against poverty; protested the Vietnam War; assassinated; has national holiday honoring him

Example extrapolation: Mahatma Gandhi was an important leader in the movement for Indian independence from Britain. As a young man, he fought for the civil rights of Indians and other victims of racism and apartheid in South Africa. He employed nonviolent protest strategies and encouraged others to do the same. He was assassinated in 1948, but his birthday is still a national holiday in India.

Archaeopteryx was a type of small dinosaur that lived in the late Jurassic time period in what would now be considered southern Germany. These dinosaurs could grow to be slightly more than a foot in length and had sharp teeth, claws, and a long bony tail. After examining fossils of *Archaeopteryx*, scientists believe that the dinosaur was covered in feathers and probably one of the first dinosaurs capable of gliding or flight.

Example generalized characteristics: dinosaur; lived in late Jurassic period; lived in Germany; extinct; around a foot in length; sharp teeth; claws; long tail; covered in feathers; could fly

Example extrapolation: The raven is a bird that is common across most of the northern hemisphere. It is about a foot long and covered in all-black feathers. Like most birds, it can fly. It has claws on its feet.

———

A *cryptid* is a creature or a plant that is described in folklore or myth but whose existence has not been confirmed or documented. Examples of cryptids include the Loch Ness Monster, Bigfoot, unicorns, yetis, and El Chupacabra. The evidence for cryptids is anecdotal, and scientists are reluctant to believe it. Whether real or not, they are fun to talk about, which is probably why they are the subject of so many television shows!

Example generalized characteristics: group of creatures; may or may not exist; suggested through folklore or mythology; evidence is anecdotal; on many television shows

Example extrapolation: Although many people once worshipped the Greek gods, this is no longer the case. However, knowledge of them is still common and has endured through myths, stories, literature, and art. They continue to be a familiar subject in pop culture today.

———

Cricket is a bat-and-ball game that was first played in England, but has become particularly popular in Australia, South Africa, New Zealand, and India. Two teams of eleven play on a long pitch and try to score runs. To score a run, a player must hit the ball after it is pitched into the air or on the ground by the bowler. Because there are very detailed and specific rules about how to end a game, cricket games have been known to go on for over five days!

Example generalized characteristics: bat-and-ball game; first played in England; popular around the world; try to score runs by hitting a ball; long games

Example extrapolation: Baseball is often called America's pastime. It is played by two teams on a diamond-shaped field, and the teams take turns trying to score runs by hitting the ball with the bat. The length of the game is determined by innings; in an inning, each team takes a turn at bat until three of its players are called out. There are nine innings in a baseball game, which means that games can go on for several hours.

———

Tea is a beverage that is prepared by pouring hot water over the dried leaves of the tea plant. Besides water, tea is the most commonly drunk beverage in the entire world! It was first introduced as medicine in China. People still drink it today for its positive effects, such as wellness and weight control; caffeinated tea also helps people to stay alert. Many people enjoy the slightly bitter taste, while others prefer blends of tea that include herbs (like chamomile and mint) or fruit (like peaches or black cherries).

Example generalized characteristics: beverage; prepared with hot water; drunk by many people; first used as medicine; used to stay awake; has health benefits; slightly bitter taste; mixed with other things to make it taste better; comes from a plant

Example extrapolation: Coffee is a popular hot drink that is made by straining hot water through the dried, ground-up seeds (more commonly called the beans) of the coffee plant. Many people drink coffee for its caffeine content, either with breakfast to help wake themselves up or later in the day to stay alert. Coffee can be bitter, so it is often mixed with cream and sugar.

A smoke detector is a device that emits loud sounds when it senses smoke; those sounds alert people to the possibility of a fire. Sensitive smoke detectors can be used to deter smoking in places where it is banned, like schools or airplanes. Because two-thirds of deaths from home fires occur in households without working smoke alarms, most fire departments and insurance companies recommend that every house has at least one.

Example generalized characteristics: makes noise; detects danger; protects its owners; deters an undesirable action in specific places; is encouraged by insurance companies; powered by batteries

Example extrapolation: Some people have a pet dog to be their watchdog. A watchdog (also called a guard dog) protects its owners by barking when it sees, hears, or smells danger. A good watchdog can deter burglars from breaking into a house.

A barcode is a visual representation of data usually used to store information about products for sale in stores. The width and spacing of the lines represent numbers, which can be decoded using a barcode scanner to give computers information about a product. Barcodes are an important part of daily life and can be found everywhere: on the back of books, on concert tickets, and even on the packaging of your favorite cereal.

Example generalized characteristics: representation of data; gives information; width and spacing matter; can be analyzed; "talks" to machines; part of our daily lives; very common

Example extrapolation: DNA is the chromosomal molecule that makes up all living things. Each gene in a strand of DNA represents a little bit of data, and the exact makeup of the gene determines how it will be expressed in an organism. Modern technology allows us to analyze DNA from humans and animals. Everyone's DNA is unique, and we would not exist without it!

Frankenstein is a gothic horror novel written by Mary Shelley about a scientist who creates a monster by using science to bring a dead body back to life. It was first written when Shelley got into a competition with her husband and other writers about who could write the best horror story. Since the book's publication in 1818, the monster of Frankenstein (often just called Frankenstein) has become a familiar character in many movies, stories, and plays.

Example generalized characteristics: novel; gothic horror; written by a woman; published in the 1800s; has a monster; written because of a competition; monster is well known; monster is used in other movies, stories, and plays

Example extrapolation: Dracula is a gothic horror novel that was first published in 1897. The title character is a vampire, and his fame has spread well beyond the original book. Dracula is probably the most well-known vampire in the world and has appeared in many movies, stories, and plays.

The Etch A Sketch™ is a famous toy developed in the 1960s by André Cassagnes and manufactured by the Ohio Art Company. It has a very iconic appearance, with a red frame surrounding a gray screen. Two white knobs at the bottom manipulate the direction of a line on the screen so that whoever is playing with it can use the knobs to draw pictures. Once a picture is complete, the user can shake the toy and the image disappears. Today, the Etch A Sketch is still produced and is included on a list of the one hundred most memorable toys from the twentieth century.

Example generalized characteristics: toy; invented mid-twentieth century; very iconic appearance; can be customized by user; encourages artistry with children; shakes to erase; on list of one hundred most memorable toys from twentieth century

Example extrapolation: Mr. Potato Head™ is a toy that first became available in the 1950s. This popular and recognizable toy consists of a plastic potato body and various body and clothing parts that can be attached in any way the user chooses. It is still sold by the original maker (Hasbro) and was included on a list of the one hundred most memorable toys from the twentieth century.

Patterns (Harder)

The Chernobyl disaster was a meltdown at a nuclear power plant in Ukraine that occurred on April 26, 1986 when workers ignored warning signs and continued with a test of the reactor under dangerous conditions. The meltdown released massive amounts of radiation into the atmosphere, which spread to many of the surrounding countries. The disaster was made worse by the fact that the Soviet Union did not tell anyone about it until two days later.

Example generalized pattern: people ignore warning signs; a disaster occurs; environmentally damaging material spreads over a large area; the people in charge don't want to admit the mistake

Example extrapolation: The Exxon Valdez oil spill was a major oil spill off the coast of Alaska in 1989. The ship's radar was broken and the crew was overtired; the ship crashed into a reef. Ten million gallons of oil spilled out and covered thousands of miles of coastline and ocean. In the aftermath, Exxon apologized but did not take responsibility for the spill.

The eruption of Mount Vesuvius was one of the most catastrophic events in European history. It was particularly devastating because the citizens living near the volcano did not anticipate its eruption. In 79 AD, Mount Vesuvius spat out a deadly cloud of gas and ash while spewing molten rock and pumice at the rate of 1.5 million tons per second. The thermal energy released was thousands of times more than the release of the atomic bomb on Hiroshima and completely destroyed the city of Pompeii. There were only two surviving eyewitness testimonies to the eruption, though it is understood that a small evacuation and rescue by sea occurred after the initial explosion. Even with this rescue mission, historians believe over sixteen thousand people died from the event.

Example generalized pattern: a natural disaster occurs; cities are damaged or destroyed; citizens do not anticipate the disaster and do not have the opportunity to prepare or flee; many people die

Example extrapolation: In 2004, an undersea earthquake caused a devastating tsunami that hit Indonesia and other countries in the southern Indian Ocean. It caused billions of dollars in damage to coastal cities. There was not enough time between the earthquake and the arrival of the tsunami for citizens to evacuate, and an estimated two hundred eighty thousand people were dead or missing afterwards.

The Football War (also called the Soccer War or the 100 Hour War) was a brief war between El Salvador and Honduras in 1969. Although it is called the Football War, soccer didn't explicitly start the conflict. Economic disparity and immigration issues between the two countries had already caused tensions to mount. During the North American qualifying rounds for the 1970 FIFA World Cup, riots occurred in both countries every time El Salvador and Honduras played each other. On the day that El Salvador won the decisive third game against Honduras in Mexico City, the El Salvadorian government dissolved diplomatic ties with Honduras. Riots in both countries continued through July, when the Salvadoran military launched an attack on Honduras.

Example generalized pattern: real tensions between two groups remain unresolved; socioeconomic, immigration, and cultural issues spur conflict; sports act as a catalyst for violence

Example extrapolation: In 1971, South Africa was under apartheid. The South African rugby team went to Australia to play several matches, which were protested heavily by young Australians. The protesters took issue with South Africa's discriminatory policies and showed their anger at the sporting events. As a result of the protests, the state of Queensland declared a state of emergency and cancelled the South African cricket team's visit to Australia later that summer.

The Spanish Civil War was fought from 1936 to 1939 throughout the country of Spain. The war pitted Republicans (that is, citizens supporting the new democratically elected Republic) against the Nationalists (that is, fascists and conservatives led by General Francisco Franco). The left-leaning Republicans were supported by anarchists, communists, the Soviet Union, and Mexico, while the right-leaning Nationalists were supported by the conservative religious right, traditionalists, fascists, Italy, and Nazi Germany. Both France and the United Kingdom chose to take a conflict-avoidance stance, which severely crippled the Republicans. The Nationalists eventually won the war and put Franco in power. He disregarded and hid human rights violations that occurred during the war and his subsequent tenure.

Example generalized pattern: country divides into two sides; split creates large issues that end up being resolved by violence; nonintervention from other countries allows fascists to gain power quickly; fascists take over and commit human rights violations

Example extrapolation: Before World War II, Germany was divided politically between left-leaning groups and the far-right Nazi party. Eventually, Hitler and the Nazis seized power and used violent methods to dispose of their enemies, exterminate various ethnic groups, and invade neighboring countries. The Nazis' rise to power was expedited by the fact that other European powers like England and France initially tried to appease Hitler to avoid war.

Robert E. Lee commanded the Confederate Army of Northern Virginia during the American Civil War. When Virginia seceded from the Union, Lee supported his home state rather than staying with the Union, despite the offer of a high-ranking position in the Union army and his personal wishes that the country would remain intact. General Lee proved to be a shrewd tactician, and despite being on the losing side of the Civil War, he was a well-respected general who gained popularity in the North while maintaining popularity in the South.

Example generalized pattern: well-respected general is given a choice between his home and his nation; general chooses home over nation; general employs wise tactics; after the war, general gains respect from both sides

Example extrapolation: During the American Revolution, George Washington served as the commander of the colonial army. As the colonists were British citizens, he could have fought for the British army but chose to support the revolution instead. Washington achieved several key victories, including the reclamation of New Jersey at the Delaware River and the capture of British troops at Saratoga and Yorktown. After the war, he became the first U.S. president and negotiated peace and trade with other nations, including Britain.

Easter Island—or Rapa Nui to early inhabitants—is a small island off the coast of Chile. The most notable features of the island are the hundreds of huge carved stone figures. Anthropologists believe that in order to move these giant statues around the island, the former inhabitants used tree trunks to roll them across the island landscape. It seems that the people of Rapa Nui built these statues zealously, hoping to appease the gods. However, without forethought, they quickly destroyed all the trees on the island, making it uninhabitable and causing their culture to disappear, save for the remaining statues.

Example generalized pattern: people use natural resources to complete tasks; people abuse natural resources and are surprised when they are diminished; location becomes uninhabitable; civilization is destroyed by lack of forethought

Example extrapolation: In society today, people use fossil fuels like coal, oil, and natural gas to generate the energy that powers nearly everything, from lighting to transportation. Experts acknowledge that the supplies of these resources are limited, but most people consume them as if they will last forever. The use of fossil fuels has also been proven to be damaging to the environment. If current trends continue, current ways of life might disappear as fossil fuel supplies dwindle and environmental damage increases.

In *Hamlet*, a play by William Shakespeare, the king—Hamlet's father—has died. Claudius, who is the dead king's brother and Hamlet's uncle, marries Hamlet's mother and takes over the throne. Hamlet sees his father's ghost, who tells him that Claudius is the person who killed him and instructs Hamlet to seek revenge. In the end, Hamlet takes revenge on Claudius but loses his life in the process.

Example generalized pattern: a king is killed leaving behind a son; the brother of the king kills the king to gain power; the son of the dead king sees his father's ghost; the ghost leads his son to get revenge against his uncle

Example extrapolation: In Disney's *The Lion King*, Mufasa, the leader of the lions, is killed by his brother, Scar. Mufasa's son, Simba, is orphaned and cast out by the new regime. Simba sees a vision of his dead father in the stars one night, and the ghost of Mufasa tells him to retake his rightful place as king. Simba does this and avenges his father by killing Scar.

The brown tree snake was originally native to Australia, Indonesia, and Papua New Guinea. However, it is best known for the devastating effects it has had on the bird population of the island of Guam. The brown tree snake was brought into Guam by accident, but thrived there because of the abundance of prey and lack of predators. Brown tree snakes quickly decimated the bird population while multiplying rapidly due to the lack of predators to threaten them. Because the snakes were new to the island, the bird population had no defense against these reptiles.

Example generalized pattern: creature is accidentally transported into a new area; the new area does not have a way to keep the population of the invasive species in check; the invasive species thrives at the expense of native plants and animals

Example extrapolation: The mountain pine beetle is originally native to Japan, but was accidentally transported to the western United States—no one knows how. There, the pine beetle found over three hundred types of plants it could eat. Unchecked by predators, its population grew rapidly. The number of mountain pine beetles has quickly exploded, and native trees have suffered immensely.

The Great Depression was a severe worldwide economic depression that occurred immediately before World War II. Economists believe that there were many causes for the downturn, including the Federal Reserve printing less money, increased taxes and tariffs for the U.S., and the post–World War I Treaty of Versailles. At the time, however, the most obvious cause was the U.S. stock market crash of 1929, which was blamed on President Herbert Hoover. Approximately 25 to 30 percent of Americans lost their jobs; many of them also lost their homes. When Franklin D. Roosevelt took office, he passed a set of laws called the New Deal to provide jobs for U.S. citizens and help turn the economy around.

Example generalized pattern: economy crashes for many reasons; people search for a scapegoat to blame economic crash on; people suffer; economy bounces back after time and with help

Example extrapolation: In October 2008, the New York stock market crashed abruptly. Experts identified several causes: financial firms took on too much risk, policymakers lacked understanding of the financial system, and regulation of the financial system failed. Presidents George W. Bush and Barack Obama have been blamed for the difficulties leading to and resulting from the crash. Following the crash, unemployment and homelessness increased substantially. Eventually, the economy began to recover through the influence of both government policies and natural economic cycles.

Some people interpreted the end date of a 5,126-year-long cycle in the Long Count calendar of the Mayans to signal the end of the world entirely. Some predicted that the end date would mark a worldwide physical or spiritual transformation, while others thought that the end of the world or a humanity-altering catastrophe would occur. However, many scholars pointed to the fact that these speculations were not grounded in research, but rather alarmist conclusions. In the end, the day came and went without a hitch.

Example generalized pattern: prediction names a specific date as the end of the world; people jump to conclusions and become afraid; the day comes and goes and everything is fine

Example extrapolation: Leading up to the start of the new millennium in the year 2000, people worried that computers would malfunction when the new year began, because at that time they only used two digits (not four) to keep track of the year. Some people interpreted this to mean that technology would become useless and humanity would be thrown back into the Stone Age. However, when the clock struck midnight on January 1, 2000, computers continued functioning as normal.

The eight-track tape was popular from the late 1960s through the 1970s. Eight-track tapes were a type of magnetic sound-recording technology that existed before cassette tapes were invented in the late 1980s. Cassette tapes ultimately became the dominant music-playing format because they could be rewound, were half the size of eight-track tapes, and were less likely to jam or skip. Today, however, cassettes are also obsolete, as most people listen to music on MP3 players or CDs.

Example generalized pattern: technology is designed and receives commercial success for a while; other technology is developed that improves upon the initial design; new technology receives commercial success and old technology fades away; the cycle continues

Example extrapolation: When home telephones first became common, most of them had rotary dials. A wheel was used to dial numbers instead of individual push-buttons. In the mid-twentieth century, however, the touch-tone dialing system was invented. Touch-tone phones have individual keys for each number, which allows people to dial much faster. Within a short span of time, touch-tone phones almost completely replaced rotary phones. In the first two decades of the twenty-first century, however, more and more people have begun moving away from landline phones entirely and using cell phones instead (which often have electronic keypads).

Napoleon invaded Russia on June 24, 1812, hoping to stop Czar Alexander I from trading with the British Empire. Napoleon's plan did not succeed. Rather than fighting with Napoleon's large army, the Russian army continued to retreat further and further into Russia. As he pursued them, Napoleon and his army eventually ended up in the center of Russia in the middle of winter without necessary winter clothing or adequate food. After deciding to retreat, Napoleon's army suffered large casualties due to exposure and hunger. By the time they retreated across the Berezina River, Napoleon's army had lost three hundred eighty thousand men and the Russian army had captured one hundred thousand men. Napoleon's army never fully recovered from this failed campaign.

Example generalized pattern: a powerful nation decides to invade Russia in June; plan takes longer than expected; invader expects a quick victory; winter comes and invading leader has to give up; failed invasion of Russia acts as a turning point

Example extrapolation: On June 22, 1941, the German army, under the command of Adolf Hitler, invaded Russia. Hitler expected Russia to be an easy conquest; German leadership at the time generally thought of Russia as a backwater nation with limited military prowess. Although Germany won the first few battles, it failed to take Moscow and became embroiled in a long siege. Winter came and the German army was forced to retreat. This failure turned the tide of World War II against the Germans.

The Industrial Revolution started at the turn of the eighteenth century, but major changes in the standard of living for a majority of the population did not occur until the turn of the twentieth century (which is sometimes labeled the Second Industrial Revolution). The Industrial Revolution mechanized processes that had previously been done by hand (like chemical and iron manufacturing) through the use of steam and coal power. These important technological innovations facilitated further progress and innovation.

Example generalized pattern: scientific revolution innovates upon existing ideas; scientific innovations have great effect over time; society today owes a great deal to the scientific innovations of the past

Example extrapolation: The Renaissance was a broad cultural movement that began in the fourteenth century and included major innovations in both the arts and the sciences. In particular, people questioned accepted ideas about astronomy, biology, and physics, and new theories were developed. These significant innovations took time to spread, especially since the printing press was not invented until the fifteenth century. The Renaissance began the modern scientific era and laid a foundation for subsequent discoveries.

Prohibition began in 1920 when the Eighteenth Amendment to the United States Constitution went into effect. The amendment ceased the legal sale of alcoholic beverages in the United States, but it had many unintended consequences. First, the justice system was flooded with cases involving illegal alcohol, but didn't have enough time or resources to process all the cases. Second, organized crime increased, leading to gang violence and corruption in the police force. Eventually, prohibition ended with the passage of the Twenty-first Amendment, which repealed laws against selling alcohol.

Example generalized pattern: law passes that is aimed at stopping people from doing something perceived to be immoral; organized crime increases due to lack of supply and continued demand; new law overwhelms resources of justice system; law is eventually repealed

Example extrapolation: Prohibition of narcotics and other drugs in the United States, commonly called the War on Drugs, has been a particularly salient issue since the early 1970s. Laws and government programs have tried to end access to and use of illegal drugs. These laws are well intentioned but have unfortunate side effects. U.S. military initiatives designed to stop the South American drug trade may have given power to drug cartels. About half the inmates in the federal prison system are incarcerated on drug charges, straining the system's resources. In reaction to these negative outcomes of the War on Drugs, some people have begun pushing for more relaxed drug policies.

The Migration Period occurred from about 400 to 800 AD. During this time, human migration around Europe intensified. During the first phase of the Migration Period, Germanic tribes moved out of Germany and Scandinavia and entered the territory of the Roman Empire. Anthropologists believe the migration was caused by several factors, including poor weather, low crop yields, overpopulation, and displacement by other nomadic tribes. While French and Italian scholars often view the migration as the invasion and destruction of the Roman Empire, German and English historians generally consider the migration to have spurred the necessary replacement of an extravagant Mediterranean civilization with a martial Nordic one.

Example generalized pattern: humans migrate from their homes; migrations are motivated by poor conditions in previous places; people disagree about whether the migration is good or bad

Example extrapolation: In the early twenty-first century, migration from Central America into the United States has increased substantially. Immigrants often leave extreme poverty and migrate in search of work or safety for their families. Immigration has become a central political issue of the era, with constant debate about whether it should be halted or allowed.

Disney's *Pocahontas* shows a fictionalized and idealized love story that takes place in the New World after the discovery of North America. European John Smith meets Pocahontas, a beautiful Powhatan woman, and the two fall in love after spending time together. Unfortunately, Pocahontas is already betrothed to another man, and John Smith's crew has plans to attack the native people for their gold. Pocahontas and John Smith survive the ensuing battle and some members of the two cultures find a way to exist together peacefully, while the intolerant Europeans are sent home.

Example generalized pattern: man goes to new world and meets woman; woman and man fall in love; significant issues divide native and recently arrived cultures; after battle, woman and man can be together; idealistic story shows how different cultures can get along after strife

Example extrapolation: In the movie *Avatar*, soldier Jake Sully goes to a recently discovered planet called Pandora. There, he meets a woman from the native population named Neytiri and they fall in love. Unfortunately, Neytiri is already betrothed. At the same time, the people from Earth plan to kill the inhabitants of Pandora so they can mine a resource called unobtanium. After the battle, the greedy people from Earth are sent home while the ones who respect nature and the culture of Pandora stay. Jake and Neytiri live happily ever after.

The Cold War was a time of military and political tension primarily between the United States and the Soviet Union from around 1947 to 1991. After World War II, the United States and the Soviet Union were left as the two major superpowers in the world. However, the two countries had differing beliefs about government: the United States encouraged capitalist democracies and the USSR encouraged totalitarian communism. The conflict is called the Cold War because there was no large-scale direct confrontation between the two countries (though in regional wars in Korea, Vietnam, and Afghanistan, each country supported opposing sides). Nevertheless, each country increased its military during the Cold War and there was a constant threat of nuclear warfare.

Example generalized pattern: two major powers exist in the world after defeating a common enemy; the major powers have fundamental political and cultural differences; rivalry becomes intense, and threat of war looms

Example extrapolation: In the fifth century BC, Athens and Sparta were the major powers in Greece. Athens was a democracy with a culture that valued philosophy and art, while Sparta was an oligarchy with a military culture. They had worked together to defeat Persia and formed an alliance of Greek city-states. The alliance soon began to split, with individual city-states backing either Athens or Sparta; the threat of war was constant. Eventually, the Peloponnesian War broke out in 431 BC.

Madonna has been a prominent American singer and cultural icon since the early 1980s. She gained popularity by trying to push boundaries in music and music videos. However, she has never stopped at just music. Madonna has also explored acting and art, as well as entering the world of business. Her ability to repeatedly reinvent her music and her image, becoming more provocative each time, separates her from other celebrities and contributes greatly to her high level of fame.

Example generalized pattern: singer becomes popular; singer explores other creative outlets such as acting, photography, art, and so on; singer reinvents herself to be more provocative; singer becomes cultural icon

Example extrapolation: Miley Cyrus first rose to fame in the mid-2000s as an actress on the television show *Hannah Montana*. As her character on the show was a pop star, Miley Cyrus transitioned easily into pop music herself. She sang several hit songs that appealed mostly to young teenage girls—the same demographic as her television show. Around 2012, she began to transform her public image and her music, shedding the image of Hannah Montana and becoming more provocative and explicit.

In the 1950s, Senator Joseph McCarthy of Wisconsin led an initiative to identify, arrest, and try for treason communists and communist sympathizers in the United States. He claimed to have a list of names of all the known communists and communist sympathizers working for the U.S. State Department. These accusations were often made with little to no evidence, a practice which came to be known as *McCarthyism*. The number of arrests quickly increased as those under scrutiny or on trial often made further accusations to win favor.

Under McCarthyism, hundreds of U.S. citizens were imprisoned, and somewhere between ten and twelve thousand individuals lost their jobs.

Example generalized pattern: community members make accusations that others are doing something wrong; the accusations are unsubstantiated; the nature of the "crime" capitalizes on a common fear; the accused are persecuted

Example extrapolation: In 1692 and 1693 in Massachusetts, there was mass hysteria that members of the community were using witchcraft. A number of people were brought to trial. Most of the evidence was "spectral," meaning the witnesses claimed to have seen a ghost that looked like the person being accused. The trials happened during a time when New England was dominated by strict conservative Puritanism. This belief system viewed witchcraft as closely associated with the devil and punishable by death. Twenty people, mostly women, were put to death as a result of the proceedings.

Hurricane Katrina was a deadly and destructive tropical cyclone that occurred in 2005. Katrina was considered to be the most costly natural disaster in the history of the United States. The hurricane is most associated with the damage it inflicted on the metropolitan area of New Orleans, Louisiana. Hours after it hit New Orleans, the system of levees surrounding the city failed, allowing water to flood almost 80 percent of the city. Afterwards, critics suggested that the city's location in a valley prone to flooding was not a good idea, especially in a coastal area known for its large storms. Despite these drawbacks, members of the community still returned to rebuild the city after the water levels receded.

Example generalized pattern: natural disaster damages metropolitan area; failure of human engineering exacerbates natural disaster; critics question placement of metropolitan area; residents of metropolitan area return home despite the risks

Example extrapolation: A major earthquake struck San Francisco in 1906. The city sustained heavy damage which was made worse by the fact that ruptured gas mains caused fires to spread throughout the city. Firefighters tried to contain the blazes by demolishing buildings with dynamite, but they ended up igniting more buildings instead. In recent years, scientists have noted that San Francisco lies on the San Andreas Fault, an area particularly prone to earthquakes. Nevertheless, San Francisco continues to be a major metropolis.

In the Winter Olympic Games of 1988, Jamaica sent a team to Alberta, Canada, to compete in the international bobsledding competition. The Jamaican team quickly became fan favorites in the competition because of their underdog status; they came from a country without snow or bobsled tracks. In one of their four runs, they lost control and crashed, keeping them from placing. However, they continued to train and competed in subsequent Olympic Games, even placing ahead of the United States, Russia, Australia, and France in 1994.

Example generalized pattern: team goes to the Olympics despite poor odds; team gains popularity due to underdog status; in the end, they succeed

Example extrapolation: In 1980, the U.S. Men's Hockey team went to the Olympics despite having only one returning veteran and mostly college-aged players. The team was an obvious underdog, with the Soviet Union being the major hockey powerhouse at the time. In a game now known as the "Miracle on Ice," the U.S. team surprisingly defeated Russia and went on to win the gold medal.

In *Romeo and Juliet*, a play by William Shakespeare, the two protagonists engage in a love affair destined for tragedy. Juliet and Romeo fall in love, despite coming from feuding families who wish to stop their involvement. Romeo and Juliet get married in secret, but their hope for eventual acceptance is ruined once Romeo accidentally kills Juliet's cousin and Romeo is banished from the city where they all live. In the end, Romeo and Juliet take their own lives, thinking that life is not worth living without each other.

Example generalized pattern: two young people fall in love despite differing backgrounds; their families try to stop their romance; their romance leads to main characters' deaths

Example extrapolation: In the musical *West Side Story*, the main characters, Tony and Maria, live in New York City but come from different ethnic backgrounds. They fall in love, but their respective friends and other members of their ethnically divided gangs discourage their relationship. In the end, Tony is shot by a rival gang member.

Billy Mitchell was a United States Army general who served as a pilot in World War I. After World War I, he illustrated that well-timed aerial attacks could decimate naval units. In a report issued in 1924, he predicted a future war with Japan. Within that prediction, he noted the exposure and vulnerability of Pearl Harbor and brought attention to the fact it could be a viable target. However, the report was ignored, and on December 7, 1941, the Japanese used aerial attacks to bomb Pearl Harbor.

Example generalized pattern: expert makes a prediction; prediction is ignored or laughed off; years later prediction comes true

Example extrapolation: In 2005, Russ Tice, a National Security Agency (NSA) agent, raised concerns that the NSA was reading the emails and listening to the phone conversations of American citizens. People didn't believe his claims; some television pundits even suggested he should be arrested for making treasonous accusations. In 2013, however, Tice's claims were validated when Edward Snowden came forward and confirmed the NSA's violation of the privacy of U.S. citizens.

The Swine Flu outbreak of 2009 was considered a pandemic because there were cases of the virus in almost every country in a relatively short amount of time. The strain of influenza moved quickly because it was a combination of three existing viruses (including traditional human flu, pig flu, and avian flu). By June of 2009, the World Health Organization (WHO) raised the alert level to indicate the danger caused by the speed at which the virus was transmitted. During this time, uncertainties about the virus and lack of vaccinations caused some people to panic. By 2010, the disease had run its course and the WHO considered the pandemic over.

Example generalized pattern: disease breaks out in a country; disease quickly spreads around the world; people panic; disease runs its course and everything is okay

Example extrapolation: In 2002, severe acute respiratory syndrome (SARS) broke out in southern China. In a matter of weeks, the disease spread to thirty-seven countries. Panic ensued due to the rate of transmission and resulting fatalities. Happily, the SARS pandemic was contained in less than one year.

The Indian Removal Act of 1830 displaced over forty-six thousand First Nations peoples (including sixteen thousand Cherokees). The law led to the Trail of Tears, during which Native Americans who were forced to leave their homelands to move west risked death due to the harsh conditions of the long journey. Native people who chose not to move were forced to assimilate into the dominant culture and give up their cultural and religious traditions.

Example generalized pattern: group of people live in a specific area; discriminatory laws or practices are established; people forced from their homes

Example extrapolation: In the nineteenth century, Muslims were a significant minority in the Balkan states of southeastern Europe. Over time, the ethnic and religious majority in those areas established discriminatory practices against Muslims and other minorities. This led to forced migration of Muslims, which culminated during the Balkan Wars with tens of thousands of people leaving their homes because of their status as ethnic or religious minorities.

The 1979 oil crisis occurred because of decreased oil exportation after the Iranian Revolution. Even though the decrease in oil supply was minimal, people panicked, thinking that supplies were dwindling. Thus, the price of oil became much higher than what should have been caused by the reduction in supply. Oil prices spiked to $39.50 a barrel, and long lines formed at gas stations. Eventually, prices fell as other countries began or expanded oil production.

Example generalized pattern: oil supply is decreased; public panics thinking oil is gone forever; price and wait time for gas is driven up; oil crisis ends

Example extrapolation: The 1973 oil crisis occurred because the Organization of Arab Petroleum Exporting Countries (OAPEC) placed an embargo on oil. The public panicked, thinking that the oil supply would be permanently limited or become extremely expensive. The price of barrels of oil quadrupled, and long lines formed at gas stations as gas was rationed. The crisis ended when the embargo was lifted in 1974.

The Watergate scandal occurred while Richard Nixon was president, and ultimately resulted in his resignation from office in 1974. Investigators discovered a conspiracy in 1972 in which the Nixon administration planted recording devices in the offices of his political opponents and other people they suspected of doing things that might be detrimental to Nixon's re-election. After Nixon's resignation, forty-three other individuals associated with the Nixon administration were sent to jail.

Example generalized pattern: person in power spies on rivals; person in power is caught spying; person in power is penalized for spying

Example extrapolation: The National Football League (NFL) taping scandal occurred in 2007 when the New England Patriots were caught videotaping the New York Jets' defensive coaches' signals. The NFL Commissioner deemed this to be a violation of league rules, and Patriots head coach Bill Belichick was fined $500,000—the maximum allowed by the league. The Patriots also lost their first-round selection in the next year's draft.

The women's suffrage movement in the United States began in 1848. *Suffrage* is the right to vote and hold political office. In 1848, the Liberty Party made women's suffrage a point in their presidential campaign and the Seneca Falls Convention issued a formal demand by U.S. women for the right to vote. However, women didn't gain these rights until 1920 when the Nineteenth Amendment to the U.S. Constitution was passed.

Example generalized pattern: a group is denied a right that others have; the group protests to gain equal rights; after much struggle, the group succeeds in taking positive steps forward

Example extrapolation: After the Civil War, African Americans in the South were denied the right to vote and were often victims of segregation and hate crimes. Between 1954 and 1968, members of the civil rights movement used civil resistance and disobedience to protest discrimination and segregation. This led to the establishment of the Civil Rights Act of 1964 and the Voting Rights Act of 1965.

The Lewis and Clark Expedition was one of the first exploratory journeys across the western section of the United States. The expedition was commissioned by President Thomas Jefferson to explore the land on the west side of the Mississippi River. Meriwether Lewis and William Clark, volunteers from the military, led the party. The expedition's goals were to establish an American presence across the continent before other world powers tried to claim it and to study the new territory's biology and geography.

Example generalized pattern: volunteers from the military explore an unknown area; expedition claims space for the United States; information from expedition is used to increase scientific understanding

Example extrapolation: In 1969, two NASA astronauts (both former military pilots) explored the surface of the moon. They were the first humans ever to walk there. The expedition greatly increased scientific knowledge in many ways. Having the first men on the moon is still a source of pride for many Americans.

The French Revolution was a time of profound social and political upheaval in France from 1789 to 1799. The lower class resented the privileges given to members of the church and the aristocracy during a financial crisis caused by war and poor harvests. The lower class sought equality by removing their oppressors from power, executing many of them by guillotine.

Example generalized pattern: lower class resents upper class for the benefits they receive from the government; lower class protests this injustice; lower class changes the way the culture is organized

Example extrapolation: After the 2008 economic crash, public attention focused on wealth disparity in the United States. The Occupy Wall Street movement promoted awareness of the fact that the wealthiest 1% of Americans control a disproportionate amount of money. The Occupiers, representing the lower class (or the other 99%) protested in public parks during the day and camped there at night. The movement brought political and cultural attention to issues around income inequality and federal economic policy.

5 Riddle Me This

For upper elementary through high school students

Riddle Me This uses physical representations of various riddles to help students practice using models to support their thinking when engaging in hypothetical reasoning.

Setup

The exact setup for this game varies depending on the chosen riddle (see pages 117–124). For each riddle, you will need to provide a few items that represent the elements involved in the riddle. For example, if the riddle involves figuring out how far apart two nails are with a string hanging between them (see "Where's the Nail?", page 117), you will need a string of the appropriate length, two nails or thumbtacks, and a surface such as a bulletin board for students to work on. Students will also need a copy of the text of the riddle for reference as they plan and try out different solutions.

The riddles listed on pages 117–124 are designed to be worked on primarily by small groups or individuals (a few work best with the whole class; these are noted). If you choose to have students work in small groups, plan to vary the groups fairly often so students get the chance to work with a variety of peers. Additionally, if students are working in groups, you can set up stations around the room, each with a different riddle, and have groups rotate between them.

Play

Present a riddle and its corresponding physical model to students. For beginners, allow students to manipulate

Reasoning Skills

- Hypothetical reasoning

Materials

- Printed copies of riddles (see pages 117–124 and online reproducible)
- Other materials will vary and are listed with specific riddles (see pages 117–124)
- Projector to display riddles (optional)
- Note-taking materials (optional)

the model as much as they want as they try to work out the answer. For a more challenging version, tell them they have to plan out their solution mentally before demonstrating it with the model. For riddles that work best with the whole class (see the whole-class activities on pages 117, 119, and 122), write the riddle on the board or display it with a projector and assign roles to students as described in the riddle so the class can act it out and solve the riddle as a group.

If students are rotating between stations, let them know how much time they will have at each station and give periodic time checks (for example, a five-minute warning). Allow students to work on the riddles for the prearranged amount of time before rotating to the next station. The riddles in this game are designed to be challenging and require persistence from students. Therefore, we recommend at least ten minutes per riddle. However, the appropriate amount of time per riddle varies according to students' age and attention span, and students can become frustrated if they feel "stuck" on a riddle for too long. In light of this, we recommend watching your students carefully during their first few experiences with this game to discover a time limit that helps students develop persistence while avoiding frustration.

Wrap-Up

Students may not solve a riddle in one session. This is completely acceptable. If students are unable to solve a riddle in the time allotted, encourage them to write down their thoughts about the riddle and come back and work on it individually at a later time.

Some students may also become frustrated with a riddle before the time is up. The physical engagement and group approach will help deter this problem to some extent, but often not entirely. For some students, prompting them to keep trying is enough to get them back on track. For others, you may need to suggest new approaches or strategies for them to try. For example, you might ask students to see what happens if they choose one starting action and follow its consequences as far as possible. Other productive strategies include writing down solutions they have already tried and asking, "What information do I have? What information do I need, and how can I get it?"

We also suggest that you create a "solution box" so students or groups who arrive at a solution to a riddle can submit it—either during group rotation or later at their own pace—without giving away the answer to others. Make sure students write down their names, the name(s) of the riddle(s), and their proposed solutions. You can periodically check this box for newly submitted answers, comment on the solutions, and return them to students.

Riddles

Here we list a number of riddles that can be easily modeled with physical objects. For each riddle, we include the text of the riddle itself, a list of materials you will need to create a model of the riddle, and the solution to the riddle. Note that the riddles and solutions are written so they can be read to students, while the materials sections are directed toward teachers. The riddles are sorted by age level (upper elementary, middle school, and high school); however, we suggest that students of any age start out with easier riddles. Riddles that work best with a large group are denoted by the phrase "whole-class activity." To download reproducible versions of the text of each riddle, which can be copied and given to students, visit **marzanoresearch.com/activitiesandgames**.

Upper Elementary

Troll Tolls (Whole-Class Activity)

Riddle

You are on your way to visit Grandma, who lives at the end of the valley. It's her birthday, and you want to give her the cakes you've made. Between your house and her house you have to cross seven bridges, and there is a troll under every bridge! Each troll insists you pay a troll toll. Before you can cross each bridge, you have to give each troll half of the cakes you are carrying. However, as they are all kind trolls, they each give you back a single cake. How many cakes do you have to bring with you to make sure you arrive at Grandma's with exactly two cakes?

Materials

You will need seven students to play the trolls; the rest of the class can take turns trying to arrive at Grandma's with two cakes. Items such as bean bags or paper printouts can represent the cakes.

Solution

You will need to leave home with two cakes (Best Brain Teasers, 2013).

Where's the Nail?

Riddle

Both ends of a string are nailed to a wall. The string is six feet long, and the center of the string dips down three feet from where each end of the string is nailed to the wall. How far apart are the two ends of the string nailed from each other?

Materials

You will need a six-foot-long piece of string, a measuring tape or yardstick, and two thumb tacks or pieces of tape to attach the ends of the string to the wall.

Solution

Both ends of the string must be hung in the same spot to have the dip be three feet lower than the ends of the string, because three feet is half the string's length (Zablocki, n.d.).

Socks and Shoes

Riddle

You are in a dark closet. On the floor there are six shoes of three colors (two of each color) and a heap of twenty-four socks, black and brown (twelve of each color). How many socks and shoes must you take into the light to be certain you have a matching pair of socks and a matching pair of shoes?

Materials

You will need a pile of six shoes (three pairs, each of a different color) and a pile of twenty-four socks (twelve of each color). We recommend creating paper cutouts to represent each one. You can use a bandana or piece of cloth as a blindfold to simulate darkness.

Solution

Three socks and four shoes would guarantee that you would have a matching pair of each. Since there are only two colors of socks, it doesn't matter how many are in the heap; as long as you take at least three, you are certain to have two of the same. As for the shoes, you must pick four, because selecting only three could result in one shoe in each of the three colors (Expand Your Mind, n.d.).

Playing Cards

Riddle

There are three playing cards lying face up, side by side. A five is just to the right of a two. A five is just to the left of a two. A spade is just to the left of a club, and a spade is just to the right of a spade. What are the three cards?

Materials

Give students a deck of cards (or imitation playing cards made of paper). For a simpler version, only give students the following four cards (real or imitation) to choose from: five of spades, two of spades, five of clubs, and two of clubs.

Solution

From left to right, the cards will be the five of spades, the two of spades, and the five of clubs, *or*, from left to right, the two of spades, the five of spades, and the two of clubs (Expand Your Mind, n.d.).

River Crossing

Riddle

A man needs to cross a river in a canoe. He also needs to transport a bag of grain, a chicken, and a fox across the river. He can only carry one of the three with him in the canoe at a time. If he leaves the grain and the chicken alone together anywhere, the chicken will eat the grain. If he leaves the chicken and the fox alone together anywhere, the fox will eat the chicken. How can he transport himself, the grain, the chicken, and the fox across the river without anything being left behind or eaten?

Materials

You will need stuffed animals to represent the fox and the chicken, a bean bag to represent the bag of grain, a doll or action figure to be the man, a basket or other vehicle to be the boat, and a piece of blue paper or a space between desks to represent the river. All items could also be represented by paper cutouts, particularly if they can be held up by magnets and moved around on a whiteboard or other surface.

Solution

The man takes the chicken across first, leaving it on the other side of the river. He returns alone in the canoe and picks up the bag of grain. After bringing across the grain, he takes the chicken back to the original side, dropping him off, and picking up the fox. After bringing the fox to the other side and leaving it with the grain, the man returns to the original side, retrieves the chicken, and makes his third and final trip across the river (Expand Your Mind, n.d.).

Coin Shuffle

Riddle

Line up five coins in the following order: quarter, penny, quarter, penny, quarter. In three moves (a move consists of swapping two adjacent coins), rearrange the coins so the three quarters are together and the two pennies are together with no empty spaces in between each coin. At the end of each move, the coins are always in line as in the original configuration. That is, the coins must be in a line with no spaces between them after each move.

Materials

You will need three quarters and two pennies; you can also use slips of paper with *Q* or *P* written on them to represent coins.

Solution

Switch a quarter on the end with its adjacent penny. Switch the center quarter with the penny from the opposite side of the first movement. Now switch the center penny with the quarter from the first movement to separate out the coins fully into quarters and pennies (Expand Your Mind, n.d.).

Pennies

Riddle

Mary has a coin purse with fifty coins, totaling exactly one dollar. One of the coins is a quarter. What are the other forty-nine coins?

Materials

You'll need an assortment of coins (at least sixty) that includes at least fifty pennies, four dimes, five nickels, and a quarter.

Solution

Mary has forty-five pennies, two dimes, two nickels, and one quarter (adapted from Expand Your Mind, n.d.).

Middle School

A Liar and a Truth-Teller (Whole-Class Activity)

Riddle

You are standing in front of two identical doors. Behind one of them is something good, and behind the other is something bad. You don't know which door leads to which. In front of the doors are two guards who know which door leads to the good thing and which leads to the bad thing. One of the guards always lies, and the other always tells the truth. You don't know which guard is the liar and which is the truth-teller. What question should you ask to find out which door leads to the good thing?

Materials

For the physical representation of this riddle, draw two doors on the board. Have two students act as the guards. Let them know (privately) which doors lead where and assign one to be the liar and one to be the truth-teller. Have them respond to the inquiries from the rest of the class according to their role (liar or truth-teller). The class can only ask yes/no and either/or questions about the contents of the doors, and must direct each question to a specific guard. To make this riddle more challenging, the class must agree on a single question they will ask to determine which door is which.

Solution

The best type of question asks one guard to tell what the other guard would say. For example, "Which door would the other guard say leads to the good thing?" This question, if posed to the truth-teller, will cause him or her to point to the door that the liar would indicate, which is the door that leads to the bad thing. If posed to the liar, the same question would prompt him or her to point to the door that the truth-teller would *not* indicate (the door to the bad thing), since he or she is lying. Either way, students know that the door either guard points to when asked this question is the door to the bad thing (Big Riddles, 2009).

Milk Jugs

Riddle

A milkman has two empty jugs: a three-gallon jug and a five-gallon jug. How can he measure exactly one gallon without wasting any milk?

Materials

You will need two jugs—perhaps pitchers or empty milk containers—with markings to delineate three and five gallons. These scales do not need to be actual gallons, but should be in proportion to each other (for example, using three cups and five cups is fine). Use water to represent the milk and have towels available in case students spill.

Solution

The milkman fills the three-gallon jug and then empties the contents into the five-gallon jug. He then fills the three-gallon jug again and continues to fill the five-gallon jug until it is full. The milk remaining in the three-gallon jug is precisely one gallon (Expand Your Mind, n.d.).

Monkey Mayhem!

Riddle

Three humans, one big monkey, and two small monkeys need to cross a river, meeting the following conditions:

- Only humans and the big monkey can row the boat.
- At all times, the number of humans on either side of the river must be greater than or equal to the number of monkeys on that side (or else the humans will be eaten by the monkeys).
- The boat only has room for two (monkeys or humans).
- Monkeys can jump out of the boat when it is banked; that is, a human can drop off a monkey without getting out of the boat and risking being eaten.

Materials

Similar to the "River Crossing" riddle, humans and monkeys can be represented by stuffed animals or figures. A basket can represent the boat. Alternatively, humans, monkeys, and the boat can be represented by paper cutouts, but in either case it needs to be clear which are humans, which is the big monkey, and which are the small monkeys.

Solution

The big monkey escorts both of the small monkeys to the other side one at a time, then returns to the starting side. Two humans cross. One human returns with one of the small monkeys, while the other human stays on the opposite bank with the other small monkey. The human that just returned crosses with the large monkey, leaves him on the opposite bank with the human, and takes back a small monkey. The two humans cross, leaving two small monkeys on the initial side, and end up with all three humans and the big monkey on the opposite side. The big monkey sails back and ferries the smaller monkeys across to the ending side one at a time, as in the beginning (Adamovic, 2012).

Apples and Oranges

Riddle

There are three covered baskets. One contains only apples, one contains only oranges, and one contains a mixture of both. The baskets are labeled, but they are all labeled incorrectly. You must determine the true contents of each basket, but you can reach into only one basket and take only one piece of fruit. Which basket do you reach into, and how does that tell you the contents of all the baskets?

Materials

Fill three cups or baskets with a few small balls or slips of paper that say either *apple* or *orange* on them. One basket should only have oranges, one should have only apples, and one should have a mixture of both. Label each cup, but ensure that no cup's label matches its actual contents. Encourage students to ask, "If I draw from this basket and get an apple, what will I know? What can I conclude from that? What if I get an orange?" Note-taking materials are also helpful for keeping track of possibilities.

Solution

Take an item from the basket labeled *Apples and Oranges*. Because of the incorrect labels, you know that this basket does not contain both types of fruit. If you get an apple, that basket has apples in it. You have then eliminated apples as a choice, and the basket labeled *Oranges* cannot have apples or oranges in it, so it must have apples *and* oranges. Therefore, the basket labeled *Apples* has oranges in it.

If, when you reach into the *Apples and Oranges* basket, you get an orange, the logic works similarly. The *Apples and Oranges* basket has oranges in it, the basket labeled *Apples* therefore has apples and oranges in it, and the basket labeled *Oranges* has apples in it.

The Hat Game

Riddle

Four men are given hats to wear. There are two black hats and two white hats, and the men know this. The first man is behind a screen and cannot see or be seen by anyone else. The second, third, and fourth men are lined up so the second man can see no one, the third man can only see the second man, and the fourth man can see both the second and third men. They are not allowed to talk to one another, and no one can see the color of his own hat, but each is instructed to try to figure out the color of his hat. A minute goes by, and no one calls out. Then, one of the men correctly calls out the color of his own hat. Which man was it?

Materials

You will need four hats in two different colors—you might use actual hats, paper hats, bandanas, or anything else that will stay on students' heads. Students then line up as described in the riddle: one student is out of the room or otherwise obscured from the rest of the group, and the others are in a line, all facing the same direction. The students in the line can only look straight ahead.

Solution

The third man yells out the color of his hat, because he figures out the following: all four men know there are two black hats and two white hats. The fourth man can see the second and third men. If the fourth man had seen the second and third men wearing the same color hats, he would have known for certain that he was wearing the other color and would have called it out. Since he did not yell it out, it is obvious that the second and third man are wearing different-colored hats. Therefore, the third man simply looks at the color of the second man's hat and calls out the opposite color—which is the color of his own hat (Royal, n.d.).

Twelve Marbles

Riddle

You have twelve marbles that are identical in size, shape, and color, but one of them weighs slightly more than the others. You need to determine which single marble is heavier in weight than the others. You are supplied with a balance (two pans on opposite sides of a fulcrum; the side with heavier things in it will tilt lower than the other side), but you can only use it three times. How can you figure out which marble is heavier?

Materials

You will need twelve marbles (the actual weights do not matter). A balance is not necessary, since students only need to figure out which groupings should be placed on the balance during each of the three weigh-ins.

Solution

First, weigh all twelve marbles, six on each side of the balance (weigh-in 1). From whichever side is heavier, take those six marbles and weigh three on each side (weigh-in 2). Again, from whichever side is heavier, take those three marbles. For the third weigh-in, place one marble to the side, and weigh the other two—one on each side of the balance (weigh-in 3). During this weigh-in, if one marble is heavier than the other, the answer is obvious. If they balance perfectly, then the marble you put to the side is the heavier one (Expand Your Mind, n.d.).

High School

Night Crossing (Whole-Class Activity)

Riddle

Four people need to cross a dark river at night. They have only one flashlight and the river is too risky to cross without it. If all the people cross simultaneously, the light will not be sufficient—only two people can cross at the same time. The speed of each person crossing the river is different. When two people cross together, they travel at the speed of the slower person. Each of the four people takes one minute, two minutes, seven minutes, and ten minutes to cross, respectively. What is the shortest time needed for all four people to cross the river?

Materials

Similar to "Troll Tolls" and "A Liar and a Truth-Teller," the best way to represent this riddle is to have students act it out. Four students act as the four people, passing a flashlight (a pencil or similar item works fine) between them to represent the torch. It should be clear how long each person takes to cross, so students should wear nametags or hold signs showing their required time (one, two, seven, or ten minutes). It is also helpful if students have note-taking materials to keep track of the time elapsed.

Solution

One and two go across (two minutes). Two comes back (two minutes). Seven and ten go across (ten minutes). One comes back (one minute). One and two go across (two minutes). The shortest time is seventeen minutes (2 + 2 + 10 + 1 + 2 = 17) (Best Brain Teasers, 2013).

Weight Watch

Riddle

There are three machines designed to produce one-ounce ball bearings. However, one machine is defective and produces 1.1-ounce ball bearings. Each machine has a cup of ball bearings that it produced sitting in front of it. You may take any combination of ball bearings from these cups (for example, you can take one from each cup, three from one cup, two from one cup, or none from a cup, and so on). Once you select a combination of ball bearings, you can weigh that combination once on a scale. What combination of ball bearings should you select to weigh to figure out which machine is defective? Keep in mind that you select one combination of ball bearings and weigh it once; you do not get to choose multiple combinations or weigh multiple times.

Materials

Label three cups A, B, and C to represent the machines. Put several (at least three) marbles in each cup to represent the ball bearings produced by that machine (the actual weights do not matter). Students should also have pencils and paper to write down various possibilities. As in "Twelve Marbles" (page 122), a scale is not necessary since students only need to figure out what combination of ball bearings (if weighed) would reveal which machine is defective. To help students think this through, ask them questions like "If you weigh this many ball bearings from this machine and it is working, what will the weight be? What if it is defective?"

Solution

Weigh two ball bearings from A and one from B. If the combined weight is three ounces, then you know C is defective. If the combined weight is 3.2 ounces, you know that A is defective. If the combined weight is 3.1 ounces, you know B is defective (Royal, n.d.).

Heads and Tails

Riddle

There are twenty coins sitting on a table. Ten are turned so the heads side is facing up, and ten are turned so the tails side is facing up. You are sitting at the table with a blindfold and gloves on. You are able to feel where the coins are but are unable to see or feel if they are heads or tails. You must create two sets of coins. Each set must have the same number of heads and tails as the other group. You can only move or flip the coins, but you do not know which coins are currently heads up or tails up. How do you create two even groups of coins with the same number of heads and tails in each group?

Materials

You will need twenty coins of any denomination and a blindfold. Although gloves are not required, it *is* possible to feel whether a coin is heads up or tails up with bare fingers; therefore, we recommend having students wear thin gloves.

Solution

Split the coins into two groups of ten. Group A will have x heads, and $10 - x$ tails; that is, among the ten coins in group A, an unknown number (x) of them will be facing heads up, while the remainder ($10 - x$) will be facing tails up. Because the entire set of coins includes ten heads and ten tails, the number of each in group B will be the opposite of group A: group B will have x tails, and $10 - x$ heads. Flip every coin in group B. Both groups now have x heads and $10 - x$ tails (Guthrie, 2010).

Cards in the Dark

Riddle

You are standing in a completely dark room. A friend walks up and hands you a normal deck of fifty-two cards. He tells you that thirteen of the fifty-two cards are face up, and the rest are face down. These face-up cards are distributed randomly throughout the deck. Your task is to split up the deck into two piles using all the cards, so each pile has the same number of face-up cards. The room is completely dark, so you can't see the deck as you do this. How can you accomplish this seemingly impossible task?

Materials

You will need a full deck of cards with thirteen of them flipped upside down, and a blindfold.

Solution

The solution to this riddle is similar to the solution for "Heads and Tails" (see page 123), except that the deck of cards is unequally split into face-up and face-down cards. Knowing that there are thirteen face-up cards in the deck, you should split the deck into a group of thirteen (group A) and a group of thirty-nine (group B). Group A will have x (an unknown number) face-up cards and $13 - x$ (the remainder of group A) face-down cards. Because there are thirteen total face-up cards in the deck, group B will have $13 - x$ face-up cards (thirteen total face-up cards minus the face-up cards that ended up in group A) and the rest face down. Flip over all the cards in group A to end up with $13 - x$ face-up cards in both groups (Big Riddles, 2009).

6 Never Tells

For middle school and high school students

Never Tells are fun activities that help students practice using inductive reasoning to identify rules and patterns. They are called Never Tells because people who know the answer should *never* just *tell* it to someone else—each person has to figure it out for himself or herself. Although Never Tells are a classic rainy-day activity at many summer camps, the concept of identifying a rule is vital to everyday reasoning and has been the focus of reasoning research.

In one of his studies of inductive reasoning, Peter C. Wason (1966) presented a series of three numbers, such as *2, 4, 6*, and asked participants to figure out the rule being used to generate the series by trying to generate other series of three numbers that also fit the rule. For each series the person gave, the experimenter would tell the person whether or not it fit the rule. The vast majority of participants came up with a hypothesis (what they thought the rule was) as quickly as possible, continually presented examples that fit the suspected rule, and only changed the hypothesis when he or she happened to present a series that led the experimenter to say it did not fit the original rule—a strategy that Wason called *successive scanning*. This strategy is both inefficient and illogical, as it depends on the participants' randomly guessing an example that fits their hypothesis but not the experimenter's rule. Stumbling onto a counterexample can be very difficult to do, especially if the actual rule being used by the experimenter is extremely general. For example, if the experimenter starts by giving the positive (correct) example *2, 4, 6*, most participants immediately guess that the rule is

Reasoning Skills

- Identifying rules and patterns
- Applying rules and patterns
- Asking questions to challenge assumptions

Materials

- Materials will vary and are listed with specific Never Tells (see pages 128–137) "even numbers increasing by two" and give examples such as *12, 14, 16* to try to confirm their hypothesis. The secret rule is actually much more general—increasing numbers. To figure out this more general rule, the participant needs to give examples that do not fit his or her hypothesis, such as *1, 2, 3*. If the participant guesses *1, 2, 3* expecting that to break the rule, he or she gains significant information when the experimenter still affirms it. Wason pointed out that "the subject must systematically generate instances which are inconsistent with different aspects of his hypothesis in order to see whether the rule holds for them" (Wason, 1966, p. 141). The same holds true for Never Tells: students must avoid confirmation bias (see the introduction, page 32) and remember to refine their hypothesis by giving instances that can disprove their proposed rule (that is, counterexamples).

Setup

Most Never Tells require no setup whatsoever, just your knowledge of the rule and an explanation of the basic idea of how to solve it. A few of the Never Tells require simple props (such as two sticks). Most Never Tells work best if you can have the class sit in a circle so that everyone can see everyone else. This also facilitates going around the circle as students give examples so that all students participate equally.

Play

Each Never Tell has a rule, which the person leading the game (usually the teacher) knows but the rest of the group does not. Each person in the group has to try to figure out the rule by presenting specific examples to the leader, who tells that person if his or her example fits the rule or not. By generating examples, getting a response, and listening to the examples and responses of the rest of the group, students try to identify the rule using inductive reasoning. They must look for patterns in the responses from the teacher to first hypothesize a rule about the qualities that make their examples correct. Then—the step that many people forget to do—they must test their hypothesized rule by providing instances that they predict will *not* fit the rule (counterexamples). When a student thinks they have figured out the correct rule—that is, he or she can reliably predict whether an example is right or wrong—the student confirms it with the teacher. To do this, the student must whisper (or go out of earshot of the rest of the group) so the rule remains secret. Students could also write their guesses on slips of paper, fold them, and hand them to the teacher. Students who know the rule can then help the rest of the group by giving positive (correct) examples, which help other students recognize patterns.

 Some of your students may have encountered one or more of the Never Tells at summer camp, in an after-school program, or with friends. As such, they may already know the rule. Before introducing a Never Tell, remind all students that if they know the rule they should not give away the answer, but can give correct examples to help their classmates figure it out.

To illustrate, consider the Never Tell called "Green Glass Door." The teacher introduces the game by telling the group that there is a magical green glass door. Some things can go through the green glass door, while others cannot. The group's task is to figure out the rule that defines which things can go through the door. The rule for "Green Glass Door" is that things with double letters in their names can go through—but the teacher keeps this a secret. Start the game by giving a positive (correct) example and a negative (incorrect) example. For example, the teacher might say, "Trees can go through the green glass door, but plants cannot." Students then take turns asking whether various things can go through the door. The first few examples that students give might be:

Joey: Can a computer go through the door?

Teacher: No.

Megan: Can a cat go through?

Teacher: No.

Teresa: What about a softball mitt?

Teacher: Yes! A softball mitt can go through the green glass door.

People are hardwired to look for patterns, so students may start identifying potential rules very quickly. In this example, based on the examples tried, a student might think, "Hmm, maybe the rule is that only things that don't start with *C* can go through the door." Instead of asking the teacher directly, the student should first test his or her rule by purposely giving examples that could disprove it. If a student asks if a canteen, caterpillar, or cookie will go through the green glass door, he or she will quickly discover that his or her speculation about the rule was incorrect. Students are unlikely to do this naturally, so remind them at the beginning of the game that they should try several times to disprove their hypothesized rule using counterexamples before checking it directly with the teacher.

 An important part of Never Tells is that every student gets a chance to figure out the rule on his or her own! You must emphasize to students that the rule is a secret they must keep to themselves. Even if figuring out the rule is frustrating, finally getting it can be very rewarding; being told the answer is far less satisfying. It may also help to remind students that Never Tells are challenging—even adults often need lots of time to figure out each rule. In sum, ensure that Never Tells remain lighthearted, fun activities and do not become objects of contention or vehicles for teasing.

When a student has hypothesized a rule and tested it with several counterexamples, he or she can whisper the hypothesized rule to you or write it down and hand it to you, and you will either confirm that the student has figured it out or send the student back to try more examples. As students begin to figure out the rule, there will be more and more positive examples given, which can make it easier for other students to figure out the correct rule. It can often take quite a while for the first person to figure out the rule, but typically other students subsequently figure it out at a quicker pace.

If students are having a very difficult time figuring out the rule, it is acceptable to give hints. Targeted hints for specific Never Tells are provided in the items at the end of this chapter. General hints that work for all Never Tells include the following:

◆ Give positive and negative examples that are very similar but differ just enough that one fits the rule and the other breaks it. For example, for "Green Glass Door," a princess can go through the door, but a prince cannot.

◆ Point students in the right direction by telling them what to look for. For example, for "Green Glass Door," say, "It's not about the thing itself, but about the name of the thing."

◆ Emphasize the defining factor in increasingly obvious ways. For example, for "Green Glass Door," draw out the pronunciation of double letters.

Another way to help students see patterns and figure out the rule is to visually keep track of the examples given by students and whether they are positive or negative examples. For "Green Glass Door," you could make a T-chart that lists things that can go through the door on one side and things that cannot on the other.

Hints can be especially important for students who are struggling to discover the rule. If a student is the last one in the class who is not in the know, he or she may feel isolated. Keep an eye out for this and be prepared to pull an individual student aside to help him or her figure out the rule.

Wrap-Up

Never Tells are easily played as long-term games. Once you introduce a Never Tell, students can give examples during any appropriate extra time. For example, if there are a few minutes left in class, students can give a few examples to work on figuring out the rule. Playing a Never Tell for too long at one time can become boring for those who already know the rule, and frustrating for those who haven't figured it out. Avoid this by limiting the time spent with the whole class focused on the game to perhaps fifteen

Students can also continue working on Never Tells during extra time with each other. Once one student knows the rule, he or she can become a leader of the game who can confirm or deny examples given by other students.

Sometimes the title of a Never Tell gives a hint about its solution. You can let students know this when introducing Never Tells, or you can see how long it takes them to figure out that particular pattern on their own!

minutes, and then let students know they will have opportunities to ask you about it during breaks and extra time. You might say, "We are going to move on to something else now, but you can keep thinking about this and ask me about specific examples at the beginning of class tomorrow or if you see me in the hallway."

Sample Never Tells

The following Never Tells are listed in order of increasing difficulty. Each one gives the name of the Never Tell, instructions for presenting it to students, the rule that students must figure out, and correct and incorrect examples. Some Never Tells also include notes about tricky situations to look out for and specific hints that you can give when needed.

The Umbrella Game

Tell students that the class is going on a picnic, and students must take turns asking if they can bring various items.

Rule: They can bring any item as long as they say "umm" or another hesitation word in front of it.

Correct: "Can I bring . . . umm . . . a picnic blanket?"

Incorrect: "Can I bring a picnic blanket?"

Potential Problems: Students might pause silently as they try to think of an object to bring; if they don't actually say "umm," it is not a correct example.

Hints: Overpronounce your "umms." If a student gives a negative example, repeat the same item he or she just used, but with an "umm" to help show that the item itself doesn't matter.

Green Glass Door

Tell students that there is a magical green glass door. Some things can go through the door, but others cannot. Students take turns guessing what can go through.

Rule: Only words with double letters can go through the door.

Correct: feet, trees, books, pepper, vacuum, Jillian

Incorrect: water, desk, Tim, shoes, cake

Potential Problems: Students might guess two-word items where one word has double letters but the other doesn't (for example, water bottle). Decide in advance whether you will accept these items.

Hints: Tell students not to think about the thing itself, but the word. Give two very similar examples, one positive and one negative. Enunciate double letter sounds.

Crossed or Uncrossed

With two sticks (or pencils, rulers, or something similar), show the group either an X or parallel lines and say, "These sticks are _____ [crossed/uncrossed]" according to the rule. Then pass the sticks to a student, ask him or her to arrange the sticks as either an X or parallel lines, and have the student say, "These sticks are _____ [crossed/uncrossed]." Tell the student if he or she is right or wrong, and then continue with another student.

Rule: The shape made by the sticks doesn't matter at all; you say "crossed" or "uncrossed" based on how your legs are positioned at that moment.

Correct: Legs crossed and sticks crossed → "Crossed."

Legs crossed and sticks uncrossed → "Crossed."

Legs uncrossed and sticks crossed → "Uncrossed."

Legs uncrossed and sticks uncrossed → "Uncrossed."

Incorrect: Legs crossed and sticks crossed → "Uncrossed."

Legs crossed and sticks uncrossed → "Uncrossed."

Legs uncrossed and sticks crossed → "Crossed."

Legs uncrossed and sticks uncrossed → "Crossed."

Hints: Change the position of your legs right before you make your statement, first subtly and then more obviously.

Phantom

Tell students there is a phantom in the room, and they have to figure out whom it is standing behind. Have them all mill about for a few seconds, and then say, "Freeze!" Then ask, "Where's the phantom?" Let students guess a few locations before telling them the right answer, and repeat.

Rule: The phantom is behind whoever speaks first.

Correct: You ask, "Where's the phantom?" Sara makes the first guess. Several guesses later, Patrick asks, "Is it behind Sara?" He is correct.

Incorrect: You ask, "Where's the phantom?" Sara makes the first guess. Then Kevin guesses, "Is it behind Nate?" He is incorrect.

Potential Problems: If the first student to make a guess says, "Is it behind me?" he or she is correct.

Yellow Frying Pan

Tell the class that you have several items in your yellow frying pan, and those items indicate who is coming over for dinner. Say, "In my yellow frying pan, I have _____, _____, and _____ [select random items]. Who is coming over for dinner?" Allow students to guess several different people before telling them who is coming to dinner.

Rule: Whoever speaks first is coming over for dinner; that is, the first person to make a guess becomes the answer. Items in the frying pan don't have to be food, and you can create a false causal link between the items and the answer in students' minds by picking items that the group might associate with a specific person (for example, what someone is wearing, things related to their favorite hobby, and so on).

Correct: You say, "In my yellow frying pan I have cheese, a baseball cap, and pencils. Who is coming over for dinner?" Bobby makes the first guess. Several guesses later, Corinne asks, "Is it Bobby?" She is correct.

Incorrect: You say, "In my yellow frying pan I have cheese, a baseball cap, and pencils. Who is coming over for dinner?" Bobby makes the first guess. Then Jerri guesses, "Is it Jason?" She is incorrect.

Potential Problems: The only way for someone to answer first and be correct is to say, "I am."

Mystery Sticks

You need two or more sticks, pencils, straws, or similar items. Explain to students that you've invented a code in which the pattern of sticks on the ground corresponds to a number. Arrange the sticks on the ground and ask the group what number they think it is. Let them guess a few numbers before you tell them the correct answer. Rearrange the sticks and repeat.

Rule: The arrangement of the sticks is meaningless. After arranging them, subtly display a number with your fingers—that's the number that students have to say.

Correct: You arrange the sticks on the ground in a shape that happens to look similar to a *4*; then cross your arms and subtly display three fingers on one hand as you ask students what number it is (see figure 6.1). The answer is three.

Arrangement of Sticks

Teacher's Arms

Figure 6.1: Example for Mystery Sticks.

Incorrect: You arrange the sticks on the ground in a box shape. You put your hands on your hips, but with one finger sticking out, indicating the answer is one. Students who guess zero, four, twenty-three, or any other number besides one are incorrect.

I Can See the Moon in This Cup

For this Never Tell, you will need a cup, mug, water bottle, or similar vessel. Hold the cup, look down into it, and say, "I can see the moon in this cup; can you?" Then offer the cup to someone in the group so he or she can try to copy you. The next person looks into the cup and says the phrase, and you tell that person whether he or she is right or wrong. This pattern continues with the cup being passed around the circle or at random to anyone in the group.

Rule: The person receiving the cup must say "Thank you" to the person handing it to them before he or she says, "I can see the moon in this cup; can you?" This doubles as a fun way to reinforce politeness and show how easily we forget our manners when focused on something else.

Correct: Devin hands the cup to Dana, Dana says "Thank you," and then she looks into the cup and says, "I can see the moon in this cup; can you?"

Incorrect: Dana takes the cup from Devin and immediately says, "I can see the moon in this cup; can you?"

Hints: Take the cup back and demonstrate again, even if it hasn't gone all the way around the circle, so the group sees more positive examples.

The Broom Dance

For this active Never Tell, you will need a broom or other random object to dance with. Do a silly dance with the broom (or other object) while singing, "I can do the broom dance, broom dance, broom dance" (substitute the name of the object for *broom*) several times. Students take turns trying to imitate you, and you indicate after each dance whether it was correct or incorrect.

Rule: You say a specific word or make a specific sound before beginning the dance (for example, saying "Okay" or clearing your throat). Students must copy the word or sound or their dance will not be correct. The dance itself doesn't matter.

Correct: You say "Okay" and then begin doing a silly dance that involves waving one arm above your head. Annie goes next. She says "Okay," and then does the same dance. Aisha goes third, and she says "Okay" before doing a completely different dance that involves spinning in circles. Both students are correct.

Incorrect: You say "Okay" and then begin doing a silly dance that involves waving one arm above your head. Neela goes next, and she immediately copies the dance. She is incorrect.

Hints: Make your specific word or sound progressively more obvious. A second person who knows the rule can copy the key word and then do a completely different dance to help students understand that the dance itself is irrelevant.

Open or Closed

Simulate a door with your hands and have it alternate open and closed several times before stopping in either position and asking, "Open or closed?"

Rule: The answer to "Open or closed?" depends not on the shape of your hands, but on your mouth.

Correct: If your mouth is open and a student says "Open," he or she is correct. If your mouth is closed and a student says "Closed," he or she is correct.

Incorrect: If a student says the opposite of what your mouth is doing, he or she is incorrect.

Hints: Start with your mouth only slightly parted for open, but progressively open it wider.

Whoops Johnny

This is another Never Tell that involves the group trying to imitate you exactly. Hold one hand up with all five fingers splayed. Starting on the pinky, use the pointer finger of your other hand to touch the ends of each of your fingers, and say "Johnny" as you touch each one. After touching your first finger, the space between your first finger and thumb acts like a slide and you say "Whoops Johnny" as your pointer finger slides down the side of your hand and up onto your thumb. Then the pattern reverses and goes back the other way, ending again with the pinky (see figure 6.2 for an illustration). The whole pattern is "Johnny [pinky], Johnny [ring finger], Johnny [middle finger], Johnny [first finger], whoops [slide] Johnny [thumb], whoops [slide the other way] Johnny [first], Johnny [middle], Johnny [ring], Johnny [pinky]." Then subtly cross your arms across your chest and ask students to copy what you just did.

Rule: Crossing your arms at the end is the key.

Correct: A student does the pattern correctly and crosses his arms at the end.

Incorrect: A student does the pattern incorrectly, or a student does the pattern correctly but fails to cross her arms at the end.

Hints: Cross your arms more obviously.

The Man in the Moon

You draw in the air with your finger while saying, "The man in the moon [draw a circle] has two eyes [add two dots for eyes], a nose [add a nose], and a mouth [add a smile]." Then, give students (one at a time) the chance to copy you exactly.

Rule: Add a small motion to the beginning of the sequence, such as scratching your nose or tucking your hair behind your ear—this is the key to the sequence.

Correct: You scratch your nose and do the sequence. A student scratches his nose and does the sequence (even if he draws the moon differently)—he is correct.

Incorrect: You scratch your nose and do the sequence. A student does the sequence without first scratching his nose—he is incorrect.

Hints: Make your added motion more obvious. You can also change the way you draw your moon (use a different hand, draw the circle clockwise instead of counterclockwise, and so on).

My Aunt Likes Coffee but Not Tea

Tell the class that you all have an aunt who is very picky. After you give an example, students take turns guessing what your aunt likes and doesn't like. Responses always take the form, "My aunt likes _____ but not _____."

Rule: Your aunt does not like things that have the letter *T* in their names.

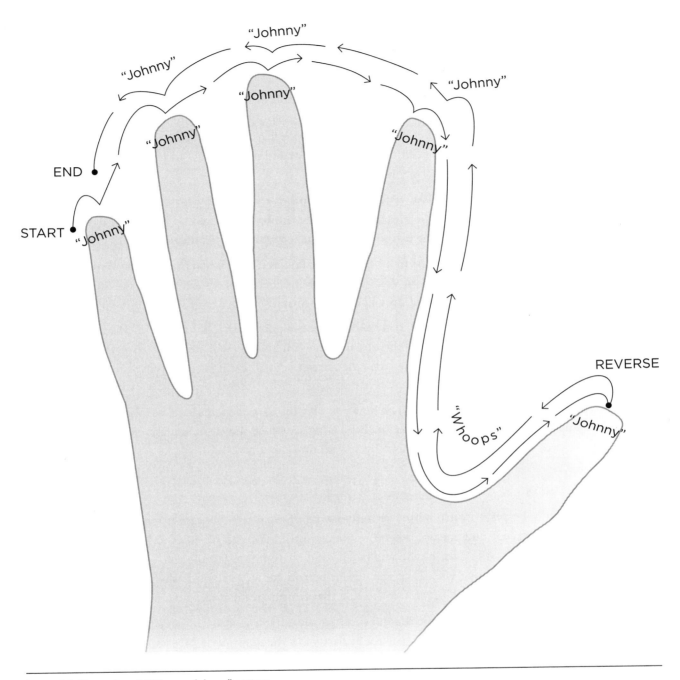

Figure 6.2: Illustration of "Whoops Johnny" pattern.

Correct: My aunt likes cream but not butter. My aunt likes books but not computers. My aunt likes sons but not daughters. My aunt likes moms but not mothers. My aunt likes pizza but not Italian food.

Incorrect: My aunt likes biscuits but not cookies. My aunt likes trays but not tables.

Hints: Give examples that are very similar, or even synonyms for the same thing, such as baseball and basketball, moms and mothers, and so on. Tell students that the rule is not about the objects being named, but about the names themselves. You can also enunciate *T* sounds more clearly to draw attention to them.

What Number Is This?

Begin by holding up your first finger and pointing at students as you say, "This is how you play the game." Then go to two fingers and say, "This is one." Then hold up three fingers and say, "This is two." Then four fingers and say, "This is three." Then five fingers and say, "This is four." Finally, hold up a fist and say, "This is five." Do this sequence at a moderate pace. Then show any random number of fingers and ask, "What is this?" Students try to guess what number it is. Let them guess a few numbers before telling them the correct answer. Then switch to a different random number of fingers and ask students to guess again. After several iterations, start over with the beginning sequence.

Rule: The answer to "What is this?" is always whatever number you held up previously. The sequence at the beginning follows this rule as well, and it means that the first number you hold up and ask about will always have the answer "zero" since you end the introductory sequence with a fist (indicating zero).

Correct: If you hold up three fingers the first time you ask (answer: zero), then the second number of fingers you hold up will have the answer "three." If you hold up five fingers the second time you ask (answer: three), then the third number of fingers you hold up will have the answer "five."

Incorrect: After the beginning sequence, you hold up one finger and ask, "What is this?" A student guesses, "Is it five?" She is incorrect, as the answer to the first number you hold up will always be zero. Then you switch to holding up four fingers. A student guesses that the answer is four. He is incorrect, as you previously held up one finger.

Hints: Keep your hand still as you say "This is how you play the game," so students will realize it is a number one rather than a "pay attention" gesture. Say the beginning sequence slower so students will have more time to process it. Repeat the number that you hold up several times in a row.

The Right Party

This game can only be played once with a group with its original rule because it requires that the whole group knows the rule except one person; however, you can invent alternative rules to keep the game going. One member of the group—the person who will be "it" and try to figure out the rule—leaves the room, and you explain the game to everyone else. Then the absent person comes back and asks yes or no questions to various people in the circle to try to figure out the rule that people in the group are using to answer.

Rule: Everyone in the circle, when asked a question by the person who is "it," must answer as if they are the person to their right (hence the name, "The Right Party"). If the question is "Are you wearing a red shirt?" then the student's answer depends on whether the person to his or her right is wearing a red shirt. You can limit the types of questions that can be asked to make the game easier or harder. Questions about physical appearance are the simplest. You may also choose to allow questions about likes and dislikes, hobbies and activities, and so on. Questions with answers that can't be seen (and therefore may be answered incorrectly) introduce the second twist in the game. If someone answers a question incorrectly for the person to his or her right, the person to their right calls out "Switch!" and everyone gets up and moves to a new spot in the circle. For example, Julien is sitting to the right of Ryan. The questioner asks Ryan, "Is math your favorite subject?" Ryan must answer as if he were Julien, but he doesn't know Julien very well, so he guesses "No." Julien hears this, and math is actually his favorite subject, so he calls out "Switch!" and everyone in the circle gets up and sits in a new spot. This is both confusing and helpful to the questioner, because he or she won't know what's happening at first but may eventually notice that it is always the person to the right who says "Switch!"

Correct: The questioner asks Freya, "Are you wearing a dress?" Lucy is sitting to the right of Freya, and Lucy is wearing pants, so Freya says "No" regardless of what she herself is wearing. The questioner then asks Rob, "Is your birthday in July?" Niall is sitting to the right of Rob, but Rob is not sure when Niall's birthday is, so he guesses "Yes." Niall's birthday is actually in March, so Niall calls out "Switch!"

Incorrect: The questioner asks Freya, "Are you wearing a dress?" Lucy is sitting to the right of Freya, and Lucy is wearing pants, but Freya says "Yes." Lucy does not say "Switch." Incorrect responses should not actually occur in The Right Party; that is, if someone answers a question incorrectly, it should always be followed by a "Switch." You should periodically remind students that they need to pay attention to all questions and responses.

Alternative Rules: Alternative rules are only limited by what the group can come up with. For example, everyone could answer for the person to their left, or for the person two (or three or any number) away from them. Everyone could answer as if they were one specific person in the group, or everyone can answer as if they were the questioner (this only works with visible questions or if the group knows each other very well, since the questioner can't say "Switch!"). A final alternative could be that everyone answers as if they were the previous person who answered a question.

The Story Game

This Never Tell can only be played once with a group because it requires all but one person to know the rule. However, you can divide up the class into small groups and send a member of each group out of the room. This increases participation, as well as the mileage you get out of the game. Explain to the whole class that one person (or one person from each group) will leave and the rest of the group will make up a story while that student is gone. Then, the student will come back and ask yes-or-no questions to try to figure out the story. Send one person (per group) out of the room, and then explain the rule to the rest of the students.

Rule: There is no story. The group's response to each question depends on the last letter of the question asked. If the question ends in a consonant, the answer is no. If the question ends in a vowel, the answer is yes. If the question ends in the letter *y*, the answer is maybe.

Correct: The person trying to guess the story (that doesn't exist) says, "Are there monkeys in the story?" The group says "Maybe." The guesser asks, "Does it take place on the moon?" The group says "No." The guesser asks, "Does it take place under the sea?" The group says "Yes."

Incorrect: The person trying to guess the story says, "Are there monkeys in the story?" The group says "Yes." The guesser asks, "Does it take place on the moon?" The group says "Maybe." The guesser asks, "Does it take place under the sea?" The group says "No." As with "The Right Party," incorrect answers should not actually occur, because the whole group knows the rule.

This Can Has Five Sides

You need a can or similar item for this Never Tell. Explain to the group that the number of sides on the can is always changing, and they have to figure out how many sides it has. Holding the can, say "This can has five sides." Pass it to the next person, who then makes a statement about how many sides it has; you must identify that statement as correct or incorrect.

Rule: The number of sides on the can must match the number of words in the statement.

Correct: This can has five sides.

Two sides.

Now the can has six sides.

It has three.

Incorrect: Four sides.

This can has twelve sides.

Potential Problems: It can be a bit difficult to count the number of words in sentences as people say them. It is acceptable to take a moment to count before telling students whether their answers are right or wrong. If necessary, ask students to repeat their sentences.

Hints: Particularly long or short sentences (such as "One" or "I counted the sides on the can and there are eleven") can draw the group's attention to sentence length as an important factor. If the group is having a very hard time, try subtly counting on your fingers as you talk and listen to students' examples. Writing students' examples on a whiteboard or chart paper can also help them recognize patterns for this Never Tell.

Around the World

The group sits in a circle and takes turns saying, "I'm going to _____ [place name]." You tell each person whether they are allowed to go or not, based on the rule.

Rule: The first letter of each place must spell out, in order, A-R-O-U-N-D-T-H-E-W-O-R-L-D.

Correct: You say, "I'm going to Albania."

Student 1 says, "I'm going to Rwanda."

Student 2 says, "I'm going to Oslo."

Student 3 says, "I'm going to Uganda."

Incorrect: You say, "I'm going to Albania."

Student 1 says, "I'm going to Cairo."

Potential Problems: Only correct answers count toward the spelling; that is, do not move on to the next letter until someone has said a place that starts with the previous one, no matter how many people get it wrong in between (see the following).

You say, "I'm going to Albania."

Student 1 says, "I'm going to Rwanda." [Correct]

Student 2 says, "I'm going to Ireland." [Wrong]

Student 3 says, "I'm going to Poland." [Wrong]

Student 4 says, "I'm going to Oslo." [Correct]

Student 5 says, "I'm going to Uganda." [Correct]

Be sure to keep track of where in the spelling the group is! When you get to the end of the word *world*, start over again with the letter *A*.

Hints: Writing down the correct examples is very helpful. This Never Tell is fairly challenging if you are the only one who knows the rule, but more people usually catch on quickly once the first few people figure it out.

Petals Around the Rose

You need five dice for this Never Tell, which is popular in mathematics and computer science circles. Roll the dice and then ask, "How many petals around the rose?" Students make guesses about how many petals there are, and you identify each guess as correct or incorrect. You should announce the correct answer before rolling again.

Rule: The center of the rose is the center dot on a die, and the petals around it are the surrounding dots. The number of petals around the rose in each roll is the sum of the petals on each individual die. Only die faces with three or five dots have a center dot; therefore, only dice that show three or five will increase the number of petals. A roll of three has two petals and a roll of five has four petals, so the answer will always be an even number or zero (if no threes or fives are rolled). Add the number of petals on each individual die to get the total answer for the roll.

Correct: You roll a one, two threes, a five, and a six (see figure 6.3). Katie guesses that there are eight petals around the rose. She is correct.

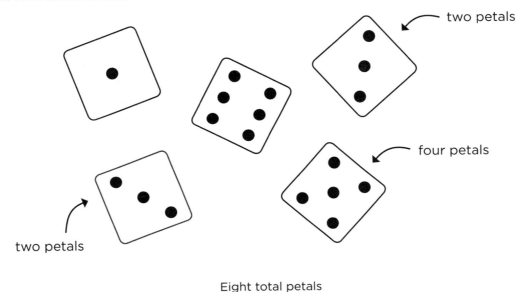

Eight total petals

Figure 6.3: Example dice roll for "Petals Around the Rose."

Incorrect: You roll a one, two threes, a five, and a six. Matt guesses that there are five petals around the rose. He is incorrect.

Hints: It is helpful to write down rolls and their corresponding numbers of petals. Roll fewer dice to create an easier version of the game.

7 Valid or True

For middle school and high school students

Valid or True gives students practice evaluating deductive conclusions and (in the more challenging version) standardizing reasoning. As explained in the introduction (page 22), a syllogism is a set of two premises and a corresponding conclusion. In the basic version of this game, students practice evaluating syllogisms for validity and truth. In the more challenging version, students are only given a statement which they must standardize into a syllogism before evaluating it for validity and truth. The goal of the game is to help students realize that conclusions are not necessarily valid or true; they must be evaluated. When conclusions are presented as statements (which happens often in daily conversations), they often contain implicit premises, which must be explicitly stated and standardized before the conclusion can be evaluated.

Setup

The only setup required for this game is the creation of syllogisms (for the basic version) or statements (for the more challenging version). This book includes sets of each type of item (see pages 142–179), but teachers may also create their own. To play this game, students need to be familiar with evaluating deductive conclusions for validity and truth (and with standardizing reasoning for the more challenging version).

Divide the class into groups of two to three students. Students will need note-taking materials to do scratch work and write down their final answers.

Reasoning Skills

- Standardizing reasoning
- Evaluating deductive conclusions

Materials

- Syllogisms or statements (see pages 142–179)
- Note-taking materials
- Whiteboard or projector to display syllogisms or statements
- Timer (optional)

Play

Begin the game by presenting an item to students. You might write it on the board or display it using a document camera or projector. If you are playing the basic version of the game, the item should be a syllogism (see pages 142–160) like the following.

Foundational premise: People who miss the bus are late to school.

Minor premise: Jeffy missed the bus.

Deductive conclusion: Jeffy is late to school.

Students evaluate the syllogism and decide if they think the argument is valid and true. Students should keep in mind that a conclusion can be valid but not true if one of the premises is untrue. Students should also remember that if a syllogism is invalid, whether or not it is true is irrelevant. Therefore, if a syllogism is invalid, there is no need to evaluate it for truth. In this example, the conclusion is valid (that is, it follows logically from the premises). Students will also probably judge it to be true. When your students are evaluating premises for truth, you should be aware that while some premises are clearly true or false, others may be statements of opinion. If a premise states an opinion, students may rightfully believe it (and therefore the syllogism) to be true or false—polite disagreement is acceptable in this situation. Confusion may arise, however, between opinions (for example, "Reality television is not entertaining") and untrue universal statements (for example, "Children who are homeschooled are shy"). The former is certainly an opinion, as the entertainment value of reality television is a matter of personal preference. The latter, however (although people may have differing perceptions about the shyness of homeschooled students), purports that *all* children who are homeschooled are shy. Homeschooled children who are not shy certainly exist. This statement is false because it states something about *all* members of a group that is only true for *some*. In general, statements about the quality or value of things are more likely to be opinions than statements that broadly describe categories of objects or groups of people. (For further discussion of facts and opinions, see Rogers & Simms, 2015.)

For the more challenging version of the game, present students with statements (see pages 161–179) instead of syllogisms. Students must first standardize the statement into a syllogism (two premises and a conclusion) before evaluating for validity and truth. For example, you might present students with the statement:

Dolphins are fish because they live in the ocean.

Students should think about the underlying assumptions of this statement and come up with a syllogism that consists of a foundational premise (general assumption), a minor premise (specific instance or observation), and a conclusion. For this example, students might generate a syllogism like the following.

Foundational premise: Things that live in the ocean are fish.

Minor premise: Dolphins live in the ocean.

Deductive conclusion: Dolphins are fish.

As explained in the introduction (page 23), there is often more than one way to standardize the reasoning behind a conclusion. As long as students' standardization is appropriately derived from the information in the statement, it is acceptable. Once a statement has been standardized, students evaluate their syllogisms and decide if the conclusion is valid and if it is true. Prompt students to use Euler diagrams to help them determine the validity of syllogisms and assess the truth of the premises. Different standardizations of the same statement may yield different answers about validity and truth. Here, the conclusion that dolphins must be fish is valid but not true, since the foundational premise is clearly untrue. Recall that if a conclusion is invalid, students do not need to evaluate its truth.

Ask students to quietly raise their hands or give another predetermined signal when they have finished working and would like you to check their answer. The goal is to avoid disrupting other students' work. If a group that signals to you has arrived at the correct answer and students have shown their work, they win a bonus point for finishing first. If they are incorrect, they keep working. Therefore, other groups should not stop working if they see another group signal because (1) the first group could be wrong, and (2) finishing first earns that group a bonus point, but points are also awarded to all groups who arrive at a correct answer.

Once one group has successfully evaluated the syllogism (or standardized and evaluated the statement), give other groups a few moments to finish up. Alternatively, you can use a set amount of time for every round (for example, two minutes).

Wrap-Up

After you let students know time is up, give all groups a chance to share their answers either by going quickly around the room or by using hand signals or other response strategies. Discuss the correct answer with the whole class. The depth of this discussion will depend on the success rate of the groups—that is, if all groups got the correct answer, a short discussion is likely sufficient, but if many groups had difficulty, you will want to make sure everyone understands before moving on.

As discussed previously, there may be disagreement about the truth of some premises—for example, the statement "She is healthier than everyone else because she is vegetarian" assumes the premise "Vegetarians are healthier than everyone else." Some students may think this premise is true while others might believe it to be false, as it is a statement of opinion. In this case and others like it, discussion can be productive and polite disagreement is acceptable. If students mistakenly identify a false statement as an opinion, you should review the difference.

 You can customize this game by using syllogisms and statements that are relevant to your class, school, or subject area. Statements about topical issues, such as "Students should get longer lunch periods because they need time to relax," can serve as the foundation for productive discussions about the evidence that supports them (premises), as well as the validity and truth of these conclusions.

To finish, give every group that arrived at the correct answer one point, give a bonus point to the group that was first to finish, and then move on to the next item.

Variation

You can also use the items at the end of this chapter individually during short periods of extra time at the beginning and end of class, or as a brain break during transitions. Present students with an item, ask them to evaluate it (or standardize and evaluate it) either individually or in pairs, and—after a set amount of time— check students' answers and award a point for correct ones. You could keep track of students' points in your gradebook or divide the class into larger teams (for easier tracking) and award points to each team based on how many of its members give correct answers.

Syllogisms and Statements for Valid or True

Here we provide a number of syllogisms and statements that teachers can use for Valid or True. The first set of items contains complete syllogisms which students must evaluate for validity and truth. The second set contains statements that students must standardize into syllogisms (with two premises and a conclusion) before evaluating. We also include answers (in italics) for each item to guide teachers as they check students' work. For syllogisms, the answer states if the conclusion is valid and (if applicable) true. For statements, we provide a suggested standardized syllogism (though students could come up with others), along with whether the conclusion is valid based on that syllogism and (if applicable) true. Reproducible versions of the syllogisms and statements, with blank spaces for students to fill in their evaluations (and their foundational premises, minor premises, and conclusions for statement items), can be downloaded at **marzanoresearch .com/activitiesandgames**.

Evaluating Syllogisms (Easier)

Please note that some syllogisms list "Answers will vary" in regard to their truth value. This is because those syllogisms include at least one statement of opinion, which could be considered true or not true. Additionally, if an argument is invalid, it does not have a truth value (this is denoted by —) because the "trueness" of invalid arguments is irrelevant. Statements about fictitious individuals (such as Jeffy or Marianne) are assumed to be true.

Foundational premise: People who miss the bus are late to school.

Minor premise: Jeffy missed the bus.

Deductive conclusion: Jeffy is late to school.

    Valid: Yes   *True: Yes*

Foundational premise: People who miss the bus are late to school.

Minor premise: Marianne did not miss the bus.

Deductive conclusion: Marianne is not late to school.

    Valid: No   *True: —*

Foundational premise: People who go to soccer practice will play in the weekend game.

Minor premise: Tayla went to soccer practice.

Deductive conclusion: Tayla played in the weekend game.

    Valid: Yes   *True: Yes*

Foundational premise: People who go to soccer practice will play in the weekend game.

Minor premise: Freddie didn't go to soccer practice.

Deductive conclusion: Freddie didn't play in the weekend game.

    Valid: No   *True: —*

Foundational premise: Some professional athletes are felons.

Minor premise: Peyton Manning is a professional athlete.

Deductive conclusion: Peyton Manning is a felon.

> *Valid: No*   *True: —*

Foundational premise: Some professional athletes are felons.

Minor premise: George Clooney is not a professional athlete.

Deductive conclusion: George Clooney is not a felon.

> *Valid: No*   *True: —*

Foundational premise: All snakes are cold blooded.

Minor premise: This animal is cold blooded.

Deductive conclusion: This is a snake.

> *Valid: No*   *True: —*

Foundational premise: All snails are cold blooded.

Minor premise: This animal is a snail.

Deductive conclusion: This animal is cold blooded.

> *Valid: Yes*   *True: Yes*

Foundational premise: No one who smokes has completely clean lungs.

Minor premise: I smoke.

Deductive conclusion: I do not have completely clean lungs.

> *Valid: Yes*   *True: Yes*

Foundational premise: No one who smokes has completely clean lungs.

Minor premise: I do not smoke.

Deductive conclusion: I have completely clean lungs.

> *Valid: No*   *True: —*

Foundational premise: Paying attention prevents accidents.

Minor premise: I am paying attention.

Deductive conclusion: There will not be an accident.

> *Valid: Yes*   *True: No*

Foundational premise: Paying attention prevents accidents.

Minor premise: I am not paying attention.

Deductive conclusion: There could be an accident.

    Valid: Yes   *True: No*

Foundational premise: All students have after-school jobs.

Minor premise: Terri is a student.

Deductive conclusion: Terri has an after-school job.

    Valid: Yes   *True: No*

Foundational premise: All students have after-school jobs.

Minor premise: Deion is not a student.

Deductive conclusion: Deion does not have an after-school job.

    Valid: No   *True: —*

Foundational premise: No cars made by Honda are also made by Toyota.

Minor premise: He drives a Honda.

Deductive conclusion: He does not drive a Toyota.

    Valid: Yes   *True: Yes*

Foundational premise: All green foods are healthy.

Minor premise: Broccoli is green.

Deductive conclusion: Broccoli is healthy.

    Valid: Yes   *True: No*

Foundational premise: All green foods are healthy.

Minor premise: Carrots are not green.

Deductive conclusion: Carrots are not healthy.

    Valid: No   *True: —*

Foundational premise: Some green foods are healthy.

Minor premise: Spinach is green.

Deductive conclusion: Spinach is healthy.

    Valid: No   *True: —*

Foundational premise: Some green foods are healthy.

Minor premise: Cookies are not green.

Deductive conclusion: Cookies are not healthy.

    Valid: No   *True: —*

Foundational premise: No hot pink foods are healthy.

Minor premise: Bubble gum is hot pink.

Deductive conclusion: Bubble gum is not healthy.

   Valid: Yes   *True: No*

Foundational premise: No hot pink foods are healthy.

Minor premise: Broccoli is not hot pink.

Deductive conclusion: Broccoli is healthy.

   Valid: No   *True: —*

Foundational premise: Products that require animal testing are bad.

Minor premise: This product requires animal testing.

Deductive conclusion: This product is bad.

   Valid: Yes   *True: Answers will vary*

Foundational premise: Homework doesn't help kids learn.

Minor premise: This is homework.

Deductive conclusion: This doesn't help kids learn.

   Valid: Yes   *True: Answers will vary*

Foundational premise: The stuffed animal is free.

Minor premise: This is free.

Deductive conclusion: This is the stuffed animal.

   Valid: No   *True: —*

Foundational premise: All cats are brown.

Minor premise: Taffy is brown.

Deductive conclusion: Taffy is a cat.

   Valid: No   *True: —*

Foundational premise: Some adults have cell phones.

Minor premise: I have a cell phone.

Deductive conclusion: I am an adult.

   Valid: No   *True: —*

Foundational premise: Superficial people get cosmetic surgery.

Minor premise: Raul had cosmetic surgery.

Deductive conclusion: Raul is superficial.

   Valid: No   *True: —*

Foundational premise: Our school doesn't sell junk food.

Minor premise: I bought junk food.

Deductive conclusion: I didn't buy it from our school.

    Valid: Yes   *True: Yes*

Foundational premise: Our city doesn't have a zoo.

Minor premise: Bronwyn and Keri are at the zoo.

Deductive conclusion: Bronwyn and Keri are not in our city.

    Valid: Yes   *True: Yes*

Foundational premise: The Internet has a lot of useless information on it.

Minor premise: I am surfing the Internet.

Deductive conclusion: I am looking at useless information.

    Valid: No   *True: —*

Foundational premise: Supporting the death penalty is wrong.

Minor premise: I support the death penalty.

Deductive conclusion: I am wrong.

    Valid: Yes   *True: Answers will vary*

Foundational premise: Jordan dislikes some things about socialism.

Minor premise: Socialism involves working together.

Deductive conclusion: Jordan dislikes working together.

    Valid: No   *True: —*

Foundational premise: Reality television is not entertaining.

Minor premise: I am watching reality television.

Deductive conclusion: I am not being entertained.

    Valid: Yes   *True: Answers will vary*

Foundational premise: Students do not learn at single-sex schools (all boys or all girls).

Minor premise: I go to a single-sex school.

Deductive conclusion: I am not learning.

    Valid: Yes   *True: Answers will vary*

Foundational premise: Students who wear uniforms get along.

Minor premise: Students at my school wear school uniforms.

Deductive conclusion: Students at my school get along.

    Valid: Yes   *True: Answers will vary*

Foundational premise: Stay-at-home moms love their children.

Minor premise: I am not a stay-at-home mom.

Deductive conclusion: I do not love my children.

> *Valid: No*   *True: —*

Foundational premise: Teenagers under the age of eighteen cannot drive.

Minor premise: I am twenty years old.

Deductive conclusion: I can drive.

> *Valid: No*   *True: —*

Foundational premise: Some scientists make important discoveries.

Minor premise: I am a scientist.

Deductive conclusion: I make important discoveries.

> *Valid: No*   *True: —*

Foundational premise: Advertising makes you want to buy products.

Minor premise: I watch advertising.

Deductive conclusion: I want to buy products.

> *Valid: Yes*   *True: No*

Foundational premise: Boxing is a harmful sport.

Minor premise: Sam is a boxer.

Deductive conclusion: Sam is being harmed.

> *Valid: Yes*   *True: Yes*

Foundational premise: Boxing is a harmful sport.

Minor premise: Sam is a boxer.

Deductive conclusion: Sam is harming others.

> *Valid: Yes*   *True: Yes*

Foundational premise: All drivers are organ donors.

Minor premise: Rita is an organ donor.

Deductive conclusion: Rita is a driver.

> *Valid: No*   *True: —*

Foundational premise: Smoking is not allowed in public spaces.

Minor premise: Leigh is smoking.

Deductive conclusion: Leigh is not in a public space.

> *Valid: Yes*   *True: No*

Foundational premise: You are vain if you compete in beauty contests.

Minor premise: Gessie is in a beauty contest.

Deductive conclusion: Gessie is vain.

> *Valid: Yes*   *True: Answers will vary*

Foundational premise: Performance-enhancing drugs are harmless.

Minor premise: Lance uses performance-enhancing drugs.

Deductive conclusion: Lance is not being harmed.

> *Valid: Yes*   *True: Answers will vary*

Foundational premise: All citizens vote.

Minor premise: Rachel is a citizen.

Deductive conclusion: Rachel votes.

> *Valid: Yes*   *True: No*

Foundational premise: All citizens vote.

Minor premise: Rachel voted.

Deductive conclusion: Rachel is a citizen.

> *Valid: No*   *True: —*

Foundational premise: Some children play video games.

Minor premise: Maurice is a child.

Deductive conclusion: Maurice plays video games.

> *Valid: No*   *True: —*

Foundational premise: Chameleons change color to blend in with their surroundings.

Minor premise: My pet is a chameleon.

Deductive conclusion: My pet changes color to blend in with his surroundings.

> *Valid: Yes*   *True: Yes*

Foundational premise: Chameleons change color to blend in with their surroundings.

Minor premise: My pet changes color to blend in with his surroundings.

Deductive conclusion: My pet is a chameleon.

> *Valid: No*   *True: —*

Foundational premise: Every student in this school has to take physical education.

Minor premise: Betts has to take physical education.

Deductive conclusion: Betts is a student in this school.

> *Valid: No*   *True: —*

Foundational premise: All Republicans own guns.

Minor premise: Gordon is a Republican.

Deductive conclusion: Gordon owns a gun.

    Valid: Yes   *True: No*

Foundational premise: All Republicans own guns.

Minor premise: Gordon owns a gun.

Deductive conclusion: Gordon is a Republican.

    Valid: No   *True: —*

Foundational premise: Peace-loving countries send representatives to the United Nations Summit.

Minor premise: Russia did not send a representative to the United Nations Summit.

Deductive conclusion: Russia is not a peace-loving country.

    Valid: Yes   *True: Answers will vary*

Foundational premise: Peace-loving countries send representatives to the United Nations Summit.

Minor premise: Switzerland did not send a representative to the United Nations Summit.

Deductive conclusion: Switzerland is not a peace-loving country.

    Valid: Yes   *True: Answers will vary*

Foundational premise: Peace-loving countries send representatives to the United Nations Summit.

Minor premise: North Korea sent a representative to the United Nations Summit.

Deductive conclusion: North Korea is a peace-loving country.

    Valid: No   *True: —*

Foundational premise: All serious athletes play football.

Minor premise: Janelle does not play football.

Deductive conclusion: Janelle is not a serious athlete.

    Valid: Yes   *True: No*

Foundational premise: All serious athletes play football.

Minor premise: Robert plays football.

Deductive conclusion: Robert is a serious athlete.

    Valid: No   *True: —*

Foundational premise: All serious athletes play football.

Minor premise: Robert is a serious athlete.

Deductive conclusion: Robert plays football.

    Valid: Yes   *True: No*

Foundational premise: All serious athletes play football.

Minor premise: Ralph is not a serious athlete.

Deductive conclusion: Ralph does not play football.

   Valid: No   *True: —*

Foundational premise: All gymnasts are small.

Minor premise: Ophelia is a gymnast.

Deductive conclusion: Ophelia is small.

   Valid: Yes   *True: No*

Foundational premise: All gymnasts are small.

Minor premise: Ophelia is small.

Deductive conclusion: Ophelia is a gymnast.

   Valid: No   *True: —*

Foundational premise: Some gymnasts are small.

Minor premise: Patrick is a gymnast.

Deductive conclusion: Patrick is small.

   Valid: No   *True: —*

Foundational premise: Prisoners are not allowed to vote.

Minor premise: Mary is a prisoner.

Deductive conclusion: Mary is not allowed to vote.

   Valid: Yes   *True: No*

Foundational premise: Prisoners are not allowed to vote.

Minor premise: Mary is not allowed to vote.

Deductive conclusion: Mary is a prisoner.

   Valid: No   *True: —*

Foundational premise: Prisoners go to rehabilitation after they serve their term.

Minor premise: Arthur is in rehabilitation.

Deductive conclusion: Arthur was a prisoner.

   Valid: No   *True: —*

Foundational premise: If you live in the United States, you have to vote.

Minor premise: I live in the United States.

Deductive conclusion: I have to vote.

   Valid: Yes   *True: No*

Foundational premise: If you live in the United States, you have to vote.

Minor premise: I have to vote.

Deductive conclusion: I live in the United States.

   Valid: No   *True: —*

Foundational premise: Gambling makes you lazy.

Minor premise: Rochelle gambles.

Deductive conclusion: Rochelle is lazy.

   Valid: Yes   *True: No*

Foundational premise: Gambling makes you lazy.

Minor premise: Rochelle is lazy.

Deductive conclusion: Rochelle is a gambler.

   Valid: No   *True: —*

Foundational premise: Cloning humans is wrong.

Minor premise: I am human.

Deductive conclusion: I should not be cloned.

   Valid: Yes   *True: Answers will vary*

Foundational premise: Cloning animals is sometimes okay.

Minor premise: Dolly is an animal.

Deductive conclusion: Cloning Dolly is okay.

   Valid: No   *True: —*

Foundational premise: My school conducts random drug testing.

Minor premise: I go to my school.

Deductive conclusion: I may be drug tested.

   Valid: Yes   *True: Yes*

Foundational premise: My school conducts random drug testing.

Minor premise: I am not going to school today.

Deductive conclusion: I will not be drug tested today.

   Valid: No   *True: —*

Foundational premise: The United Nations is composed of peace-loving nations.

Minor premise: Our nation loves peace.

Deductive conclusion: Our nation is in the United Nations.

   Valid: No   *True: —*

Foundational premise: Bad parents have children who misbehave.

Minor premise: Tommy misbehaves.

Deductive conclusion: Tommy's parents are bad parents.

   Valid: No   *True: —*

Foundational premise: Bad parents have children who misbehave.

Minor premise: Tommy's parents are bad parents.

Deductive conclusion: Tommy misbehaves.

   Valid: Yes   *True: No*

Foundational premise: Marriage is outdated.

Minor premise: People shouldn't do outdated things.

Deductive conclusion: People shouldn't get married.

   Valid: Yes   *True: Answers will vary*

Foundational premise: Advertisers should not target children.

Minor premise: Ursula is a child.

Deductive conclusion: Advertisers should not target Ursula.

   Valid: Yes   *True: Answers will vary*

Foundational premise: Hosting the Olympics is a good investment.

Minor premise: Canada hosted the Olympics.

Deductive conclusion: Canada made a good investment.

   Valid: Yes   *True: Answers will vary*

Foundational premise: Hosting the Olympics is a good investment.

Minor premise: Egypt has never hosted the Olympics.

Deductive conclusion: Egypt does not make good investments.

   Valid: No   *True: —*

Foundational premise: All teenagers have curfews.

Minor premise: Aaron is a teenager.

Deductive conclusion: Aaron has a curfew.

   Valid: Yes   *True: No*

Foundational premise: All teenagers have curfews.

Minor premise: Leslie is not a teenager.

Deductive conclusion: Leslie does not have a curfew.

   Valid: No   *True: —*

Foundational premise: Convicted terrorists have forfeited certain rights.

Minor premise: Paul is a convicted terrorist.

Deductive conclusion: Paul has forfeited certain rights.

> *Valid: Yes*   *True: Yes*

Foundational premise: Convicted terrorists have forfeited certain rights.

Minor premise: Paul has not forfeited his rights.

Deductive conclusion: Paul is not a convicted terrorist.

> *Valid: Yes*   *True: Yes*

Foundational premise: Homework is a waste of time.

Minor premise: Susan is required to do homework.

Deductive conclusion: Susan is required to waste her time.

> *Valid: Yes*   *True: Answers will vary*

Foundational premise: Homework is not a waste of time.

Minor premise: Susan is required to do homework.

Deductive conclusion: Susan is not wasting her time.

> *Valid: No*   *True: —*

Foundational premise: All nations have a right to possess nuclear weapons.

Minor premise: Iran is a nation.

Deductive conclusion: Iran has a right to possess nuclear weapons.

> *Valid: Yes*   *True: Answers will vary*

Foundational premise: Some nations have a right to possess nuclear weapons.

Minor premise: The United States is a nation.

Deductive conclusion: The United States has a right to possess nuclear weapons.

> *Valid: No*   *True: —*

Foundational premise: Some nations have a right to possess nuclear weapons.

Minor premise: North Korea is a nation.

Deductive conclusion: North Korea does not have a right to possess nuclear weapons.

> *Valid: No*   *True: —*

Foundational premise: Animals have rights.

Minor premise: Frisky is an animal.

Deductive conclusion: Frisky has rights.

> *Valid: Yes*   *True: Answers will vary*

Foundational premise: Animals have rights.

Minor premise: Rusty has rights.

Deductive conclusion: Rusty is an animal.

   Valid: No   *True: —*

Foundational premise: Vegetarians are healthier than omnivores.

Minor premise: Meghan is a vegetarian.

Deductive conclusion: Meghan is healthier than omnivores.

   Valid: Yes   *True: Answers will vary*

Foundational premise: Vegetarians are healthier than omnivores.

Minor premise: Eric is an omnivore.

Deductive conclusion: Eric is less healthy than any vegetarian.

   Valid: Yes   *True: Answers will vary*

Foundational premise: Teachers should carry guns.

Minor premise: Mrs. Ross is a teacher.

Deductive conclusion: Mrs. Ross should carry a gun.

   Valid: Yes   *True: Answers will vary*

Foundational premise: Teachers should carry guns.

Minor premise: Mrs. Alvarado should carry a gun.

Deductive conclusion: Mrs. Alvarado is a teacher.

   Valid: No   *True: —*

Foundational premise: Fatty or sugary foods should be subject to an additional tax.

Minor premise: Avocados are fatty.

Deductive conclusion: Avocados should be subject to an additional tax.

   Valid: Yes   *True: Answers will vary*

Foundational premise: Fatty or sugary foods should be subject to an additional tax.

Minor premise: Diet Coke is not sugary or fatty.

Deductive conclusion: Diet Coke should not be subject to an additional tax.

   Valid: No   *True: —*

Foundational premise: Diamonds are expensive.

Minor premise: This is a diamond.

Deductive conclusion: This is expensive.

   Valid: Yes   *True: Yes*

Foundational premise: Diamonds are expensive.

Minor premise: This is expensive.

Deductive conclusion: This is a diamond.

> *Valid: No*   *True: —*

Foundational premise: Horses like to run.

Minor premise: Skye is a horse.

Deductive conclusion: Skye likes to run.

> *Valid: Yes*   *True: No*

Foundational premise: Horses like to run.

Minor premise: Ryder likes to run.

Deductive conclusion: Ryder is a horse.

> *Valid: No*   *True: —*

Foundational premise: Rabbits are furry.

Minor premise: Fancy is a rabbit.

Deductive conclusion: Fancy is furry.

> *Valid: Yes*   *True: Yes*

Foundational premise: Porcupines are prickly.

Minor premise: Spiny is a porcupine.

Deductive conclusion: Spiny is prickly.

> *Valid: Yes*   *True: Yes*

Foundational premise: Cougars are wild cats.

Minor premise: Leon is a wild cat.

Deductive conclusion: Leon is a cougar.

> *Valid: No*   *True: —*

Foundational premise: Crocodiles have lots of teeth.

Minor premise: Lyle is a crocodile.

Deductive conclusion: Lyle has lots of teeth.

> *Valid: Yes*   *True: Yes*

Foundational premise: Dentists brush their teeth three times a day.

Minor premise: Walter brushes his teeth three times a day.

Deductive conclusion: Walter is a dentist.

> *Valid: No*   *True: —*

Foundational premise: Farmers like the smell of hay.

Minor premise: Ferdinand likes the smell of hay.

Deductive conclusion: Ferdinand is a farmer.

    Valid: No   *True: —*

Foundational premise: All children wear mittens.

Minor premise: Jasmine is a child.

Deductive conclusion: Jasmine wears mittens.

    Valid: Yes   *True: No*

Foundational premise: Children who are homeschooled are shy.

Minor premise: Bella is homeschooled.

Deductive conclusion: Bella is shy.

    Valid: Yes   *True: No*

Foundational premise: Children who are homeschooled are shy.

Minor premise: Bella is shy.

Deductive conclusion: Bella is homeschooled.

    Valid: No   *True: —*

Foundational premise: Developed countries are responsible for fighting climate change.

Minor premise: The United States is a developed country.

Deductive conclusion: The United States is responsible for fighting climate change.

    Valid: Yes   *True: Answers will vary*

Foundational premise: Developed countries are responsible for fighting climate change.

Minor premise: India is not a developed country.

Deductive conclusion: India is not responsible for fighting climate change.

    Valid: No   *True: —*

Foundational premise: Our class has a pet hamster.

Minor premise: Swimmy is our class's pet.

Deductive conclusion: Swimmy is a hamster.

    Valid: No   *True: —*

Foundational premise: Snakes live in trees.

Minor premise: Tweety lives in a tree.

Deductive conclusion: Tweety is a snake.

    Valid: No   *True: —*

Foundational premise: Horseback riders have good balance.

Minor premise: Gymnasts have good balance.

Deductive conclusion: Horseback riders are gymnasts.

    Valid: No   *True: —*

Foundational premise: Freedom of speech means you can say anything you want.

Minor premise: I have freedom of speech.

Deductive conclusion: I can say anything I want.

    Valid: Yes   *True: No*

Foundational premise: Freedom of speech means you can say anything you want.

Minor premise: Freedom of speech is your right.

Deductive conclusion: It is your right to say anything you want.

    Valid: Yes   *True: No*

Foundational premise: People who watch violent movies commit violent crimes.

Minor premise: Richie is watching a violent movie.

Deductive conclusion: Richie will commit a violent crime.

    Valid: Yes   *True: No*

Foundational premise: Genetically modified foods are not healthy.

Minor premise: This spinach has been genetically modified.

Deductive conclusion: This spinach is not healthy.

    Valid: Yes   *True: Answers will vary*

Foundational premise: People who keep wild animals as pets are cruel.

Minor premise: Sally's pet is a wild animal.

Deductive conclusion: Sally is cruel.

    Valid: Yes   *True: Answers will vary*

Foundational premise: People who keep wild animals as pets are cruel.

Minor premise: Edwin is cruel.

Deductive conclusion: Edwin keeps wild animals as pets.

    Valid: No   *True: —*

Foundational premise: Laughing is healthy.

Minor premise: Jess is healthy.

Deductive conclusion: Jess is laughing.

    Valid: No   *True: —*

Foundational premise: Cell phones make life very convenient.

Minor premise: Bob has a cell phone.

Deductive conclusion: Bob's life is very convenient.

    Valid: Yes   *True: Answers will vary*

Foundational premise: Cell phones make life very convenient.

Minor premise: Bob's life is very convenient.

Deductive conclusion: Bob has a cell phone.

    Valid: No   *True: —*

Foundational premise: Parents who attend parenting classes are good parents.

Minor premise: Gregg and Marla attended parenting classes.

Deductive conclusion: Gregg and Marla are good parents.

    Valid: Yes   *True: Answers will vary*

Foundational premise: Parents who attend parenting classes are good parents.

Minor premise: Gregg and Marla are good parents.

Deductive conclusion: Gregg and Marla attended parenting classes.

    Valid: No   *True: —*

Foundational premise: People who drive too fast get traffic tickets.

Minor premise: Mario got a traffic ticket.

Deductive conclusion: Mario drives too fast.

    Valid: No   *True: —*

Foundational premise: People who drive too fast get traffic tickets.

Minor premise: Stella did not get a traffic ticket.

Deductive conclusion: Stella does not drive too fast.

    Valid: Yes   *True: No*

Foundational premise: People who drive too fast get traffic tickets.

Minor premise: Emile drives too fast.

Deductive conclusion: Emile got a traffic ticket.

    Valid: Yes   *True: No*

Foundational premise: People who park in the wrong place get traffic tickets.

Minor premise: Hollie got a traffic ticket.

Deductive conclusion: Hollie parked in the wrong place.

    Valid: No   *True: —*

Foundational premise: People who park in the wrong place get traffic tickets.

Minor premise: Jacqui parked in the wrong place.

Deductive conclusion: Jacqui got a traffic ticket.

> *Valid: Yes*   *True: No*

Foundational premise: Monarchies are useless.

Minor premise: The queen of England is part of a monarchy.

Deductive conclusion: The queen of England is useless.

> *Valid: Yes*   *True: Answers will vary*

Foundational premise: Telling people they are wrong is mean.

Minor premise: Soli told Gavriel that she was wrong.

Deductive conclusion: Soli is mean.

> *Valid: Yes*   *True: No*

Foundational premise: Using social media is a waste of time.

Minor premise: Therese is wasting her time.

Deductive conclusion: Therese is using social media.

> *Valid: No*   *True: —*

Foundational premise: Using social media is a waste of time.

Minor premise: Jerrie is not using social media.

Deductive conclusion: Jerrie is not wasting time.

> *Valid: No*   *True: —*

Foundational premise: Leatherback turtles are an endangered species.

Minor premise: Flipper is a leatherback turtle.

Deductive conclusion: Flipper is endangered.

> *Valid: Yes*   *True: Yes*

Foundational premise: Leatherback turtles are an endangered species.

Minor premise: This tiger is not a leatherback turtle.

Deductive conclusion: This tiger is not endangered.

> *Valid: No*   *True: —*

Foundational premise: Leatherback turtles are an endangered species.

Minor premise: This tiger is an endangered species.

Deductive conclusion: This tiger is a leatherback turtle.

> *Valid: No*   *True: —*

Foundational premise: All blueberries are blue.

Minor premise: This is a blueberry.

Deductive conclusion: This is blue.

> *Valid: Yes*   *True: Yes*

Foundational premise: Backpacks are spacious.

Minor premise: My bag is spacious.

Deductive conclusion: My bag is a backpack.

> *Valid: No*   *True: —*

Foundational premise: Backpacks are spacious.

Minor premise: My bag is not spacious.

Deductive conclusion: My bag is not a backpack.

> *Valid: Yes*   *True: No*

Foundational premise: Artists are crazy.

Minor premise: Picasso was an artist.

Deductive conclusion: Picasso was crazy.

> *Valid: Yes*   *True: No*

Foundational premise: Artists are crazy.

Minor premise: Crazy people are unproductive.

Deductive conclusion: Artists are unproductive.

> *Valid: Yes*   *True: No*

Foundational premise: Genetically modified organisms (GMOs) make you sick.

Minor premise: The pulled pork has GMOs in it.

Deductive conclusion: The pulled pork will make you sick.

> *Valid: Yes*   *True: Answers will vary*

Foundational premise: GMOs make you sick.

Minor premise: The pulled pork does not have GMOs in it.

Deductive conclusion: The pulled pork will not make you sick.

> *Valid: No*   *True: —*

Evaluating Statements (Harder)

To use this set of items, give students only the statement (for example, "Dolphins are fish because they live in the ocean") and ask them to standardize and evaluate it. Here, suggested standardized arguments (in italics) are provided below each statement as an answer guide for teachers, though students may standardize the statement differently. A list of the statements, along with blank spaces for students to fill in foundational premises, minor premises, and conclusions, can be found at **marzanoresearch.com/activitiesandgames**. The following items also include answers regarding validity and truth. Please note that, in some cases, "Answers will vary" is listed regarding truth value. This is because the syllogism includes at least one statement of opinion, which could be true or not true. Additionally, if a syllogism is invalid, it does not have a truth value (this is denoted by —) because the "trueness" of invalid syllogisms is irrelevant.

Statement: Dolphins are fish because they live in the ocean.

Foundational premise: Things that live in the ocean are fish.

Minor premise: Dolphins live in the ocean.

Deductive conclusion: Dolphins are fish.

Valid: Yes   *True: No*

Statement: She is healthier than everyone else because she is a vegetarian.

Foundational premise: Vegetarians are healthier than everyone else.

Minor premise: She is a vegetarian.

Deductive conclusion: She is healthier than everyone else.

Valid: Yes   *True: Answers will vary*

Statement: Carla is short because she drinks coffee.

Foundational premise: Drinking coffee makes people short.

Minor premise: Carla drinks coffee.

Deductive conclusion: Carla is short.

Valid: Yes   *True: No*

Statement: Ronnie has bad skin because he eats chocolate.

Foundational premise: If you eat chocolate, you will have bad skin.

Minor premise: Ronnie eats chocolate.

Deductive conclusion: Ronnie has bad skin.

Valid: Yes   *True: No*

Statement: College is useless because you can get a job without going to college.

Foundational premise: Useful things help you get a job.

Minor premise: You can get a job without going to college.

Deductive conclusion: College is useless.

Valid: No   *True: —*

Statement: Althea caught a cold because she went outside with wet hair.

> *Foundational premise:* Going outside with wet hair makes you catch a cold.
>
> *Minor premise:* Althea went outside with wet hair.
>
> *Deductive conclusion:* Althea caught a cold.
>
> *Valid:* Yes   *True:* No

Statement: Natalie is running around because she ate sugar.

> *Foundational premise:* Eating sugar makes you run around.
>
> *Minor premise:* Natalie ate sugar.
>
> *Deductive conclusion:* Natalie is running around.
>
> *Valid:* Yes   *True:* No

Statement: Olivia is cold because she is not wearing a hat.

> *Foundational premise:* Not wearing a hat makes you cold.
>
> *Minor premise:* Olivia is not wearing a hat.
>
> *Deductive conclusion:* Olivia is cold.
>
> *Valid:* Yes   *True:* No

Statement: Hanson is tired because he didn't drink enough water.

> *Foundational premise:* Not drinking enough water makes you tired.
>
> *Minor premise:* Hanson did not drink enough water.
>
> *Deductive conclusion:* Hanson is tired.
>
> *Valid:* Yes   *True:* Answers will vary

Statement: Grace has arthritis because she cracked her knuckles when she was younger.

> *Foundational premise:* Cracking your knuckles gives you arthritis.
>
> *Minor premise:* Grace cracked her knuckles.
>
> *Deductive conclusion:* Grace has arthritis.
>
> *Valid:* Yes   *True:* No

Statement: Gunther got a cavity because he drinks water without fluoride in it.

> *Foundational premise:* Drinking water without fluoride gives you cavities.
>
> *Minor premise:* Gunther drinks water without fluoride.
>
> *Deductive conclusion:* Gunther will get cavities.
>
> *Valid:* Yes   *True:* No

Statement: Jane lost weight because she drank lots of water.

    Foundational premise: Drinking lots of water will make you lose weight.

    Minor premise: Jane drank lots of water.

    Deductive conclusion: Jane lost weight.

    Valid: Yes   *True:* Answers will vary

Statement: Ivy got a stomachache because she drank water before she ran.

    Foundational premise: If you drink water before running, you get a stomachache.

    Minor premise: Ivy drank water before running.

    Deductive conclusion: Ivy will get a stomachache.

    Valid: Yes   *True:* Answers will vary

Statement: Frank is smart because he's been to six countries.

    Foundational premise: Going to many different countries makes you smart.

    Minor premise: Frank has been to many different countries.

    Deductive conclusion: Frank is smart.

    Valid: Yes   *True:* No

Statement: Iceland is the best place to live because it is the greenest country in the world.

    Foundational premise: Green countries are better places to live.

    Minor premise: Iceland is the greenest country in the world.

    Deductive conclusion: Iceland is the best place to live.

    Valid: Yes   *True:* Answers will vary

Statement: Marcia should drink milk because she is a woman.

    Foundational premise: Women should drink milk.

    Minor premise: Marcia is a woman.

    Deductive conclusion: Marcia should drink milk.

    Valid: Yes   *True:* Answers will vary

Statement: Don't eat quinoa because it is expensive.

    Foundational premise: Don't eat things that are expensive.

    Minor premise: Quinoa is expensive.

    Deductive conclusion: Don't eat quinoa.

    Valid: Yes   *True:* Answers will vary

Statement: Mika doesn't speak English because he was born in Asia.

> *Foundational premise:* People in Asia don't speak English.
>
> *Minor premise:* Mika was born in Asia.
>
> *Deductive conclusion:* Mika doesn't speak English.
>
> *Valid:* Yes   *True:* No

Statement: People should eat organic foods because they don't want toxins in their bodies.

> *Foundational premise:* People should eat things that don't put toxins in their bodies.
>
> *Minor premise:* Organic foods don't have toxins.
>
> *Deductive conclusion:* People should eat organic foods.
>
> *Valid:* Yes   *True:* Answers will vary

Statement: Thomas has a strong sense of family because of his Native American heritage.

> *Foundational premise:* Having Native American heritage gives you a strong sense of family.
>
> *Minor premise:* Thomas has Native American heritage.
>
> *Deductive conclusion:* Thomas has a strong sense of family.
>
> *Valid:* Yes   *True:* No

Statement: Paul is a hippie because he is in a rock band.

> *Foundational premise:* People in rock bands are hippies.
>
> *Minor premise:* Paul is in a rock band.
>
> *Deductive conclusion:* Paul is a hippie.
>
> *Valid:* Yes   *True:* No

Statement: You shouldn't eat cake because butter is bad for you.

> *Foundational premise:* You shouldn't eat butter because it's bad for you.
>
> *Minor premise:* Cake has butter in it.
>
> *Deductive conclusion:* You shouldn't eat cake.
>
> *Valid:* Yes   *True:* Answers will vary

Statement: Kelli shouldn't fly on airplanes because sometimes they crash.

> *Foundational premise:* Kelli shouldn't ride on things that crash.
>
> *Minor premise:* Some airplanes crash.
>
> *Deductive conclusion:* Kelli shouldn't fly on airplanes.
>
> *Valid:* No   *True:* —

Statement: Chichen Itza is the most important Mayan ruin because it is the largest.

> *Foundational premise: Large things are the most important.*
>
> *Minor premise: Chichen Itza is the largest Mayan ruin.*
>
> *Deductive conclusion: Chichen Itza is the most important Mayan ruin.*
>
> **Valid:** *Yes*   **True:** *Answers will vary*

Statement: Bengal tigers shouldn't be a protected species because they are so fierce.

> *Foundational premise: Fierce animals shouldn't be protected.*
>
> *Minor premise: Bengal tigers are fierce.*
>
> *Deductive conclusion: Bengal tigers shouldn't be protected.*
>
> **Valid:** *Yes*   **True:** *Answers will vary*

Statement: Sasha has diabetes because she ate too much sugar.

> *Foundational premise: Eating too much sugar gives you diabetes.*
>
> *Minor premise: Sasha ate too much sugar.*
>
> *Deductive conclusion: Sasha has diabetes.*
>
> **Valid:** *Yes*   **True:** *No*

Statement: Mark shouldn't live in Denver because severe hailstorms often occur there.

> *Foundational premise: People shouldn't live where there are severe hailstorms.*
>
> *Minor premise: Denver has severe hailstorms.*
>
> *Deductive conclusion: Mark shouldn't live in Denver.*
>
> **Valid:** *Yes*   **True:** *Answers will vary*

Statement: Texas is miserable because it is so hot.

> *Foundational premise: Heat is miserable.*
>
> *Minor premise: Texas is hot.*
>
> *Deductive conclusion: Texas is miserable.*
>
> **Valid:** *Yes*   **True:** *Answers will vary*

Statement: Maria needs to learn to write well because she wants to be a famous author when she grows up.

> *Foundational premise: Famous authors must write well.*
>
> *Minor premise: Maria wants to be a famous author.*
>
> *Deductive conclusion: Maria needs to learn to write well.*
>
> **Valid:** *Yes*   **True:** *Answers will vary*

Statement: You shouldn't trust anything you read on the Internet because some people write untrue things there.

> *Foundational premise:* You shouldn't trust sources that have untrue information.
>
> *Minor premise:* People write untrue things on the Internet.
>
> *Deductive conclusion:* You shouldn't trust things you read on the Internet.
>
> *Valid:* Yes   *True:* Answers will vary

Statement: Don't listen to what your teacher says because some teachers give incorrect information.

> *Foundational premise:* Don't listen to people who give incorrect information.
>
> *Minor premise:* Some teachers give incorrect information.
>
> *Deductive conclusion:* Don't listen to your teacher.
>
> *Valid:* No   *True:* —

Statement: Jamison shouldn't go on vacation to South America because he doesn't like hot weather.

> *Foundational premise:* South America has hot weather.
>
> *Minor premise:* Jamison doesn't like to go on vacation where there is hot weather.
>
> *Deductive conclusion:* Jamison shouldn't go to South America.
>
> *Valid:* Yes   *True:* Answers will vary

Statement: Patti has a lot of money because she has an after-school job.

> *Foundational premise:* After-school jobs earn you a lot of money.
>
> *Minor premise:* Patti has an after-school job.
>
> *Deductive conclusion:* Patti has a lot of money.
>
> *Valid:* Yes   *True:* No

Statement: George can't legally drive on public roads because he's only twelve.

> *Foundational premise:* Twelve-year-old children can't legally drive on public roads.
>
> *Minor premise:* George is twelve.
>
> *Deductive conclusion:* George can't legally drive on public roads.
>
> *Valid:* Yes   *True:* Yes

Statement: Dane doesn't have any siblings because he's an only child.

> *Foundational premise:* An only child does not have siblings.
>
> *Minor premise:* Dane is an only child.
>
> *Deductive conclusion:* Dane doesn't have siblings.
>
> *Valid:* Yes   *True:* Yes

Statement: Marty will go to college because his parents are rich.

> ***Foundational premise:*** *People with rich parents go to college.*
>
> ***Minor premise:*** *Marty has rich parents.*
>
> ***Deductive conclusion:*** *Marty will go to college.*
>
> ***Valid:*** *Yes*   ***True:*** *No*

Statement: Celia will like this restaurant because it doesn't have a jukebox.

> ***Foundational premise:*** *Celia does not like restaurants with jukeboxes.*
>
> ***Minor premise:*** *This restaurant does not have a jukebox.*
>
> ***Deductive conclusion:*** *Celia will like this restaurant.*
>
> ***Valid:*** *No*   ***True:*** *—*

Statement: Rodney is such a good swimmer; I bet he is a lifeguard.

> ***Foundational premise:*** *Lifeguards are good swimmers.*
>
> ***Minor premise:*** *Rodney is a good swimmer.*
>
> ***Deductive conclusion:*** *Rodney is a lifeguard.*
>
> ***Valid:*** *No*   ***True:*** *—*

Statement: Dwayne doesn't like animals because he didn't want to go to the zoo.

> ***Foundational premise:*** *People who don't like animals don't want to go to the zoo.*
>
> ***Minor premise:*** *Dwayne didn't want to go to the zoo.*
>
> ***Deductive conclusion:*** *Dwayne doesn't like animals.*
>
> ***Valid:*** *No*   ***True:*** *—*

Statement: Wanda doesn't read newspapers because the ink turns her fingers black.

> ***Foundational premise:*** *Wanda doesn't do things that turn her fingers black.*
>
> ***Minor premise:*** *Reading newspapers turns your fingers black from the ink.*
>
> ***Deductive conclusion:*** *Wanda doesn't read newspapers.*
>
> ***Valid:*** *Yes*   ***True:*** *Yes*

Statement: Louise won't watch that movie because it shows violence against women.

> ***Foundational premise:*** *Louise won't watch things that show violence against women.*
>
> ***Minor premise:*** *The movie shows violence against women.*
>
> ***Deductive conclusion:*** *Louise won't watch the movie.*
>
> ***Valid:*** *Yes*   ***True:*** *Yes*

Statement: Flamingos are pink because they eat shrimp.

> *Foundational premise: Eating shrimp turns some animals pink.*
>
> *Minor premise: Flamingos eat shrimp.*
>
> *Deductive conclusion: Flamingos are pink.*
>
> *Valid: No*   *True: —*

Statement: Shakespeare probably didn't write his plays because we can't prove he did.

> *Foundational premise: Things you can't prove probably didn't happen.*
>
> *Minor premise: We can't prove Shakespeare wrote his plays.*
>
> *Deductive conclusion: Shakespeare probably didn't write his plays.*
>
> *Valid: Yes*   *True: No*

Statement: Marjorie hates cats because she is allergic to them.

> *Foundational premise: Marjorie hates things she is allergic to.*
>
> *Minor premise: Marjorie is allergic to cats.*
>
> *Deductive conclusion: Marjorie hates cats.*
>
> *Valid: Yes*   *True: Yes*

Statement: Euan hates cats because they hate him.

> *Foundational premise: Euan hates things that hate him.*
>
> *Minor premise: Cats hate Euan.*
>
> *Deductive conclusion: Euan hates cats.*
>
> *Valid: Yes*   *True: Yes*

Statement: The person on the phone hung up without speaking because he is a burglar seeing if we are home.

> *Foundational premise: If a person is a burglar, he calls your house without speaking.*
>
> *Minor premise: The person on the phone called without speaking.*
>
> *Deductive conclusion: The person on the phone was a burglar.*
>
> *Valid: No*   *True: —*

Statement: Green is the best color because it is my favorite.

> *Foundational premise: My favorite things are the best.*
>
> *Minor premise: Green is my favorite color.*
>
> *Deductive conclusion: Green is the best color.*
>
> *Valid: Yes*   *True: No*

Statement: Children shouldn't stay up past 10 p.m. because they will be groggy for school.

Foundational premise: Children shouldn't do things that make them groggy for school.

Minor premise: Staying up past 10 p.m. makes children groggy for school.

Deductive conclusion: Children shouldn't stay up past 10 p.m.

Valid: Yes   *True: Answers will vary*

Statement: College students are cool because they're in college.

Foundational premise: Being in college is cool.

Minor premise: College students are in college.

Deductive conclusion: College students are cool.

Valid: Yes   *True: Answers will vary*

Statement: You shouldn't eat spinach because some spinach has *E. coli* on it.

Foundational premise: You shouldn't eat things with E. coli on them.

Minor premise: Some spinach has E. coli on it.

Deductive conclusion: You shouldn't eat spinach.

Valid: No   *True: —*

Statement: Greek yogurt is not as good because it is too thick.

Foundational premise: Thicker yogurt is not as good as regular yogurt.

Minor premise: Greek yogurt is thick.

Deductive conclusion: Greek yogurt is not as good as regular yogurt.

Valid: Yes   *True: Answers will vary*

Statement: Homemade cookies aren't as good as store-bought cookies because they are not convenient.

Foundational premise: Things that are convenient are good.

Minor premise: Homemade cookies are not convenient.

Deductive conclusion: Homemade cookies aren't good.

Valid: No   *True: —*

Statement: You shouldn't buy lottery tickets because they are a waste of money.

Foundational premise: You shouldn't buy things that are a waste of money.

Minor premise: Lottery tickets are a waste of money.

Deductive conclusion: You shouldn't buy lottery tickets.

Valid: Yes   *True: Answers will vary*

Statement: You should give your lottery winnings to me because I told you which numbers to choose.

    Foundational premise: *The person who chooses the lottery numbers should get the winnings.*

    Minor premise: *I told you which lottery numbers to choose.*

    Deductive conclusion: *You should give your lottery winnings to me.*

    Valid: *Yes*   *True:* *Answers will vary*

Statement: School should start later in the morning because students will be more attentive.

    Foundational premise: *Students are more attentive later in the morning.*

    Minor premise: *School should start when students are more attentive.*

    Deductive conclusion: *School should start later in the morning.*

    Valid: *Yes*   *True:* *Answers will vary*

Statement: Clarissa hates going to 3-D movies because the glasses make her look silly.

    Foundational premise: *Clarissa hates doing things that make her look silly.*

    Minor premise: *Clarissa looks silly wearing the glasses at 3-D movies.*

    Deductive conclusion: *Clarissa hates going to 3-D movies.*

    Valid: *Yes*   *True:* *Yes*

Statement: Jordan has good taste in music because he doesn't listen to the radio.

    Foundational premise: *People who don't listen to the radio have good taste in music.*

    Minor premise: *Jordan doesn't listen to the radio.*

    Deductive conclusion: *Jordan has good taste in music.*

    Valid: *Yes*   *True:* *Answers will vary*

Statement: My dad shouldn't make me mow the lawn because he doesn't pay me.

    Foundational premise: *People should get paid for the work they do.*

    Minor premise: *My dad doesn't pay me to mow the lawn.*

    Deductive conclusion: *My dad shouldn't make me mow the lawn.*

    Valid: *Yes*   *True:* *Answers will vary*

Statement: Liz hates the taste of peanut butter because she is allergic to it.

    Foundational premise: *If you are allergic to something, you hate the taste of it.*

    Minor premise: *Liz is allergic to peanut butter.*

    Deductive conclusion: *Liz hates the taste of peanut butter.*

    Valid: *Yes*   *True:* *No*

Statement: Professional athletes are not allowed to vote because some professional athletes are felons.

> ***Foundational premise:*** *Felons are not allowed to vote.*
>
> ***Minor premise:*** *Some professional athletes are felons.*
>
> ***Deductive conclusion:*** *Professional athletes are not allowed to vote.*
>
> ***Valid:*** *No*   ***True:*** *—*

Statement: Ferrets aren't good pets because they smell horrible.

> ***Foundational premise:*** *Things that smell horrible aren't good pets.*
>
> ***Minor premise:*** *Ferrets smell horrible.*
>
> ***Deductive conclusion:*** *Ferrets aren't good pets.*
>
> ***Valid:*** *Yes*   ***True:*** *Answers will vary*

Statement: Turtles aren't good pets because they're not fun to hold.

> ***Foundational premise:*** *Things that aren't fun to hold aren't good pets.*
>
> ***Minor premise:*** *Turtles aren't fun to hold.*
>
> ***Deductive conclusion:*** *Turtles aren't good pets.*
>
> ***Valid:*** *Yes*   ***True:*** *Answers will vary*

Statement: Libraries are fun because they have a lot of books.

> ***Foundational premise:*** *Places that have a lot of books are fun.*
>
> ***Minor premise:*** *Libraries have a lot of books.*
>
> ***Deductive conclusion:*** *Libraries are fun.*
>
> ***Valid:*** *Yes*   ***True:*** *Answers will vary*

Statement: Ethan is illiterate because he failed his English test.

> ***Foundational premise:*** *People who are illiterate fail English tests.*
>
> ***Minor premise:*** *Ethan failed an English test.*
>
> ***Deductive conclusion:*** *Ethan is illiterate.*
>
> ***Valid:*** *No*   ***True:*** *—*

Statement: Whitney always chews gum so her breath must smell really good.

> ***Foundational premise:*** *Chewing gum makes your breath smell really good.*
>
> ***Minor premise:*** *Whitney chews gum.*
>
> ***Deductive conclusion:*** *Whitney's breath must smell really good.*
>
> ***Valid:*** *Yes*   ***True:*** *Answers will vary*

Statement: Emma is very cultured because she lives in London.

> *Foundational premise: People who live in London are very cultured.*
>
> *Minor premise: Emma lives in London.*
>
> *Deductive conclusion: Emma is very cultured.*
>
> *Valid: Yes*   *True: No*

Statement: Lela is selling her clothes at a yard sale so she must be poor.

> *Foundational premise: Poor people sell their clothes at yard sales.*
>
> *Minor premise: Lela sells her clothes at a yard sale.*
>
> *Deductive conclusion: Lela must be poor.*
>
> *Valid: No*   *True: —*

Statement: Brent has long hair because he skateboards.

> *Foundational premise: All skateboarders have long hair.*
>
> *Minor premise: Brent skateboards.*
>
> *Deductive conclusion: Brent has long hair.*
>
> *Valid: Yes*   *True: No*

Statement: Justin hates vegetables because he won't eat salad.

> *Foundational premise: People who won't eat salad hate vegetables.*
>
> *Minor premise: Justin won't eat his salad.*
>
> *Deductive conclusion: Justin hates vegetables.*
>
> *Valid: Yes*   *True: No*

Statement: Caitlyn is a bad pet owner because she lost her turtles.

> *Foundational premise: People who lose their pets are bad pet owners.*
>
> *Minor premise: Caitlyn lost her turtles.*
>
> *Deductive conclusion: Caitlyn is a bad pet owner.*
>
> *Valid: Yes*   *True: Answers will vary*

Statement: Frances is embarrassed because she has a weird haircut.

> *Foundational premise: People get embarrassed when they have weird haircuts.*
>
> *Minor premise: Frances has a weird haircut.*
>
> *Deductive conclusion: Frances is embarrassed.*
>
> *Valid: Yes*   *True: Answers will vary*

Statement: Plants shouldn't be kept indoors because they won't get natural light.

> *Foundational premise: No indoor places get natural light.*
>
> *Minor premise: Plants need natural light to grow.*
>
> *Deductive conclusion: Plants won't grow indoors.*
>
> *Valid: Yes*   *True: No*

Statement: Bears are the scariest predators because they live in our state.

> *Foundational premise: The scariest predators are the ones that live in our state.*
>
> *Minor premise: Bears live in our state.*
>
> *Deductive conclusion: Bears are the scariest predators.*
>
> *Valid: Yes*   *True: Answers will vary*

Statement: I hate loud noises because they're startling.

> *Foundational premise: Loud noises are startling.*
>
> *Minor premise: I hate being startled.*
>
> *Deductive conclusion: I hate loud noises.*
>
> *Valid: Yes*   *True: Answers will vary*

Statement: Will isn't a good boyfriend because he doesn't buy gifts for Alex.

> *Foundational premise: Good boyfriends buy gifts.*
>
> *Minor premise: Will doesn't buy gifts.*
>
> *Deductive conclusion: Will is not a good boyfriend.*
>
> *Valid: Yes*   *True: No*

Statement: Lia is going to be a doctor because she's going to medical school.

> *Foundational premise: People who go to medical school will become doctors.*
>
> *Minor premise: Lia is going to medical school.*
>
> *Deductive conclusion: Lia is going to become a doctor.*
>
> *Valid: Yes*   *True: No*

Statement: College is worth the price because you get an education.

> *Foundational premise: Education is worth the price.*
>
> *Minor premise: College provides an education.*
>
> *Deductive conclusion: College is worth the price.*
>
> *Valid: Yes*   *True: Answers will vary*

Statement: You shouldn't write on yourself with marker because it will stay there forever.

> *Foundational premise: You shouldn't permanently mark your body.*
>
> *Minor premise: If you write on yourself with marker, it will stay there forever.*
>
> *Deductive conclusion: You shouldn't write on yourself with marker.*
>
> *Valid: Yes*   *True: No*

Statement: Dora hides trash because she is a spiteful dog.

> *Foundational premise: Hiding trash is spiteful.*
>
> *Minor premise: Dora is spiteful.*
>
> *Deductive conclusion: Dora hides trash.*
>
> *Valid: No*   *True: —*

Statement: Danny is happy because he hit a home run in the baseball game.

> *Foundational premise: Hitting home runs makes people happy.*
>
> *Minor premise: Danny hit a home run.*
>
> *Deductive conclusion: Danny is happy.*
>
> *Valid: Yes*   *True: Yes*

Statement: I should go to the movies tonight because there's a new movie out that I want to see.

> *Foundational premise: People should go see movies that they want to see.*
>
> *Minor premise: There is a movie that I want to see.*
>
> *Deductive conclusion: I should go to the movies tonight.*
>
> *Valid: Yes*   *True: Answers will vary*

Statement: Don't be afraid of change because it is inevitable.

> *Foundational premise: Don't be afraid of things that are inevitable.*
>
> *Minor premise: Change is inevitable.*
>
> *Deductive conclusion: Don't be afraid of change.*
>
> *Valid: Yes*   *True: Answers will vary*

Statement: That animal can jump so it must be a frog.

> *Foundational premise: Frogs are animals that can jump.*
>
> *Minor premise: This animal can jump.*
>
> *Deductive conclusion: This animal is a frog.*
>
> *Valid: No*   *True: —*

Statement: That Olympic athlete will win a gold medal because she is so fast.

    Foundational premise: Athletes who are fast will win a gold medal.

    Minor premise: That Olympic athlete is fast.

    Deductive conclusion: That Olympic athlete will win a gold medal.

    Valid: Yes   *True:* No

Statement: Treat other people nicely so they will treat you nicely back.

    Foundational premise: Treating other people nicely will make them treat you nicely back.

    Minor premise: You treat other people nicely.

    Deductive conclusion: Other people will treat you nicely.

    Valid: Yes   *True:* Answers will vary

Statement: Donald must be unfriendly because he is so quiet.

    Foundational premise: All people who are quiet are unfriendly.

    Minor premise: Donald is quiet.

    Deductive conclusion: Donald is unfriendly.

    Valid: Yes   *True:* No

Statement: She must not be very nice because she is very beautiful.

    Foundational premise: Beautiful people are not nice.

    Minor premise: She is beautiful.

    Deductive conclusion: She is not nice.

    Valid: Yes   *True:* No

Statement: That man is corrupt because he's a politician.

    Foundational premise: Politicians are corrupt.

    Minor premise: That man is a politician.

    Deductive conclusion: That man is corrupt.

    Valid: Yes   *True:* No

Statement: Becky was in a car accident; she must have been texting while driving.

    Foundational premise: Texting while driving can cause car accidents.

    Minor premise: Becky was in a car accident.

    Deductive conclusion: Becky was texting while driving.

    Valid: No   *True:* —

Statement: He has white hair because he is so old.

> *Foundational premise:* Old people have white hair.
>
> *Minor premise:* He is old.
>
> *Deductive conclusion:* He has white hair.
>
> *Valid:* Yes   *True:* No

Statement: The plant is withering because it doesn't have enough water.

> *Foundational premise:* Lack of water makes plants wither.
>
> *Minor premise:* The plant doesn't have enough water.
>
> *Deductive conclusion:* The plant is withering.
>
> *Valid:* Yes   *True:* No

Statement: Beware of strangers because they could hurt you.

> *Foundational premise:* Beware of things that could hurt you.
>
> *Minor premise:* Strangers could hurt you.
>
> *Deductive conclusion:* Beware of strangers.
>
> *Valid:* Yes   *True:* Yes

Statement: Bananas are the least tasty fruit because they have the weirdest texture.

> *Foundational premise:* The weirder the texture, the less tasty the fruit is.
>
> *Minor premise:* Bananas have the weirdest texture.
>
> *Deductive conclusion:* Bananas are the least tasty fruit.
>
> *Valid:* Yes   *True:* Answers will vary

Statement: He's an expert so he must be right.

> *Foundational premise:* Experts are always right.
>
> *Minor premise:* He is an expert.
>
> *Deductive conclusion:* He must be right.
>
> *Valid:* Yes   *True:* No

Statement: She knows a lot of information, so she must be powerful.

> *Foundational premise:* Information is power.
>
> *Minor premise:* She knows a lot of information.
>
> *Deductive conclusion:* She must be powerful.
>
> *Valid:* Yes   *True:* Answers will vary

Statement: Books are better than movies because you can use your imagination.

> *Foundational premise: Things that make you use your imagination are better.*
>
> *Minor premise: Books make you use your imagination, but movies do not.*
>
> *Deductive conclusion: Books are better than movies.*
>
> *Valid: Yes*   *True: Answers will vary*

Statement: Riddles are difficult because they take a long time to figure out.

> *Foundational premise: Things that take a long time to figure out are difficult.*
>
> *Minor premise: Riddles take a long time to figure out.*
>
> *Deductive conclusion: Riddles are difficult.*
>
> *Valid: Yes*   *True: Answers will vary*

Statement: Capitalism is great because there's so much money in the system.

> *Foundational premise: Lots of money in a system is great.*
>
> *Minor premise: Capitalism has lots of money in its system.*
>
> *Deductive conclusion: Capitalism is great.*
>
> *Valid: Yes*   *True: Answers will vary*

Statement: Nickels are worth more than dimes because they are bigger.

> *Foundational premise: Coins that are bigger are worth more.*
>
> *Minor premise: Nickels are bigger than dimes.*
>
> *Deductive conclusion: Nickels are worth more than dimes.*
>
> *Valid: Yes*   *True: No*

Statement: Microwaves cause cancer because of radiation.

> *Foundational premise: Radiation can sometimes cause cancer.*
>
> *Minor premise: Microwaves use radiation.*
>
> *Deductive conclusion: Microwaves cause cancer.*
>
> *Valid: No*   *True: —*

Statement: Obama is the best president because he's the most recent president.

> *Foundational premise: More recent things are better.*
>
> *Minor premise: Obama is the most recent president.*
>
> *Deductive conclusion: Obama is the best president.*
>
> *Valid: Yes*   *True: Answers will vary*

Statement: Barbeque is better than sushi because it has more calories.

> ***Foundational premise:*** *Things with more calories are better.*
>
> ***Minor premise:*** *Barbeque has more calories than sushi.*
>
> ***Deductive conclusion:*** *Barbeque is better than sushi.*
>
> ***Valid:*** *Yes*   ***True:*** *Answers will vary*

Statement: Raw meat is dangerous because it makes you sick.

> ***Foundational premise:*** *Things that make you sick are dangerous.*
>
> ***Minor premise:*** *Raw meat makes you sick.*
>
> ***Deductive conclusion:*** *Raw meat is dangerous.*
>
> ***Valid:*** *Yes*   ***True:*** *No*

Statement: January is the best month because it's when my birthday occurs.

> ***Foundational premise:*** *The month when my birthday occurs is the best.*
>
> ***Minor premise:*** *My birthday is in January.*
>
> ***Deductive conclusion:*** *January is the best month.*
>
> ***Valid:*** *Yes*   ***True:*** *No*

Statement: You should go camping because the weather is great.

> ***Foundational premise:*** *You should go camping when the weather is great.*
>
> ***Minor premise:*** *The weather is great.*
>
> ***Deductive conclusion:*** *You should go camping.*
>
> ***Valid:*** *Yes*   ***True:*** *Answers will vary*

Statement: She would be a great basketball player because she is so tall.

> ***Foundational premise:*** *All tall people are good at basketball.*
>
> ***Minor premise:*** *She is tall.*
>
> ***Deductive conclusion:*** *She would be a great basketball player.*
>
> ***Valid:*** *Yes*   ***True:*** *No*

Statement: Chopsticks are better eating utensils because they are fun to use.

> ***Foundational premise:*** *Things that are fun are better.*
>
> ***Minor premise:*** *Chopsticks are fun to use.*
>
> ***Deductive conclusion:*** *Chopsticks are better eating utensils.*
>
> ***Valid:*** *Yes*   ***True:*** *Answers will vary*

Statement: Earth is my favorite planet because I live here.

> ***Foundational premise:*** *My favorite planet is the one I live on.*
>
> ***Minor premise:*** *I live on Earth.*
>
> ***Deductive conclusion:*** *My favorite planet is Earth.*
>
> ***Valid:*** *Yes*   ***True:*** *Yes*

Statement: Take an umbrella with you because it is raining.

> ***Foundational premise:*** *People should take an umbrella with them when it is raining.*
>
> ***Minor premise:*** *It is raining.*
>
> ***Deductive conclusion:*** *Take an umbrella.*
>
> ***Valid:*** *Yes*   ***True:*** *Yes*

Statement: Unicycles are cool because they only have one wheel.

> ***Foundational premise:*** *Vehicles with one wheel are cool.*
>
> ***Minor premise:*** *Unicycles have one wheel.*
>
> ***Deductive conclusion:*** *Unicycles are cool.*
>
> ***Valid:*** *Yes*   ***True:*** *Answers will vary*

Proverb Pairs

For middle school and high school students

8

In Proverb Pairs, students discover the premises and conclusions behind common sayings and proverbs and then evaluate them for validity and truth.

Setup

For this game, you will need enough pairs of proverb and syllogism cards so that each student will have one card (for example, in a class of thirty, you would need fifteen pairs of cards). In each pair, one card states a common saying or proverb, and the other card lists an underlying syllogism—that is, two premises and a conclusion—for the saying or proverb. This chapter includes premade pairs of proverbs and syllogisms (see pages 184–194; for reproducible cards with the proverbs and syllogisms, visit **marzanoresearch.com /activitiesandgames**), but teachers may also elect to create their own. Shuffle the set of cards and randomly distribute one card to each student. Each student should also receive copies of the summary sheet (see reproducible on page 195) that he or she can use to evaluate the proverb-syllogism pairs. Each student will need one copy of the organizer for each proverb-syllogism pair he or she evaluates (see the next section).

Play

Students read their cards. Then, taking their cards with them, students stand up and mingle with each other, trying to find the person with the card that matches their own. If a student has a card with a proverb on it, he or she has to find the student who has the set of premises and a conclusion (syllogism) that

Reasoning Skills

- Standardizing reasoning
- Evaluating deductive conclusions
- Asking questions to challenge assumptions

Materials

- Pairs of proverb and syllogism cards (see pages 184–194 and online reproducibles)
- Copies of summary sheet (one per student per round; see reproducible on page 195)
- Pen or pencil for each student
- Timer (optional)

corresponds to that proverb, and vice versa. Students with syllogism cards might not immediately know what proverb is referenced by the set of premises and conclusion but should be able to figure it out by conferring with their classmates and comparing their syllogism with various proverbs.

For example, one student might receive a card that states the syllogism shown in figure 8.1.

Foundational premise: If you eat healthy food, you won't get sick.

Minor premise: If you get sick, you need to see the doctor.

Conclusion: If you eat healthy food, you won't need to see the doctor.

Figure 8.1: Syllogism card for Proverb Pairs.

The matching card would state the corresponding proverb, as shown in figure 8.2.

An apple a day keeps the doctor away.

Figure 8.2: Proverb card for Proverb Pairs.

Once two students have paired up, they discuss the syllogism related to the proverb to determine whether the reasoning behind the proverb is sound (valid and true). If they find that it is not, they should brainstorm ways to restate either the syllogism or the proverb in a way that is valid and true.

 Some proverbs and sayings are fairly well known, so students will likely not have difficulty connecting the standardized argument to the proverb. If students are having difficulty with more obscure sayings, encourage them to look for words that appear in both the proverb and the syllogism, and have them check to see if the conclusion is a different way of expressing the message of the proverb.

To scaffold the evaluation process and to facilitate later discussion, students should record their work on a summary sheet, such as the one provided at the end of this chapter (see example on page 183 and blank reproducible on page 195).

As shown in figure 8.3, students should first copy down the proverb and matching syllogism. This step is important because they will have different cards during the next round of the game and may not remember which syllogism they were evaluating. Students should next evaluate the validity of the standardized argument using the strategies that they have previously learned, such as drawing Euler diagrams. If they decide the conclusion is valid, they should also evaluate the truth of the argument by examining the premises. As in Valid or True (pages 142–179), students' answers regarding the truth of some premises may vary.

Based on their evaluation of the syllogism's validity and truth, students should decide if the conclusion is sound. If the syllogism is valid and the premises are true, the conclusion is sound. If the syllogism is invalid or one or both premises are not true, the conclusion cannot be considered sound. If they judge the conclusion to be unsound, students should decide which factor (validity or truth) makes it unsound and brainstorm ways to revise the proverb or the syllogism so that it is sound. Even if the conclusion is sound, students might come up with exceptions or improvements to the proverb, which they can also record.

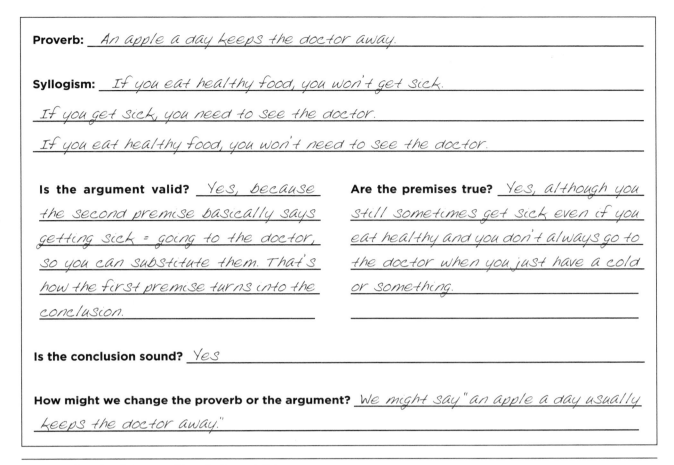

Proverb: _An apple a day keeps the doctor away._

Syllogism: _If you eat healthy food, you won't get sick._
If you get sick, you need to see the doctor.
If you eat healthy food, you won't need to see the doctor.

Is the argument valid? _Yes, because the second premise basically says getting sick = going to the doctor, so you can substitute them. That's how the first premise turns into the conclusion._

Are the premises true? _Yes, although you still sometimes get sick even if you eat healthy and you don't always go to the doctor when you just have a cold or something._

Is the conclusion sound? _Yes_

How might we change the proverb or the argument? _We might say "an apple a day usually keeps the doctor away."_

Figure 8.3: Completed Summary Sheet for Proverb Pairs.

Once all students have finished discussing and recording their evaluations of validity and truth, they trade cards with someone other than their current partner and the next round begins. For the third round (and subsequent rounds), students should make sure that they trade for a card they have not seen before. You might choose to give a time limit (perhaps five minutes or so) for evaluation once all students have found their partners, to keep the game moving.

Wrap-Up

After playing several rounds of the game, bring the whole class together for a discussion. It is impractical to discuss the proverbs following each round, as this would break up the game and prevent further rounds by giving students the answers to proverb-syllogism pairs they have not seen yet. Instead, play several rounds of the game before coming together as a class to discuss. Students can refer back to their summary sheets as various proverbs are discussed.

If any of the proverb pairs were particularly difficult for multiple pairs of students, make sure to discuss and talk through them with the whole class to clear up any lingering confusion. Other topics of discussion could include the following:

◆ With regard to the processes of evaluating validity and truth, what were some common mistakes or especially difficult proverbs?

◆ Regarding proverbs that were not sound, are they still good advice?

- ◆ Did any of the standardized syllogisms make you think about that proverb differently?

- ◆ Do most people think about the reasons behind common sayings? Why or why not? Should they?

It is not necessary to discuss every proverb, nor do students need to have seen and evaluated every pair before whole-class discussion (although it is fine if that is the case). We do recommend reviewing enough proverb pairs to allow each student to contribute to the discussion at least once. At the end of the game, you might choose to collect students' summary sheets to use as an unobtrusive assessment.

Proverbs and Syllogisms for Proverb Pairs

This section lists a number of proverbs and their corresponding syllogisms, as well as answers regarding the validity and truth of each syllogism. Please note that the syllogisms presented here may not represent the only standardization of a specific proverb. Additionally, some proverb pairs list "Answers will vary" in regard to their truth value. These syllogisms include at least one statement of opinion, which students may evaluate to be true or not true. For printable versions of the proverbs and syllogisms in card form, visit **marzanoresearch .com/activitiesandgames**.

Proverb: Haste makes waste.

Foundational premise: When you do things quickly, you don't do a good job.

Minor premise: When you don't do a good job, you get bad results.

Conclusion: When you do things quickly, you get bad results.

     Valid: Yes   *True: Answers will vary*

Proverb: A stitch in time saves nine.

Foundational premise: Early attention to a problem prevents problems from getting worse.

Minor premise: Preventing problems from getting worse saves time later.

Conclusion: Early attention to a problem saves time later.

     Valid: Yes   *True: Answers will vary*

Proverb: Ignorance is bliss.

Foundational premise: Not knowing things means you won't worry about them.

Minor premise: Not worrying makes you happy.

Conclusion: Not knowing things makes you happy.

     Valid: Yes   *True: Answers will vary*

Proverb: Don't cry over spilled milk.

Foundational premise: When you make a mistake, do something to fix it.

Minor premise: Being sad doesn't fix mistakes.

Conclusion: Don't be sad when you make a mistake.

     Valid: No   *True: —*

Proverb: You can catch more flies with honey than with vinegar.

Foundational premise: If you are sweet, people will respond to you.

Minor premise: When people respond to you, you get what you want.

Conclusion: If you are sweet, you will get what you want.

   Valid: Yes   *True: No*

Proverb: You can lead a horse to water, but you can't make him drink.

Foundational premise: Making something easy won't guarantee it will happen.

Minor premise: It is possible to make something easy.

Conclusion: You can make something easy, but you can't force it to happen.

   Valid: Yes   *True: Yes*

Proverb: Those who live in glass houses shouldn't throw stones.

Foundational premise: People shouldn't expose their own flaws.

Minor premise: Criticizing people who have the same flaws as you exposes your own flaws.

Conclusion: People shouldn't criticize people who have the same flaws as they do.

   Valid: Yes   *True: No*

Proverb: Well begun is half done.

Foundational premise: Starting a task well saves time.

Minor premise: Saving time lets you finish a task quickly.

Conclusion: Starting a task well lets you finish it quickly.

   Valid: Yes   *True: Yes*

Proverb: A little learning is a dangerous thing.

Foundational premise: Knowing a little bit makes you think you're smart when you're not.

Minor premise: Thinking you're smart when you're not can lead to bad outcomes.

Conclusion: Knowing a little bit can lead to bad outcomes.

   Valid: Yes   *True: Yes*

Proverb: A rolling stone gathers no moss.

Foundational premise: Busy people don't stay still.

Minor premise: Bad things happen to people who stay still.

Conclusion: Bad things won't happen to busy people.

   Valid: No   *True: —*

Proverb: Good things come to those who wait.

Foundational premise: Good things take time.

Minor premise: Things that take time require waiting.

Conclusion: Good things require waiting.

    Valid: Yes   *True: Yes*

Proverb: A dog is man's best friend.

Foundational premise: Dogs are loyal.

Minor premise: Being loyal makes you a good companion.

Conclusion: Dogs are good companions.

    Valid: Yes   *True: Yes*

Proverb: An apple a day keeps the doctor away.

Foundational premise: If you eat healthy food, you won't get sick.

Minor premise: If you get sick, you need to see the doctor.

Conclusion: If you eat healthy food, you won't need to see the doctor.

    Valid: Yes   *True: No*

Proverb: Honesty is the best policy.

Foundational premise: Telling the truth is a good deed.

Minor premise: Good deeds are the best things to do.

Conclusion: Telling the truth is the best thing to do.

    Valid: Yes   *True: Answers will vary*

Proverb: Slow and steady wins the race.

Foundational premise: If you work slowly but continuously, you won't make mistakes.

Minor premise: If you don't make mistakes, you will succeed.

Conclusion: If you work slowly but continuously, you will succeed.

    Valid: Yes   *True: No*

Proverb: Birds of a feather flock together.

Foundational premise: People who are similar like being together.

Minor premise: People who like being together hang out with each other.

Conclusion: People who are similar hang out with each other.

    Valid: Yes   *True: No*

Proverb: Early to bed, early to rise makes a man healthy, wealthy, and wise.

Foundational premise: If you go to bed early, you'll get good sleep.

Minor premise: If you get good sleep, you will be healthy, rich, and smart.

Conclusion: Going to bed early will make you healthy, rich, and smart.

     Valid: Yes   *True: No*

Proverb: Absence makes the heart grow fonder.

Foundational premise: Not seeing someone makes you miss that person.

Minor premise: Missing someone makes you like that person more.

Conclusion: Not seeing someone makes you like that person more.

     Valid: Yes   *True: Answers will vary*

Proverb: If at first you don't succeed, try, try again.

Foundational premise: You should keep trying until you reach an acceptable outcome.

Minor premise: You failed the first time, which is not an acceptable outcome.

Conclusion: If you fail the first time, you should try again.

     Valid: Yes   *True: Yes*

Proverb: Forgive and forget.

Foundational premise: Forgiving someone means you stop being angry at them.

Minor premise: You can't truly stop being angry unless you forget what made you mad.

Conclusion: To really forgive someone, you have to forget what they did.

     Valid: Yes   *True: Answers will vary*

Proverb: Nothing ventured, nothing gained.

Foundational premise: To get something, you have to pay the price.

Minor premise: The price of a reward is the risk you take.

Conclusion: You have to take a risk to get a reward.

     Valid: Yes   *True: Answers will vary*

Proverb: All is fair in love and war.

Foundational premise: In certain situations (like love and war), people conduct themselves differently than in regular life.

Minor premise: When people conduct themselves differently from regular life, things that are unfair in regular life become fair.

Conclusion: In certain situations (like love and war), things that are unfair in regular life become fair.

     Valid: Yes   *True: Answers will vary*

Proverb: It takes a village to raise a child.

Foundational premise: Many different people are necessary to raise a child.

Minor premise: Communities are made up of many different people.

Conclusion: A community is necessary to raise a child.

    Valid: Yes   *True:* Answers will vary

Proverb: Red sky at morning, sailors take warning. Red sky at night, sailors delight.

Foundational premise: If the sky is red in the evening, there will be good weather the next day.

Minor premise: If there is good weather, sailors will be happy.

Conclusion: If the sky is red in the evening, sailors will be happy.

    Valid: Yes   *True:* Yes

Proverb: Don't beat a dead horse.

Foundational premise: All resources will run out.

Minor premise: It is useless to try to get something if there is nothing left.

Conclusion: It is useless to try to get a resource after it runs out.

    Valid: Yes   *True:* Answers will vary

Proverb: Look before you leap.

Foundational premise: Investigating something before you do it prevents bad outcomes.

Minor premise: It is a good idea to prevent bad outcomes.

Conclusion: It is a good idea to investigate something before you do it.

    Valid: Yes   *True:* Yes

Proverb: Garbage in, garbage out.

Foundational premise: What you put into something is what you will get out of it.

Minor premise: You put bad work into a project.

Conclusion: You will get bad work out of that project.

    Valid: Yes   *True:* Yes

Proverb: Not all those who wander are lost.

Foundational premise: To be lost, you must first have an intended destination.

Minor premise: If you are wandering, you might not have an intended destination.

Conclusion: Some people who wander are not lost.

    Valid: Yes   *True:* Answers will vary

Proverb: Don't count your chickens before they hatch.

Foundational premise: Nothing is guaranteed until it actually happens.

Minor premise: You should not depend on things that are not guaranteed.

Conclusion: You should not depend on things that haven't happened yet.

      Valid: Yes   *True: Yes*

Proverb: Make hay while the sun shines.

Foundational premise: Good choices should be made right away.

Minor premise: Taking advantage of an opportunity is a good choice.

Conclusion: Take advantage of opportunities right away.

      Valid: Yes   *True: Answers will vary*

Proverb: I think, therefore I am.

Foundational premise: Everything that thinks is self-aware.

Minor premise: Everything that is self-aware is in existence.

Conclusion: Everything that thinks is in existence.

      Valid: Yes   *True: Answers will vary*

Proverb: Don't put all your eggs in one basket.

Foundational premise: Depending completely on one thing is a risky decision.

Minor premise: Risky decisions are bad choices.

Conclusion: Depending completely on one thing is a bad choice.

      Valid: Yes   *True: Answers will vary*

Proverb: He who hesitates is lost.

Foundational premise: Waiting to act causes you to miss out on an opportunity.

Minor premise: Some opportunities only occur once.

Conclusion: If you wait to act, you will miss your only chance.

      Valid: No   *True: —*

Proverb: Life is like a box of chocolates; you never know what you're going to get.

Foundational premise: Life is unpredictable.

Minor premise: Things that are unpredictable are full of surprises.

Conclusion: Life is full of surprises.

      Valid: Yes   *True: Yes*

Proverb: The bigger they are, the harder they fall.

Foundational premise: People who are powerful have more things (like money or elevated status).

Minor premise: Things can be lost.

Conclusion: People who are powerful have more to lose.

    Valid: Yes   *True: Yes*

Proverb: Murder will out.

Foundational premise: Some people are bad at keeping secrets.

Minor premise: A murder is an example of something that would be kept secret.

Conclusion: Someone will eventually expose murder.

    Valid: No   *True: —*

Proverb: Don't throw the baby out with the bathwater.

Foundational premise: Good things can be mixed in with bad things.

Minor premise: You should get rid of bad things, but keep good things.

Conclusion: You should sort out good things before throwing away bad things.

    Valid: Yes   *True: Yes*

Proverb: Easy come, easy go.

Foundational premise: Things that are acquired quickly are prone to change.

Minor premise: Things that are prone to change can leave quickly.

Conclusion: Things that are acquired quickly can leave quickly.

    Valid: Yes   *True: Yes*

Proverb: What's good for the goose is good for the gander.

Foundational premise: Things that are good for an individual are enjoyable.

Minor premise: Enjoyable things are good for everyone.

Conclusion: Things that are good for an individual are good for other people as well.

    Valid: Yes   *True: Answers will vary*

Proverb: When in Rome, do as the Romans do.

Foundational premise: Your behavior should please others.

Minor premise: Others like their own behavior.

Conclusion: Your behavior should be like the behavior of others.

    Valid: Yes   *True: Answers will vary*

Proverb: If the mountain will not come to Mohammed, Mohammed must go to the mountain.

Foundational premise: If the path to a goal is impossible, you will not achieve it.

Minor premise: You should always achieve your goals, even if it's not in the way you planned.

Conclusion: If the path to your goal is impossible, you should find a different way to get the same result.

   Valid: Yes   *True: Answers will vary*

Proverb: Do unto others as you would have them do unto you.

Foundational premise: You get what you give.

Minor premise: You treat others nicely.

Conclusion: Others will treat you nicely.

   Valid: Yes   *True: No*

Proverb: An ounce of prevention is worth a pound of cure.

Foundational premise: You can only prevent something from happening when you can take steps against it.

Minor premise: You cannot take steps against something that has already happened.

Conclusion: You cannot prevent something that has already happened.

   Valid: Yes   *True: Yes*

Proverb: A fool and his money are soon parted.

Foundational premise: Foolish people do not manage money well.

Minor premise: People who do not manage money well usually lose their money.

Conclusion: Foolish people usually lose their money.

   Valid: Yes   *True: Answers will vary*

Proverb: Don't change horses in the middle of the stream.

Foundational premise: Major changes will delay your plans.

Minor premise: Don't do things that will delay your plans once you've started an activity.

Conclusion: Don't make major changes once you've started an activity.

   Valid: Yes   *True: No*

Proverb: Don't be the pot calling the kettle black.

Foundational premise: Do not criticize someone unless he or she does something wrong.

Minor premise: You have done something wrong in the past.

Conclusion: Do not criticize someone for doing something you have done in the past.

   Valid: No   *True: —*

Proverb: You reap what you sow.

Foundational premise: You are responsible for your actions.

Minor premise: Your actions determine what happens to you.

Conclusion: You are responsible for what happens to you.

> *Valid: Yes*   *True: Answers will vary*

Proverb: A penny saved is a penny earned.

Foundational premise: If you earn money, you can spend it later.

Minor premise: If you save money, you can spend it later.

Conclusion: If you earn or save money, you can spend it later.

> *Valid: Yes*   *True: Yes*

Proverb: You can't teach an old dog new tricks.

Foundational premise: It is hard to change someone once he or she has developed habits.

Minor premise: Habits develop over a long period of time.

Conclusion: It is hard to change someone after a long time.

> *Valid: Yes*   *True: Yes*

Proverb: The pen is mightier than the sword.

Foundational premise: The effect of words can last a long time, but the effects of physical force only last a short time.

Minor premise: Things that last a long time are more powerful than things that don't.

Conclusion: The effect of words has more power than the effect of physical force.

> *Valid: Yes*   *True: Answers will vary*

Proverb: A chain is only as strong as its weakest link.

Foundational premise: A functional group does good work.

Minor premise: Good work relies on each member.

Conclusion: A functional group relies on each member.

> *Valid: Yes*   *True: Answers will vary*

Proverb: A friend in need is a friend indeed.

Foundational premise: People who need help from you want to get something.

Minor premise: When people want to get something, they are friendlier.

Conclusion: People who need help from you are friendlier.

> *Valid: Yes*   *True: Yes*

Proverb: A good man is hard to find.

Foundational premise: Nice people are rare.

Minor premise: Rare things are hard to find.

Conclusion: Nice people are hard to find.

> *Valid: Yes*   *True: No*

Proverb: A leopard cannot change its spots.

Foundational premise: You cannot change your genetic traits.

Minor premise: Your genetic traits make you who you are.

Conclusion: You cannot change who you are.

> *Valid: Yes*   *True: Answers will vary*

Proverb: A miss is as good as a mile.

Foundational premise: If you miss something by a wide margin, you have not achieved it.

Minor premise: If you miss something by a small margin, you have not achieved it.

Conclusion: If you miss something by a small margin, the end result is the same as if you miss something by a wide margin.

> *Valid: Yes*   *True: Answers will vary*

Proverb: A picture is worth a thousand words.

Foundational premise: Complex ideas should be explained in a way that is understandable.

Minor premise: One understandable way to explain things is through using simple pictures.

Conclusion: All complex ideas should be explained through simple pictures.

> *Valid: No*   *True: —*

Proverb: A thing of beauty is a joy forever.

Foundational premise: Something that is truly beautiful has appeal that will not dwindle.

Minor premise: Something with appeal that will not dwindle makes a person happy forever.

Conclusion: Something that is truly beautiful makes us happy forever.

> *Valid: Yes*   *True: Answers will vary*

Proverb: Actions speak louder than words.

Foundational premise: Saying something does not make it happen.

Minor premise: You can count on things that happen.

Conclusion: You can't count on things that people say.

> *Valid: No*   *True: —*

Proverb: All good things must come to an end.

Foundational premise: All things eventually end.

Minor premise: Good things are things.

Conclusion: All good things eventually end.

     Valid: Yes   *True: Yes*

Proverb: All that glitters is not gold.

Foundational premise: Appearances do not always reflect quality.

Minor premise: Some things have good appearances.

Conclusion: Some things that appear good are actually poor quality.

     Valid: No   *True: —*

Proverb: A bird in the hand is worth two in the bush.

Foundational premise: What you have on hand is easily accessible.

Minor premise: Things that are easily accessible have more value than what you desire and don't have.

Conclusion: What you have on hand has more value than what you desire and don't have.

     Valid: Yes   *True: Answers will vary*

Proverb: If the shoe fits, wear it.

Foundational premise: If something applies to you, you should accept it.

Minor premise: This criticism applies to you.

Conclusion: You should accept this criticism.

     Valid: Yes   *True: Yes*

Proverb: When the cat's away, the mice will play.

Foundational premise: When there's no authority figure, no one is in control.

Minor premise: When no one is in control, people do what they want.

Conclusion: When there's no authority figure, people do what they want.

     Valid: Yes   *True: Answers will vary*

Proverb: Hunger is the best spice.

Foundational premise: When you're really hungry, you become less picky.

Minor premise: When you are less picky, anything tastes good.

Conclusion: When you're really hungry, anything tastes good.

     Valid: Yes   *True: Answers will vary*

Summary Sheet for Proverb Pairs

Proverb: _____

_____

_____

_____

Syllogism: _____

_____

_____

_____

Is the argument valid?

_____

_____

_____

_____

_____

_____

Are the premises true?

_____

_____

_____

_____

_____

_____

Is the conclusion sound? _____

_____

_____

_____

_____

How might we change the proverb or the argument?

_____

_____

_____

_____

9 Premises Puzzle

For middle school and high school students

In Premises Puzzle, students practice forming valid arguments and identifying irrelevant and potentially distracting evidence. Students must choose the premises that support a conclusion from a set of options that includes one complete, valid argument and a number of decoy statements.

Setup

To set up for this game, print and cut apart sets of premises and conclusions (such as those provided on pages 202–215). In each set, there should be one complete standardized argument—a conclusion and two or more premises that logically support it—and various other premises that are irrelevant to the argument. For example, a set might be comprised of the following statements:

> All houses are painted blue.
>
> The place I live is painted red.
>
> No things that are painted red are painted blue.
>
> Therefore, the place I live is not a house.
>
> The ocean is also blue.
>
> Monika's favorite color is red.

Here, the first three statements are relevant premises, the fourth (beginning with *therefore*) is a conclusion, and the final two statements are irrelevant premises. During gameplay, each statement appears on its own

Reasoning Skills

- Evaluating deductive conclusions
- Explaining how evidence supports a conclusion

Materials

- Sets of premises and conclusions printed on slips of paper (see reproducibles, pages 202–215)
- Timer (optional)

piece of paper, and they are shuffled into random order. This book includes premade sets of standardized arguments with irrelevant statements, but teachers can also create their own.

You can adjust the difficulty of the game for age or ability by increasing or decreasing the number of decoy statements in each set. If there are only a few irrelevant premises, students will have an easier time identifying the standardized argument, whereas many irrelevant premises will create more options and therefore a more challenging game. Similar content among statements (for example, if all statements mention dogs) can also make the game more difficult.

Sets of premise puzzles can be tailored to specific content areas. For a science class, you might create sets that include a scientific theory, several pieces of evidence and data, and some distracting data. For students studying literature, you could list textual evidence from a novel they have just read, along with a conclusion about the work—students sort the evidence into those premises that support the conclusion and those that are irrelevant.

To scaffold this activity for students who have less experience with it, provide more explanation about the sets you are giving them. For instance, you might only include sets where the standardized arguments consist of two premises and a conclusion (syllogisms), explaining that the resulting arguments will take that form exactly.

The game can be played by individuals or small groups; decide in advance which way the class will be playing. Each student or group will need a set of statements for each round you plan to play, but the sets can be all the same or all different. If the sets are all the same, it allows for more whole-class assistance and discussion; if the sets are all different, you can redistribute them to play additional rounds.

With a bit of extra time and materials, you can create a magnetic version of this game (which is fun for students to play and ideal for demonstrating the game on a whiteboard or other magnetic surface). Print or write the premises and conclusions on a heavier paper, such as cardstock, and glue small magnets to the back of each statement.

Explain to students that they will be given a set of statements, but not all of them will be relevant to creating a valid argument. They will have to sift through the statements to find the premises and conclusion that create a valid standardized argument.

Play

Give each student or group of students a set of statements. Students begin by reading each statement. Remind students that the conclusion must be fully supported by the premises. If there is a term in the conclusion that does not appear anywhere else in the argument, or if there are any assumptions required to reach the conclusion, the argument is incomplete. Students may have accidentally ignored a premise, or they may have tried to create an argument that cannot be fully supported by the statements in front of them. They should also determine the appropriate order for the relevant statements. The conclusion, of course, should follow the premises, and if the premises fall clearly into the categories of foundational and minor, the foundational premise(s) should appear first.

For example, consider the set of statements in figure 9.1, which are presented in random order as they would be during the game. The conclusion can clearly be identified because it begins with the term *therefore* (this is true of all of the conclusions in the sets provided on pages 202–215). Students need to select a series of premises (often more than two) that create a complete and valid argument for the conclusion, as shown in figure 9.2.

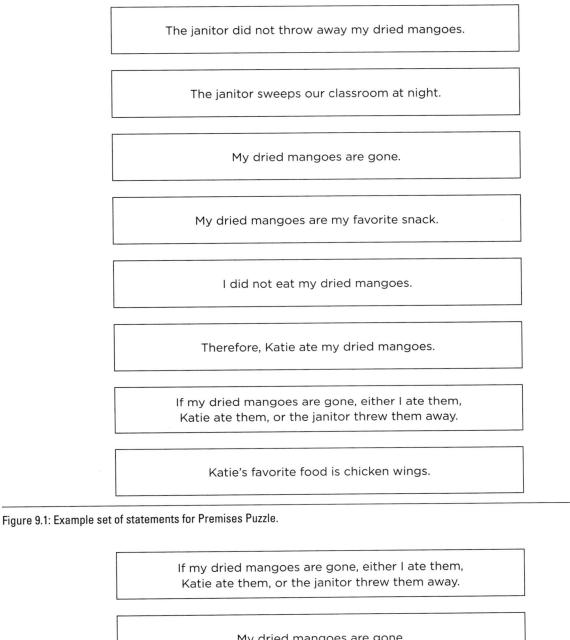

The janitor did not throw away my dried mangoes.

The janitor sweeps our classroom at night.

My dried mangoes are gone.

My dried mangoes are my favorite snack.

I did not eat my dried mangoes.

Therefore, Katie ate my dried mangoes.

If my dried mangoes are gone, either I ate them,
Katie ate them, or the janitor threw them away.

Katie's favorite food is chicken wings.

Figure 9.1: Example set of statements for Premises Puzzle.

If my dried mangoes are gone, either I ate them,
Katie ate them, or the janitor threw them away.

My dried mangoes are gone.

I did not eat my dried mangoes.

The janitor did not throw away my dried mangoes.

Therefore, Katie ate my dried mangoes.

Figure 9.2: Complete and valid argument.

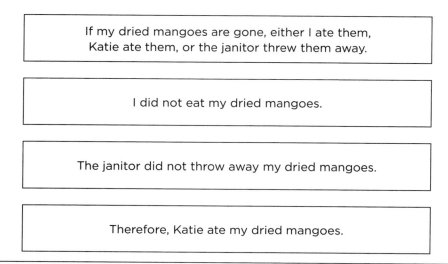

Figure 9.3: Incomplete argument.

As an example of an incomplete argument, the argument in figure 9.3 assumes that the mangoes are gone. This argument does not establish that fact as a premise; therefore, this is not the best argument students could create from the available premises.

The first time the game is played, or if students are having difficulty and aren't sure where to begin, you might offer hints or strategies for approaching the puzzle. For instance, you might suggest that they look for the conclusion first or set aside any statements that are obviously irrelevant. Once individual students or groups have selected the statements that they think form a complete argument, they must evaluate its validity before announcing that they've finished or asking you to check their work.

Wrap-Up

Premises Puzzle can either be played as a simple activity or as a game with points. If using it as an activity, check each student's or group's work as they finish or have students write down their complete argument on a separate piece of paper to be handed in. This is a good approach for students who are just beginning to practice the formation of complete and valid arguments.

To play Premises Puzzle as a game with points, begin by setting a time limit for each round—we recommend one to two minutes. Give students or groups of students sets of statements and start the timer. When the time is up, check everyone's work. This version works best if each group is given the same set of statements. If a student or group has created a complete and valid argument within the time limit, the student or group receives a point. Pass out new sets of statements to play another round.

Variation

Another version of this game is more collaborative and physically active. For this version, you will need enough space for the entire class to walk around and divide into groups. As before, create slips of paper with individual statements on them; however, do not include any irrelevant statements. That is, all premises should match and logically support a conclusion. There should be exactly as many slips of paper as students in the class. Each student draws a statement from a hat. Once all students have a statement, they confer with their classmates to find the rest of their argument. The first group to find all its members and arrange its statements properly wins. Alert students to the fact that they do not know how many statements are in their argument, and caution them against preemptively announcing that they have found their complete group when they might still be missing a member. You can also use this version of the game as a way to divide students into randomized groups for another activity.

Sets of Premises Puzzles

Here we provide thirty Premises Puzzles at the middle school level and thirty at the high school level. We suggest, however, that all students first play with the middle school sets. Each set includes a complete argument consisting of several premises and a conclusion, as well as a few irrelevant statements. The conclusion is always the statement that begins with the word *therefore*. Here, the irrelevant statements appear after the conclusion. All statements within each set should be cut apart and shuffled before giving the set to students. If you are playing the collaborative, active variation of the game, omit the irrelevant statements.

Middle School

Some fire stations have a pet Dalmatian.

All Dalmatians wear collars.

Therefore, some fire stations have a pet that wears a collar.

Jorge's dog is a German Shepherd.

Some dogs like to swim.

_____

All owls have feathers.

No lizards have feathers.

Therefore, no lizards are owls.

No monkeys have feathers.

Some owls eat mice.

_____

If there is sufficient evidence for something, then it is accepted as true.

There is sufficient evidence that Crystal jaywalked.

Therefore, it is accepted as true that Crystal jaywalked.

People are innocent until proven guilty.

Crystal never tells the truth.

_____

All pink umbrellas are made by The Umbrella Company.

Everything made by The Umbrella Company is plastic.

Therefore, all pink umbrellas are plastic.

My sister's favorite color is yellow.

Some umbrellas are made of cloth.

Everything made by The Umbrella Company is pink umbrellas.

No man is an island.

Bill is a man.

Therefore, Bill is not an island.

Jody is a woman.

This statement is a metaphor.

No people are mountains.

_____

The edge of our solar system is eighteen billion kilometers from the Sun.

The Voyager 1 spacecraft is more than eighteen billion kilometers from the Sun.

Therefore, the Voyager 1 is outside our solar system.

Life that exists outside of Earth is considered alien.

Aliens are not able to communicate with humans.

Mars is populated by robots.

_____

Do not let strangers into your house.

The babysitter is a stranger.

Therefore, do not let the babysitter into your house.

The babysitter has great recommendations.

Do not trust strangers with your children.

Babysitters often steal pizza from the refrigerator.

_____

The more information something contains, the more important it is.

The Internet contains more information than any library.

Therefore, the Internet is more important than libraries.

Some libraries contain rare books.

Some websites contain false information.

You can believe what you read in books.

The amount of information on the Internet can be measured in exabytes.

_____

Hippies smell bad.

Britta smells great.

Therefore, Britta is not a hippie.

Hippies have long hair and love drum circles.

Britta has long hair and loves drum circles.

Britta likes astrology.

Hippies are very nice.

Taking something that costs money without paying for it is stealing.

Pirating music is downloading it without paying for it.

Therefore, pirating music is stealing.

My sister says it's okay to download music off the Internet.

Downloading music off the Internet is easy and cheap.

Very few people get caught downloading music off the Internet.

Musicians do not make a lot of money.

Musicians steal when they do not make enough money.

_____

A spork is a combination of a spoon and a fork.

Spoons are useful when eating liquids.

Forks are useful when eating solids.

Therefore, sporks are useful when eating liquids or solids.

Sporks should incorporate a knife element into their design.

Sporks are very cool.

_____

Geoff is wearing a disguise.

People who wear disguises are untrustworthy.

You shouldn't associate with untrustworthy people.

Therefore, you shouldn't associate with Geoff.

The disguise is not good at hiding Geoff's identity.

Geoff enjoys wearing disguises.

_____

Everything grown-ups get to do is better than what kids get to do.

Grown-ups drink coffee.

Kids drink milk.

Therefore, drinking coffee is better than drinking milk.

Soda is worse for you than milk.

No one likes to drink tea.

_____

Things that are fast are better than things that are slow.

Movies are fast to watch.

Books are slow to read.

Therefore, movies are better than books.

Movies based on books are the best.

Some movies are longer than other movies.

Hiking is only fun when the weather is nice and warm.

The forecast for this weekend predicts over a foot of snow will fall.

A foot of snow is not nice or warm.

Therefore, this weekend, hiking would not be fun.

Sledding is fun in the snow.

It is crowded on trails when it is nice and warm.

You are exposed to radiation when you use cell phones and microwaves.

Radiation can hurt you.

No one should ever do something that could hurt him or her.

Therefore, no one should use cell phones or microwaves.

Microwave dinners are delicious.

Cell phones hurt when you drop them on your foot.

Bacon and pineapple pizza is the best kind of pizza.

Sauces make everything better.

Chipotle ranch is a sauce.

Therefore, putting chipotle ranch on a bacon and pineapple pizza would make it even better.

Chipotle ranch is not spicy enough.

The best things in life are free.

Having an after-school job builds character.

Having an after-school job earns money.

High schoolers today need to build character and earn money.

Therefore, high schoolers should get after-school jobs.

High schoolers often spend (rather than save) their money.

Having good character will make you happier in the long run.

Boys and girls distract each other in the classroom.

Single-sex classrooms consist of either all boys or all girls.

Classrooms with minimal distractions are better for learning.

Therefore, single-sex classrooms are better for learning.

Girls are too talkative.

Boys are more easily distracted than girls.

People should do what makes them happy.

Some people are happy to drink soda.

The government should make laws that make its citizens happy.

Therefore, the government should not ban soda.

Some government officials drink soda.

If you do not like something, you can choose to avoid it.

_____

The government should try to ensure that women and men are treated equally.

Men can get drafted into the army.

Women cannot get drafted into the army.

Therefore, the government should create laws that allow women to be drafted.

Men make better soldiers than women.

Women sign up for the army voluntarily.

_____

You should not spend money you do not have.

When you use a credit card, someone is loaning you money.

Money loaned to you is money you do not have.

Therefore, you should not use credit cards.

Loans are okay as long as you pay them back.

You should spend the money that you have.

_____

All houses are painted blue.

The place I live is painted red.

No things that are painted red are painted blue.

Therefore, the place I live is not a house.

The ocean is blue.

Monika's favorite color is red.

_____

If June wants a snack, then she will eat popcorn, but only in the afternoon.

June wants a snack.

It is after noon.

Therefore, June will eat popcorn.

Popcorn always gets stuck in her teeth.

June thinks popcorn is a healthy snack.

If it's morning, June eats pretzels.

Fatima is an engineer.

All engineers like math.

If people like math, then they will read books about it in their spare time.

Therefore, Fatima reads books about math in her spare time.

Fatima likes romance novels.

Books about math are expensive.

If something is expensive, then you should take care of it.

_____

The tea cup ride at the fair spins in circles.

You get dizzy if you spin in circles.

You throw up if you get dizzy.

Therefore, if you go on the tea cup ride at the fair, you will throw up.

If you are dizzy, you can spin the other way to go back to normal.

Tyler went on the tea cup ride at the fair last summer.

You can get funnel cake at the fair.

_____

If an animal has one horn, then it is a unicorn.

An Indian rhino is an animal.

An Indian rhino has one horn.

Therefore, an Indian rhino is a unicorn.

An Indian rhino is gray.

An Indian rhino is rotund.

Unicorns do not exist.

_____

Mike plays the guitar.

People who play the guitar get calluses on their fingers.

Calluses make fingers look unsightly.

Therefore, Mike's fingers are unsightly.

Mike is embarrassed by unsightly fingers.

People who garden get calluses.

Mike does not like gardens.

The best music is beautiful.

Beethoven made beautiful music.

Justin Bieber does not make beautiful music.

Therefore, Beethoven made better music than Justin Bieber.

Some music that Beethoven made was not beautiful.

Justin Bieber has a beautiful haircut.

Beethoven's haircut will never be considered beautiful.

_____

Classes that go outside are better than classes that stay inside.

The science class is going to the creek to look at tadpoles.

The creek is outside.

The math class is staying inside.

Therefore, the science class is better than the math class.

Math classes never study tadpoles.

Not all creeks have tadpoles.

High School

The constitutional right to bear arms means that American citizens have the right to own guns.

I am an American citizen.

Therefore, it is my right to own a gun.

Gun laws should be stricter.

Constitutional rights do not apply to felons.

Felons should be allowed to own guns.

_____

Colleges want to know as much about a student as possible before admittance.

SAT and ACT scores are information about a student.

Therefore, it makes sense that colleges want to see a student's SAT and ACT scores.

The SAT and ACT identify a student's strengths in subjects that are important for success.

The SAT is unfair because it is not representative of the majority of real-world work scenarios.

The ACT grading system is better than the SAT grading system.

Adults can drink alcohol.

Eighteen-year-olds cannot drink alcohol.

Therefore, eighteen-year-olds are not adults.

People in the military do not drink alcohol.

Adults can serve in the military.

Eighteen-year-olds can serve in the military.

Drinking alcohol is not a mature thing to do.

_____

Some video games depict violent acts.

Depictions of violent acts desensitize viewers to violence.

People who are desensitized to violence are more likely to commit violent crimes.

Therefore, some video games make people who play them more likely to commit violent crimes.

Some video games do not depict violent acts.

Video games that are not violent are more fun.

_____

Outside of the U.S., people agree that soccer is normally called "football."

There are more people outside of the U.S. than inside the U.S.

Whatever has the most people supporting it should be the norm.

Therefore, the U.S. should change the name of soccer to football.

We should change the name of American football.

The U.S. is not very good at soccer compared to European countries.

American football is similar to rugby.

_____

Good owners do not let their dogs attack other dogs.

Christian's dog is named Ruby.

Ruby just attacked a dog.

Therefore, Christian is not a good owner.

Ruby hates other dogs.

When Christian sees another dog, he pets it.

Good dog owners take their dogs on walks.

It is better to be smart than to have money.

College costs a lot of money.

College makes you smart.

Therefore, it is better to go to college.

Things that cost a lot of money will make you poor.

Smart people often wear glasses.

Glasses cost a lot of money.

_____

Things make Jeanna happy.

Jeanna buys things.

Jeanna needs money to buy things.

Therefore, money makes Jeanna happy.

There are other things that make people happy besides money.

Money can buy a nice fedora or a boat.

Money cannot buy true friends.

_____

Stalking is the act of secretly following an individual around and taking pictures of him or her.

The paparazzi follow movie stars around and take pictures of them.

People who stalk other people should go to jail.

Therefore, the paparazzi should go to jail.

Private investigators follow an individual around and take pictures of him or her.

No one should partake in stalking other individuals.

Private investigators can follow movie stars around and take pictures of them.

_____

Vaccinations stop the spread of diseases.

Stopping the spread of diseases helps people.

The government should make laws that help people.

Therefore, there should be laws requiring vaccinations.

Vaccinations are required in schools.

People can transmit diseases without knowing they have them.

Some laws do not help people.

Teaching Reasoning: Activities and Games for the Classroom © 2015 Marzano Research • marzanoresearch.com
Visit **marzanoresearch.com/activitiesandgames** to download this page.

Some people smoke cigarettes in public places.

Many people do not like the smell of cigarette smoke.

Laws are meant to stop things that many people do not like.

Therefore, there should be laws to stop smoking in public places.

Second-hand smoke kills.

Many people do not mind the smell of cigarette smoke.

People are allowed to smoke inside some establishments.

_____

Public transportation systems reduce traffic on highways.

Highways become clogged with traffic when a lot of people drive on them.

When highways are clogged, they are not helpful.

The government should prioritize money in order to help the most people.

Therefore, money should go to public transportation rather than building highways.

People need to get around in cities.

Public transportation systems help lots of people get around easily.

Commuting on highways costs more money than taking public transportation.

_____

I will check out either a fantasy, mystery, or romance novel from the library.

At the library, I remembered that I do not like romance novels.

Mystery novels are only written by male authors.

I do not read books by male authors.

Therefore, I will check out a fantasy novel.

Female authors write better books than male authors.

The library has a large selection of books by male authors.

_____

Henry's voice sounds like the voice of a cartoon character.

Cartoon characters sound silly.

People don't take people with silly voices seriously.

It is hard to be successful if people do not take you seriously.

Therefore, it is hard for Henry to be successful.

One cartoon character is Daffy Duck.

People in suits are very easy to take seriously.

In order to be a good driver, you must have quick reflexes.

In order to be a good driver, you must be able to see over the steering wheel.

First graders and eighth graders have quick reflexes.

First graders cannot see over the steering wheel, while most eighth graders can.

Therefore, most eighth graders would be good drivers.

Bad drivers crash their cars.

Steering wheels are often damaged in car crashes.

_____

Harman is an artist in New York.

Artists in New York are rich.

Rich people have bad attitudes.

People with bad attitudes don't have many friends.

Therefore, Harman doesn't have many friends.

It is hard to be an artist in New York.

Many people in New York have bad attitudes.

_____

Sometimes it is acceptable to do something that hurts an individual to benefit a collective group of people.

Torture hurts an individual.

Torture can help persuade someone to divulge information.

Some information can benefit a collective group of people.

Therefore, sometimes torture is acceptable.

Individuals can have information.

Some kinds of torture are far worse than other forms.

_____

People should try to avoid excluding others.

You exclude others if you publicly celebrate a holiday that others don't celebrate.

Not everyone celebrates Christmas.

Saying "Merry Christmas" to everyone is a way of publicly celebrating Christmas.

Therefore, people should try to avoid saying "Merry Christmas."

Some people don't celebrate any holidays in December.

Saying "Merry Christmas" is a gesture of good will.

Clothes are supposed to keep you decent and less exposed to the elements.

Clothes from a thrift store keep you decent and less exposed to the elements just as well as clothes from the mall.

Clothes from the mall cost more than clothes from a thrift store.

When the quality is the same, people should spend less money, not more money.

Therefore, people should buy clothes at a thrift store.

Clothes from the mall are more fashionable.

When you buy clothes at the mall, you can also go to the food court.

_____

If my dried mangoes are gone, either I ate them, Katie ate them, or the janitor threw them away.

My dried mangoes are gone.

I did not eat my dried mangoes.

The janitor did not throw away my dried mangoes.

Therefore, Katie ate my dried mangoes.

The janitor sweeps our classroom at night.

Katie's favorite food is chicken wings.

My dried mangoes are my favorite snack.

_____

Recycling is good for the environment.

The government should make people do things that are good for the environment.

The government makes laws so people will do (or not do) certain things.

A way to make people do something is to fine them when they don't do it.

Therefore, the government should make a law to fine people when they do not recycle.

It is good to make people do things they do not want to do.

Laws are always good.

Paying fines does not make people feel good.

_____

We have technology to exterminate mosquitoes.

Mosquitoes spread diseases that kill humans.

Saving human lives helps humans.

We should use technology that helps humans.

Therefore, we should exterminate mosquitoes.

Mosquitoes are the worst insects.

Only female mosquitoes bite.

Mosquitoes breed in stagnant water.

Teaching Reasoning: Activities and Games for the Classroom © 2015 Marzano Research • marzanoresearch.com
Visit **marzanoresearch.com/activitiesandgames** to download this page.

When students get distracted, it is harder for them to learn.

Schools are a place where students should learn as much as they can.

Students get distracted by fashion trends like flashy sneakers and accessories.

A dress code that mandates school uniforms does not allow flashy sneakers and accessories.

Therefore, schools should require that all students wear school uniforms.

Students can be distracted by cell phones and MP3 players.

Students do not wear school uniforms to hip-hop shows.

Some students learn more in school than other students.

_____

If you like things separately, then you like them mixed together.

Harriet loves almonds and marshmallows.

Harriet loves chocolate ice cream.

Rocky road ice cream has a chocolate base.

Rocky road ice cream has almonds and marshmallows in it.

Therefore, Harriet loves rocky road ice cream.

S'mores have marshmallows in them.

Butter pecan ice cream is for the elderly.

_____

Cheerleaders and football players are athletes.

Athletes play sports.

Cheerleaders can do flips.

Football players run, hit, throw, or catch.

It is harder to do flips than to run, hit, throw, or catch.

Therefore, cheerleaders play a harder sport than football players.

Football players are often bigger than cheerleaders.

Lacrosse is a difficult sport.

_____

If I do not go to prom, it will be because I was sick, the captain of the basketball team didn't ask me, or I did not get a dress.

I bought a great prom dress at the thrift store for ten dollars.

I have been drinking orange juice every morning.

Drinking orange juice every morning keeps you from getting sick.

The captain of the basketball team is going to prom with my best friend.

Therefore, I will not go to prom.

The captain of the basketball team loves orange juice.

The cousin of the captain of the basketball team loves thrift stores.

Guns are often used in violent crimes.

Gun laws impose waiting periods, which prevent people from impulsively buying guns right away.

If people have to wait before they react, they calm down and think about what they will do.

When people are calm, they are less likely to commit a violent crime.

Therefore, gun laws that impose waiting periods make people less likely to commit violent crimes.

Laws should mandate owners' registering their guns.

Guns can be used to hunt.

People often commit violent crimes in fits of rage.

Most people who have guns are not criminals.

_____

You must kill an animal to get its fur for a coat.

You should only support killing animals if it is for something you need.

Wearing fur coats is fashionable.

Being fashionable is not a need.

Wearing a fur coat shows that you support killing animals.

Therefore, you should not wear fur coats.

_____

Nia is vegan.

Vegans do not eat any animal products.

Eggs and milk are animal products.

There are eggs and milk in the cookies on the counter.

Nia is close to the cookies on the counter.

Nia cries when she is close to yummy things she cannot eat.

The cookies on the counter are yummy.

Therefore, Nia is crying.

Vegans are crybabies.

_____

Drugs are chemicals that have a physiological effect when introduced in the body.

Changes in mental state are a physiological effect.

Drugs should be regulated or banned by the government.

Caffeine is a chemical that makes a person more alert.

Increased alertness is a change in mental state.

Caffeine is in coffee.

Therefore, the government should regulate or ban coffee.

Coffee is not as dangerous as other drugs.

Coffee without any sugar added is superior to coffee with sugar.

Caffeine is in soda and tea.

10 Reasoning Relay
For middle school and high school students

In Reasoning Relay, teams of students work together to generate conclusions from short scenarios. Then, they standardize the reasoning behind the conclusion and evaluate it for validity and truth.

Setup

For this activity, you will need paragraphs (such as those on pages 223–230) that contain evidence leading to an unstated conclusion. For example, the following paragraph might be used.

> "Achoo!" Patti sneezed. She sneezed again and then a third time. She felt very warm and her head hurt. She dragged herself out of bed and called her boss. She told her boss she wouldn't be going to work. (Oswego City School District, 2011)

The evidence in this paragraph includes the following.

- ◆ Patti is sneezing.
- ◆ Patti feels warm.
- ◆ Patti's head hurts.
- ◆ Patti is not going to work.

These pieces of evidence, along with the knowledge that people generally don't go to work when they are sick, lead to the unstated conclusion that Patti is sick.

Reasoning Skills

- Applying rules and patterns
- Standardizing reasoning
- Evaluating deductive conclusions
- Explaining how evidence supports a conclusion
- Asking questions to challenge assumptions

Materials

- Short paragraphs for students to analyze (see reproducibles, pages 223–230)
- Copies of Reasoning Relay worksheet (see reproducible, page 222)
- Pen or pencil for each student
- Projector to display paragraphs (optional)

This book includes examples of paragraphs for use with this activity (thirty at the middle school level and thirty at the high school level), but you can also find or create your own. Passages from books and other literary or historical documents are excellent sources. Paragraphs can pertain to any subject area—from literature to scientific observations—making this activity quite versatile.

You will need one paragraph for each round of play. To create the worksheets needed for each round, copy the paragraph for the round into the blank space at the top of the worksheet (see the reproducible on page 222), creating a round 1 worksheet master. Then, make enough copies of the round 1 master so each group will have one, keeping in mind that students will be playing in teams of four or five (so a class of thirty would require six copies of the round 1 master, a class of twenty-five would require five copies, and so on). Prepare a master worksheet for each round you intend to play and make enough copies of each master for each team to have one. In lieu of copying the paragraph directly onto the worksheet, you can simply write or project each paragraph on the board so all students can read it. If this is the case, simply multiply the number of teams by the number of rounds you will be playing and make that many copies of the worksheet (there will just be a blank area where the paragraph would normally go).

Divide students into teams of four or five. Distribute the round 1 worksheet to each team and ask each team to assign a letter—A, B, C, D (and E, in groups of five)—to each member. Each student will also need something to write with.

Depending on the time available and the preexisting layout of your classroom, you might choose to rearrange students' desks to facilitate the relay element of this activity. Horizontal or vertical rows of four or five, such that each team has its own row, are ideal. Groups of desks (where students can pass the worksheet around in a circle) also work well.

Play

Give the first student in each group (student A) the group's worksheet for that round. The worksheet should have the paragraph for that round copied onto it; alternatively, you could write or project the paragraph on the board so all students can read it. The following is an example of a paragraph that could be used:

> Alice went to Jimmy's house for lunch. Jimmy's mother served them tuna fish sandwiches. Alice liked her sandwich very much and had almost finished it when, all of a sudden, her dentures fell out of her mouth. (Reder, 1980, p. 41)

Student A reads the passage to him- or herself and allows intuitive conclusions to pop into his or her head. At this step, you should encourage your students to entertain all of their ideas, even those that may seem farfetched. Then, student A writes one intuitive conclusion—for example, "Alice is old"—on the worksheet and passes it to the next student (student B).

Student B reads the story and student A's conclusion, and then tries to figure out the reasoning behind it. For example, seeing that student A has written "Alice is old," student B considers why, after reading the paragraph, student A would

 This activity asks students to take many of the skills they have learned and practiced in previous games and apply them to situations they might encounter in real life. Because this can be quite complex, we suggest emphasizing to students that this relay is not a race. Some parts will go quickly—like making intuitive inferences—but others will take more time—such as analyzing others' reasoning. The purpose of this activity is to make students aware of the snap judgments we make every day and to encourage them to slow down, challenge intuition, and take a more reasoned approach. The stress of even the most friendly competition is counterproductive to these goals. Remind students to work at their own pace and be prepared to share and discuss at the end of the round.

conclude that. Student B then records his or her reasons for the conclusion on the worksheet. For example, student B might write, "In the story, it says, 'Alice's dentures fell out,' and only old people wear dentures." In this example, student B only wrote down one reason for the conclusion but could have written more, depending on the paragraph. Student B's reasons for student A's conclusion may include general principles or specific evidence.

Student B then passes the worksheet to student C, whose job is to standardize the reasoning that students A and B have generated into an explicit argument (a set of premises that lead to a conclusion). The paragraphs in this book can be standardized into syllogisms (exactly two premises and a conclusion), and we strongly recommend that you specifically instruct students to create syllogisms the first several times they play Reasoning Relay. When students are comfortable with the structure of the game and familiar with arguments based on more than two premises (after playing Premises Puzzle, for instance), you might then choose to introduce an added challenge by allowing students to standardize reasoning into arguments with two *or more* premises that support and logically lead to the conclusion.

In the example about Alice's dentures, student C finds two premises that allow him or her to create a standardized syllogism. The foundational premise comes from student B's interpretation: only old people wear dentures. The minor premise comes directly from the story: Alice wears dentures. These premises lead to the conclusion that student A originally generated: Alice is old. Student C writes the standardized argument—in this case, a syllogism—on the worksheet and passes it to student D.

Student D evaluates student C's standardized argument for validity and truth. To evaluate the validity, he or she might draw an Euler diagram. To evaluate the truth of the argument, Student D might identify an exception to one of the premises or any other reason the conclusion might not be true. For example, he or she might write, "Sometimes people's adult teeth just don't grow in and they might have to get dentures when they're young."

If there are groups of five, student D evaluates only for validity and then passes to student E, who evaluates for truth (including identifying exceptions to the premises or other reasons the conclusion might not be true). Tables 10.1 and 10.2 (page 220) show each student's responsibilities for a four-person team and a five-person team, respectively.

Table 10.1: Team Member Responsibilities (Four-Person Team)

Student	Responsibilities
A	Reads the paragraph; writes down one intuitive conclusion
B	Reads the paragraph; reads student A's conclusion; writes down reasons for the conclusion
C	Reads the paragraph, student A's conclusion, and student B's reasons; selects from student B's reasons and the paragraph to create and write down a standardized argument (syllogism) that leads to student A's conclusion
D	Evaluates student C's standardized argument for validity and truth (including identifying exceptions to the premises or reasons the conclusion might not be true)

Table 10.2: Team Member Responsibilities (Five-Person Team)

Student	Responsibilities
A	Reads the paragraph; writes down one intuitive conclusion
B	Reads the paragraph; reads student A's conclusion; writes down reasons for the conclusion
C	Reads the paragraph, student A's conclusion, and student B's reasons; selects from student B's reasons and the paragraph to create and write down a standardized argument (syllogism) that leads to student A's conclusion
D	Evaluates student C's standardized argument for validity
E	Evaluates student C's standardized argument for truth (including identifying exceptions to the premises or reasons the conclusion might not be true)

Figure 10.1 shows a group's worksheet at the end of a complete relay based on a high-school-level paragraph taken from a news article.

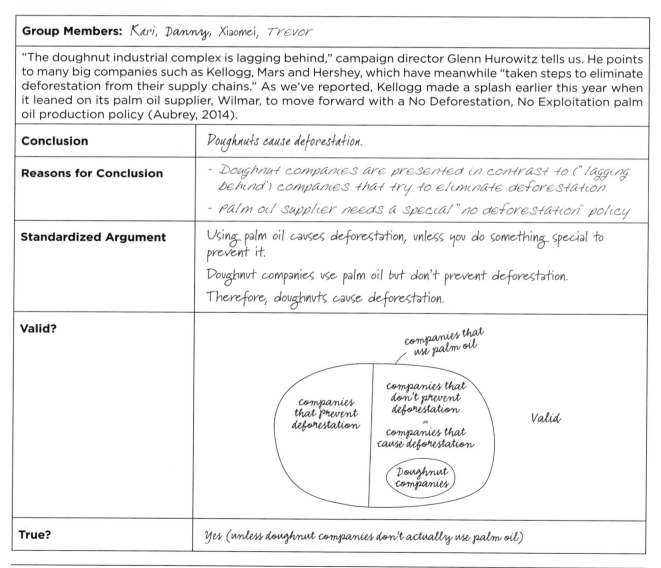

Group Members: Kari, Danny, Xiaomei, Trevor	
"The doughnut industrial complex is lagging behind," campaign director Glenn Hurowitz tells us. He points to many big companies such as Kellogg, Mars and Hershey, which have meanwhile "taken steps to eliminate deforestation from their supply chains." As we've reported, Kellogg made a splash earlier this year when it leaned on its palm oil supplier, Wilmar, to move forward with a No Deforestation, No Exploitation palm oil production policy (Aubrey, 2014).	
Conclusion	Doughnuts cause deforestation.
Reasons for Conclusion	- Doughnut companies are presented in contrast to ("lagging behind") companies that try to eliminate deforestation. - Palm oil supplier needs a special "no deforestation" policy
Standardized Argument	Using palm oil causes deforestation, unless you do something special to prevent it. Doughnut companies use palm oil but don't prevent deforestation. Therefore, doughnuts cause deforestation.
Valid?	companies that use palm oil / companies that prevent deforestation / companies that don't prevent deforestation = companies that cause deforestation / Doughnut companies / Valid
True?	Yes (unless doughnut companies don't actually use palm oil)

Figure 10.1: Completed Reasoning Relay worksheet.

Wrap-Up

Once a group has finished the relay, members can discuss their answers within their group. When every group has finished round 1, the class discusses it together. You can use the following example discussion questions when playing Reasoning Relay with your class:

- What did it feel like to generate conclusions intuitively (as student A)?

- Was it difficult to figure out (as student B) why someone else drew a certain conclusion?

- Did every group (specifically, student C in each group) come up with the same syllogism or argument, or were there different answers?

- What exceptions to the premises or additional reasons did you think of (as student D or E)?

- Did anyone think of a conclusion that was different from the rest of their group or come up with reasons that the others on your team didn't expect?

- Have you ever had to figure out what someone was thinking based on a conclusion—something they did or said without explaining themselves?

- What kinds of conclusions do people draw on a daily basis?

Additionally, you can collect each group's worksheet as an informal assessment.

After the class discusses round 1, pass out a new paragraph for round 2 and ask students to rotate roles (student A becomes student B, student B becomes student C, student C becomes student D, and so on).

 This activity could also be done "popcorn" style as a whole class. You display a paragraph on the board and then call on a student at random to complete each step of the process. One student draws a conclusion about the paragraph, a second tries to find reasons for that conclusion, and so on. This is also an excellent way to teach students how to perform each role (A, B, C, and so on) before having them play in groups.

Variation

Once students are comfortable with the structure of the game and performing each step, you can have teams work on multiple paragraphs at the same time. Give each student on the team a worksheet and a different source paragraph. (If there are four students on a team, you will need four worksheets with four different paragraphs.) Each student begins by reading the paragraph and intuitively drawing a conclusion. Then, everyone passes their worksheets to the right (or left). On the new sheet they have just been handed, they complete the second step, and then pass it on again. This repeats until every worksheet has been completely filled out. This variation engages all students at all points during the relay. However, we recommend only using it if students are very familiar with the relay structure of the game and each specific role.

Worksheet for Reasoning Relay

Group Members:	
Conclusion	
Reasons for Conclusion	
Standardized Argument	
Valid?	
True?	

Paragraphs for Reasoning Relay

Here, we provide paragraphs to be used as source material for Reasoning Relay. They are sorted into age-appropriate sets. Middle school paragraphs take the form of brief stories (some from outside sources and some that we created) and lead quite clearly to a conclusion. High school paragraphs are mostly taken from various news media and require more analysis. We suggest that students new to the game play with the middle school items first.

Middle School

Pete called Ted Tuesday afternoon and invited him to come to his house after dinner to watch a movie. It had been a long, boring day, and Ted was excited to have something to do. After dinner, he hopped on his bike and pedaled over to Pete's house. The house was dark, and when he rang the bell, there was no answer. Ted turned around, hopped back on his bike, and rode home (Oswego City School District, 2011).

_____

"Achoo!" Patti sneezed. She sneezed again and then a third time. She felt very warm and her head hurt. She dragged herself out of bed and called her boss. She told her boss she wouldn't be going to work (Oswego City School District, 2011).

_____

Mary was very proud of her garden. She'd planted the seeds early in the spring and tended to the plants every day since then. She pulled the weeds so they'd have lots of space. She knew that the plants needed plenty of water, so she watered them every day too. Last Saturday her friend Pam called early in the morning and invited Mary to spend the day at the mall. They left early and spent the day there, even taking in a movie. Pam then invited Mary to sleep over Saturday night too, and she happily accepted. When Mary arrived home on Sunday afternoon, her beautiful plants were bent and drooping (Oswego City School District, 2011).

_____

Mr. Craig was at the park with his family. He was the family cook and stood at the grill cooking the hot dogs while everyone else swam in the pool. The little boy had been standing by the tree for a few minutes before Mr. Craig really noticed him. "Do you need any help?" the boy asked. "No, I think I've got it under control!" Mr. Craig chuckled. Then he noticed the boy's dirty t-shirt and ragged pants. "I might need some help eating all of these hot dogs though," Mr. Craig said. "I think I may have cooked too many. Would you like one?" "Okay," the boy said. "I wouldn't want you to have too many" (Oswego City School District, 2011).

_____

It was the bottom of the ninth. Jeffrey, who had the highest batting average for the season, stepped up to the plate. He was working off a full count. The score was tied. The bases were loaded. The pitcher threw a curve ball. . . . There was a groan from the crowd as the runners had to return to their bases (Neuhaus Education Center, n.d.).

_____

The aroma from the cafeteria was wafting into the classroom. It smelled like a movie theater! The students filed into the cafeteria to watch the movie. They each took a bag. They had a great time, watching and munching. . . . After the movie, there was a long line at the water fountain (Neuhaus Education Center, n.d.).

Everyday after work Paul took his muddy boots off on the steps of the front porch. Alice would have a fit if the boots made it so far as the welcome mat. He then took off his dusty overalls and threw them into a plastic garbage bag; Alice left a new garbage bag tied to the porch railing for him every morning. On his way in the house, he dropped the garbage bag off at the washing machine and went straight up the stairs to the shower as he was instructed. He would eat dinner with her after he was "presentable," as Alice had often said (Morton, n.d.a).

Cassie rolled over in her bed as she felt the sunlight hit her face. The beams were warming the back of her neck when she slowly realized that it was a Thursday, and she felt a little too good for a Thursday. Struggling to open her eyes, she looked up at the clock. "9:48," she shouted, "Holy cow!" Cassie jumped out of bed, threw on the first outfit that she grabbed, brushed her teeth in two swipes, threw her books into her backpack, and then ran out the door (Morton, n.d.a).

Josh woke up early on Saturday morning and looked outside the window. The sun was out and it was hot. His dad called to Josh and said, "It is a perfect day, don't forget to bring a towel!" Josh grabbed a towel and they left the house (Hall, n.d.).

Wendy was walking down her driveway in the evening when she heard a sound coming from above her head. She looked up into the trees that surrounded her yard and saw two big round eyes staring back at her. A moment later, a large shadow swooped silently away through the forest.

Katie was excited about tonight. Happily, she put on her big, red shoes and bright, yellow outfit. Her mom helped Katie paint her face white with a big, red circle on each cheek. Just before Katie ran out the door to meet her friends, she attached her large, squeaky nose and placed a bright blue, pointy hat on top of her head. She grabbed an empty bag and went out into the night (Hall, n.d.).

Jalisa woke up early and ran down the stairs with a huge smile on her face. She had been waiting all night for Saturday to arrive. She ran into the kitchen. On the table was a large pile of hot, steaming flapjacks with a candle in them. Dante, Jalisa's brother, walked in holding a large box wrapped in pretty pink paper and tied with a shiny, purple bow. Jalisa beamed and quickly tore off the paper to reveal a box with a beautiful doll on the side. She hugged and kissed her brother and ran to call her best friend. The day was starting off wonderfully (Hall, n.d.).

At noon, Marisol tells her officemate Joey that she will be ready to go to lunch as soon as she uses the restroom, which is on the other side of their small building. Joey waits in the office, but twenty minutes go by and Marisol does not return. Finally, after another ten minutes, Marisol returns, but instead of talking to Joey and getting ready to go to lunch, she sits down at her computer and begins typing.

Siri, Amanda, Alex, and Meridith are all roommates. Siri, Amanda, and Alex decide to go for a long hike on Saturday, but Meridith has to go to choir practice instead. When Meridith gets home that afternoon, she sees Siri's car and Amanda's car parked in front of the house. Alex's car is not there.

Luisa goes to the library to get a book. As she is leaving, the anti-theft buzzer goes off and a security guard starts to approach her.

Teaching Reasoning: Activities and Games for the Classroom © 2015 Marzano Research • marzanoresearch.com
Visit **marzanoresearch.com/activitiesandgames** to download this page.

Jackson wants to make dinner, but is low on food. In the back of the refrigerator, he sees a container of macaroni and cheese from a week and a half ago. He throws it into the microwave without a second thought. After it is done heating, he smells it and frowns, then goes to throw the hot food away.

———————

At the school dance, people are dancing to the music the DJ is playing. The music stops and Principal Williams takes the microphone. He says he has something very special planned for the dance, pauses, and then starts singing showtunes. All of the students leave the dance floor.

———————

Lily turns when she hears a dog growling. When she sees the dog, it doesn't have a collar or a leash and is on the sidewalk coming toward her. Lily looks around, but there is no dog owner to be seen. She starts to back away slowly, careful not to make any sudden movements.

———————

Mrs. O'Donnell is handing back the big test from last week. When Mrs. O'Donnell returns Victor's test, he frowns. "See me after class" is scrawled across the top of the page in big red letters.

———————

Caitlyn is the fastest girl on the track team. State championships are on Friday and she's excited to show off her speed. During practice she is about to jump a hurdle, but hesitates. As she jumps, her foot hooks the hurdle and she falls and slides across the track. She starts crying.

———————

Gregor is making dinner in the kitchen. His wife and son are both in the living room watching TV. He hears his son laughing hysterically over the sound of the television, but doesn't hear his wife laughing.

———————

Juan's baby cousin, Adam, is visiting. At snack time, Juan tries to give Adam a cheese cracker, but Adam doesn't eat it. Later, Juan tries to feed Adam part of an apple, which Adam also doesn't want. Later, Juan sees his aunt feeding Adam applesauce with a spoon.

———————

Marriot is talking to a friend during lunch. After she eats her bologna sandwich, she is ready for dessert. She pulls out a box of blackberries. After eating one, her face puckers up and she spits out the blackberry.

———————

Chris was upset that the teacher made the new kid sit with him. He liked to sit by himself, and he didn't want to make any friends. While the teacher was passing out papers, the new kid made the first move, "Hi, my name's Sean." Chris replied brusquely, "That's nice," without looking up from the notebook on which he was doodling. Sean paid Chris's lack of manners no mind. Instead, he stole a glance at the notebook on which Chris was drawing. Sean noticed that Chris was drawing a guitar with skulls on it. Sean asked politely, "What's your favorite band?" Chris ignored him. Sean continued, "My favorite band is The Lords of Death." Chris looked up at him for the first time. "Hello, Sean, my name is Chris. I believe that we are going to be great friends." Sean smiled (Morton, n.d.b).

———————

I quickly packed my suitcase. I tossed in a change of clothes, a toothbrush, and a hairbrush. Glancing at my watch, I zipped the suitcase and walked to the front door. After I shut the window blinds, I pulled a heavy coat from the closet (Pearson Education, 2011).

You have just gotten a pit bull puppy from an animal shelter. He's lovable but nervous. If you raise your voice for any reason, he cowers and trembles. If you scold him, he hides. When you got him from the shelter, he had a slight limp and a deep scratch across his nose (Flemming, 2014).

———————————————

Nicolo does not like to play sports. In fact, he would much rather read a book than run around outside. Whenever he meets any of his parent's friends, they always ask whether or not he is good at basketball. He is beginning to get very frustrated each time someone asks him that.

———————————————

When Chaz comes home, his mom looks at him and immediately scolds him for not wearing sunscreen.

———————————————

Reba gets into the car. The first thing she does is roll down the windows. When she goes to buckle in, she flinches when her hand touches the metal on her seatbelt.

———————————————

Mikey does all of his carpentry in the basement. When he finishes his work and goes upstairs, he's surprised to see that it's dark outside.

———————————————

Lenaya bikes to school every day. When she is a few blocks away from her house, she sees orange signs ahead and construction workers motioning that no one can go down the road. She looks at her watch nervously before taking the detour.

High School

The food team at the Natick Soldier Research, Development & Engineering Center in Massachusetts, must meet a wide battery of requirements for these modern MREs [Meals, Ready to Eat], including: (1) Guaranteed shelf life acceptability for at least three years at 80°F or for six months at 100°F. . . . (2) Strict nutritional benchmarks (1,300 calories composed of 169 grams of carbohydrates, 41 grams of protein and 50 grams of fat, plus micronutrients such as vitamins, folic acid, calcium and zinc). (3) Durable packaging that can survive temperature swings and a 100-foot drop from a plane and ideally generates a minimal amount of waste (Sanchez, 2014).

———————————————

During the California Gold Rush of 1849, the world's supply of gold more than doubled, and hundreds of thousands of people rushed to California to find their share. Boomtowns popped up to accommodate the visitors. A boomtown is a community that receives sudden and explosive growth and development. San Francisco had around two-hundred residents in 1846, and about 36,000 in 1852. The few merchants in these boomtowns sold goods for more than ten times what they cost back East. For example, a single pound of flour sold for as much as $17. Not everyone who joined in the California Gold Rush got rich, but most of the boomtown merchants did (Morton, n.d.b).

———————————————

In a kerfuffle that hints at one of the pageant world's idiosyncrasies, a "well-placed" source says newly crowned Miss USA Nia Sanchez, representing Nevada . . . "[set] up some minimum paper trail to appear like she was in Nevada and allow her to compete," the source tells Fox News. Indeed, Sanchez competed three times for the Miss California USA crown—in 2010, 2011 and 2012—never winning before entering the Nevada pageant, which she won in January (Truesdell, 2014).

Why, my dear, you must know, Mrs[.] Long says that Netherfield is taken by a young man . . . from the north of England; that he came down on Monday in a chaise and four to see the place, and was so much delighted with it that he is to take possession before Michaelmas, and some of his servants are to be in the house by the end of next week (Austen, J., 1813, pp. 1–2).

Very long and very severe were the equinoctial gales that year. We waited long for news of the *Lone Star* of Savannah, but none ever reached us. We did at last hear that somewhere far out in the Atlantic a shattered stern-post of the boat was seen swinging in the trough of a wave, with the letters "L. S." carved upon it (Doyle, 1891, chapter 20, para. 3).

When I was three and Bailey four, we had arrived in the musty little town, wearing tags on our wrists which instructed—"To Whom It May Concern"—that we were Marguerite and Bailey Johnson Jr., from Long Beach, California, en route to Stamps, Arkansas, c/o Mrs. Annie Henderson (Angelou, 1969, p. 5).

When Bonnie Parker met Clyde Barrow, she was twenty years old. Although she had been a rebellious child and teenager, she had never broken a law in her life. The worst thing she had done in her mother's opinion was run off and get married to a shiftless womanizer who humiliated and neglected her. When Clyde came along, Bonnie was ripe for the attentions of a man who seemed to think she was both important and attractive. As long as he didn't desert her, Bonnie didn't much care about Clyde's two-year jail sentence. In jail at least, she knew where he was, and she could write him daily letters about how much she loved him. Bonnie, however, got nervous when she heard that Clyde was planning a jailbreak. To bind him more tightly to her, she smuggled him a gun and helped him escape. After he got caught and sent back to prison, Bonnie was even more determined to wait for the man she called her "one true love." Upon his release from jail, Bonnie took Clyde home to meet her folks and announced she was going to Houston, Texas to get a new job. The next time her mother heard from her, Bonnie Parker was sitting in jail (Flemming, 2014).

Consider a typical 2030 retiree—an educated Gen X woman, around 65, who has worked all her life at small and midsize companies. Those firms have created most of the new jobs in the economy for the past 50 years, but only 15% of them offer formal retirement plans. Our retiree has put away savings here and there, but she's also part of the middle class, which took the biggest wealth hit during the financial crisis of 2008. . . . [In addition,] average real wages have been virtually flat for three decades, even as living costs have risen (Foroohar, 2014).

On that day, Ng opened the steel door of a shipping container to inspect a load of organic soybeans from China and spotted a feathery little alien. "It was just kind of on top of the grain," he says. It was a black and white moth, just a half-centimeter long. As the inspection continued, Ng found a few more. "It was not a moth that we had seen before, that I recognized or that any of the other inspectors recognized," he says. He captured the insect, put it into a little glass vial, and shipped it off to experts at the U.S. Department of Agriculture (Charles, 2014).

[Dinosaurs] evolved into a world already populated with big, slow—coldblooded—reptiles. "You know, if you are a little bit . . . warmer-blooded than a reptile," he points out, "essentially your muscles fire faster; your nerves fire faster; you are a more dangerous predator." At the same time, a bit of coldbloodedness has its own charms. You burn energy more slowly, so you don't have to eat as much to grow. (Think of a crocodile or snake that can live for a month on one meal.) "And that means maybe they could get a lot bigger than a mammal could be," Grady says, "which wouldn't be able to eat enough if it was the size of a *Tyrannosaurus rex*" (Joyce, 2014).

Although it's not the first time FDA has picked a battle over bugs—mimolette, anyone?—this time, "it really put a rocket under the cheese industry," he says. "The very pillar that we built our niche business on is the ability to age our cheese on wood planks, an art that has been practiced in Europe for thousands of years," Wisconsin cheesemaker Chris Roelli told the blog Cheese Underground—one of the first to report on the issue. Cheesemakers have already gotten members of Congress involved (Fulton, 2014).

"The doughnut industrial complex is lagging behind," campaign director Glenn Hurowitz tells us. He points to many big companies such as Kellogg, Mars and Hershey, which have meanwhile "taken steps to eliminate deforestation from their supply chains." As we've reported, Kellogg made a splash earlier this year when it leaned on its palm oil supplier, Wilmar, to move forward with a No Deforestation, No Exploitation palm oil production policy (Aubrey, 2014).

What is a ticket, after all? It's "a type of temporary passport that grants a rite of passage." When you go to the theater you are slipping out of your life into someone else's imaginary world. When you get on a train, you are literally on a voyage. When you take a book out of the library, you are making a promise to bring that book back safely. These leave-takings deserve a token that says, I Am Out Of My Routine; This Is Not Ordinary; Risks Are Being Taken. . . . The usher scans our PDF code with a beam of light, and waves us through. There's no tearing, nothing to save. It's more efficient, of course (Krulwich, 2014).

There are foods that people instinctively associate with the risk of poisoning—raw chicken, raw egg, shellfish. At the time of Edwina Currie's remarks—which were perceived to have dramatically exaggerated the prevalence of the disease in eggs in the UK—there were 12,302 cases of the salmonella PT4 strand most commonly found in poultry. It dropped by 54% in the three years following the introduction of the British Lion scheme in 1998, which saw hens vaccinated against salmonella, and last year there were just 229 reported cases. But people are still mistrustful. . . . Watercress, beansprouts and curry leaves are believed to have been behind some of the most high profile outbreaks of food poisoning recently. People have died after eating contaminated celery, peanut butter and cantaloupe melon (Townsend, 2013).

Researchers in Spain followed more than 2,000 children aged 6 to 18 for three years and looked at how physical fitness, motor skills and muscle strength related to academic performance. Fitness levels were assessed based on how efficiently people's hearts and lungs respond during exercise—and when they compared the students' fitness to their grades in math and language classes, as well as their overall GPA, the researchers found that the more fit kids had higher grades (Park, 2014).

"With my scars, I am identified everywhere I go," says Fleury Yoro, who comes from Atacora in the north of the country. . . . When he studied in Benin's largest city, Cotonou, he says he was often mocked because of his scars. Some people "did not want anyone to think they could be friends with such a savage," he says. . . . Sinkeni Ntcha stopped after his first three children "because of AIDS," he says. "Blades have to be changed each time but the chiefs refused" (Adjovi, 2014).

A resolution calling for the renaming of a street outside China's embassy in Washington to Liu Xiaobo—in honor of the incarcerated Chinese Nobel Peace Prize winner—was proposed to the U.S. Congress on Wednesday, where it met positive recognition much to Beijing's dismay. . . . Liu Xiaobo, a political activist who helped write the pro-democracy manifesto *Charter 08*, was sentenced to 11 years' imprisonment in 2009 for attempted subversion of the state. . . . "Liu Xiaobo is a man who has violated Chinese laws," Chinese Foreign Ministry spokesman Hong Lei said (Hellman, 2014).

And some breeds "are not runners at all," he says. Among them: short-nosed dogs such as pugs, Boston terriers and bulldogs, as well as short-legged dogs under 15 pounds, such as Yorkies, Shih Tzus and Lhasas. Even breeds that would seem to be runners, such as greyhounds, aren't built for endurance sports, says Weitzman, a greyhound owner (Krug, 2014).

The [expansion of the marine sanctuary] designation is expected to face objections from the U.S. tuna fleet that operates in the region. Fish caught in the area account for up to 3 percent of the annual U.S. tuna catch in the western and central Pacific, according to the Pew Charitable Trusts. When Bush created the monument in 2009, he exempted sport fishing to address industry opposition (Eilperin, 2014).

The number of people for whom eliminating gluten is a medical necessity is small. About 1 percent of the population has been found to have celiac disease, a disorder in which gluten—a protein in barley, rye and wheat—can damage the small intestine. Another 6 percent of the population is more broadly classified as gluten intolerant. But the diet itself is being used by people who want to lose weight, reduce inflammation, curb fatigue and ease other conditions, or because it helps them avoid highly processed grain. Many simply say they just feel better without it, though there is not yet much scientific evidence to back up the claims (Severson, 2014).

After Clint Dempsey scored less than one minute into the game, [Tim] Howard was in charge of keeping the fleet-footed Ghanaians at bay from his spot in what could very well be the loneliest place in all of sports—the one between two white goal posts. As Ghana shot the ball toward him again and again, he did his best to create an impenetrable force field. He leapt high and wide. He rolled low and fast. He scrambled out of the box to meet oncoming shots with so much power and speed that he seemed like a freight train gone off its rails. He did everything he could to stop Ghana because there was no way, not this time, that Howard was going to feel the heartbreak he felt four years ago (Macur, 2014).

Northern Gateway has become something of backup for Canada, as approval for the Keystone XL pipeline remains mired in Washington. If built, Northern Gateway would ship about 500,000 barrels of bitumen a day to the coast compared with the 700,000-barrel-a-day capacity of Keystone XL, which would take oil sands production to the Gulf Coast of the United States. When Northern Gateway is combined with the country's other pipeline plans, Canada could expand shipments from the oil sands by three million barrels a day (Austen, I., 2014).

A [Unesco World Heritage site] designation marks a site as a place of central significance, one worthy of special measures to protect it. Countries submitting sites pledge they will follow strict conservation protocols in hopes of gaining prestige, a tourism bump and sometimes financial support. Jeffrey Quilter, director of the Peabody Museum of Archaeology and Ethnology at Harvard and an expert on Peru who just returned from a university excursion there, said placement on the heritage list clearly helps promote sites as important travel destinations. "Machu Picchu and the Galápagos are on everybody's bucket list," he said (Blumenthal, 2014).

"Some instinct told me [that you have no experience in agriculture]," said the old gentleman, putting on his spectacles, and looking over them at me with asperity, while he folded his paper into a convenient shape. "I wish to read you what must have made me have that instinct. It was this editorial. Listen, and see if it was you that wrote it: 'Turnips should never be pulled, it injures them. It is much better to send a boy up and let him shake the tree. Now, what do you think of that'?—for I really suppose you wrote it?" "Think of it? Why, I think it is good. I think it is sense. I have no doubt that every year millions and millions of bushels of turnips are spoiled in this township alone by being pulled in a half-ripe condition, when, if they had sent a boy up to shake the tree—" (Twain, 1875, pp. 234–235).

"In the final years of schools I think one should read important works and world literature, but in the years before that, it should be books that inspire you to read more," reflects Hannah Schubert, a 17-year-old German currently doing an exchange year at a secondary school outside London. . . . Rossana Cavalleri, a Milanese mother of a 15-year-old and an 18-year-old attending a science-based secondary school, lists their literature requirements: each year one part of Dante's *Divine Comedy* along with other Italian works and foreign literature, decided by the individual teacher. "I think it's adequate," she reflects. "But the kids read because they're forced to" (Braw, 2014).

While corporate profits have increased by 20 percent in the past two decades and productivity has surged, income has stagnated, suggesting people are working more and getting paid less. Forty percent of professional men and 15 percent of professional women work more than 50 hours per week, and the United States is one of only nine countries around the world that doesn't require employers to offer paid annual leave (Machado, 2014).

When her father died, it got about that the house was all that was left to her; and in a way, people were glad. At last they could pity Miss Emily. Being left alone, and a pauper, she had become humanized. Now she too would know the old thrill and the old despair of a penny more or less (Faulkner, 1930, para. 26).

One morning every spring, for exactly two minutes, Israel comes to a stop. Pedestrians stand in place, drivers pull over to the side of the road, and nobody speaks, sings, eats, or drinks as the nation pays respect to the victims of the Nazi genocide. From the Mediterranean to the Dead Sea, the only sounds one hears are sirens. "To ignore those sirens is a complete violation of the norms of our country," Daniela Schiller told me recently. Schiller, who directs the laboratory of affective neuroscience at the Mount Sinai School of Medicine, has lived in New York for nine years, but she was brought up in Rishon LeZion, a few miles south of Tel Aviv. "My father doesn't care about the sirens," she says. "The day doesn't exist for him. He moves about as if he hears nothing" (Specter, 2014).

Brazilian officials say they confiscated 39kg (86lb) of caramel spread from Uruguay's football team as it arrived in Brazil for the World Cup. [Uruguay lost in a shocking defeat to Costa Rica with a disappointing 3–1 final score.] . . . An official with the Brazilian agriculture department told Reuters news agency that the Uruguayans could have the dulce de leche back "as soon as they can produce the necessary documents." . . . Former Uruguay goalkeeper Juan Castillo said the team had also taken dulce de leche to the World Cup in South Africa, where they had not had any problems at customs [and where they fared much better in their bracket] (Uruguay squad's caramel spread confiscated in Brazil, 2014).

O'Keefe admits that 14 years ago, when he first started parenting full time, he needed "an ego of steel" because he got plenty of negative comments, primarily from men. One man, upon learning about O'Keefe's role, asked his wife, "Oh, what does he tell his buddies at the gym?" But while O'Keefe said he'd get maybe two insults a month 10 years ago, today it's down to about two a year (Wallace, 2014).

11 Are You Saying . . . ?

For high school students

Are You Saying . . . ? takes the reasoning skills that students have developed through classroom instruction and games to the next level by asking them to apply their reasoning skills to real-life situations. Reasoning in daily life is rarely cut and dried, and people often draw conclusions or make statements without thinking about or stating the reasoning behind them. The ability to listen to what others are saying and think critically about underlying assumptions is an essential skill. In Are You Saying . . . ?, students identify and challenge poor reasoning or unstated assumptions.

Setup

To play, students must be familiar with the basics of evaluating reasoning (determining validity and truth) and comfortable recognizing and generating foundational premises, minor premises, and conclusions. The only materials required for this game are some type of buzzer or bell students can use to "buzz in" when they have an answer, and paragraphs to be read aloud or displayed for students to analyze. This book includes numerous examples of paragraphs that involve unstated assumptions or potentially poor reasoning (see pages 234–258), which are drawn from various sources— debates, interviews, political speeches, and so on. In addition, teachers can find examples or write their own.

The class should be divided into at least two teams for this game. While having only two teams simplifies the competition and makes it easier for you to deter-

Reasoning Skills

- Standardizing reasoning
- Asking questions to challenge assumptions

Materials

- Buzzer, bell, or other signaling device for each team
- Paragraphs to be read aloud or displayed to the teams (see pages 234–258 and online reproducibles)
- Overhead or computer projector to display paragraphs to students (optional)

mine who buzzed in first, dividing the class into three or four teams makes the groups smaller and gives each student more opportunities to participate.

If time allows, you might also arrange the classroom to add to the competitive atmosphere. Group students' desks so each team has its own area. Teams could all face the front of the classroom, in typical game show fashion, or be turned toward each other to give the impression of a face off.

Once teams have been established, give a buzzer to each team and determine a rotation of some kind for the buzzer. Every student should get an approximately equal number of chances to be the spokesperson who hits the buzzer and answers for his or her team. The buzzer can be rotated to a new spokesperson after each paragraph.

Play

Prepare students to listen for claims by giving a bit of background information about the paragraph (for example, "This is part of a speech by John F. Kennedy" or "These are statements made about the topic of genetic engineering"). Begin reading the paragraph aloud (if you have chosen to display the paragraph on the board, do so simultaneously). When a student hears a statement or conclusion that is based on hidden reasoning, the current spokesperson for that team hits the buzzer. If the spokesperson hears a conclusion based on hidden reasoning, he or she can hit the buzzer immediately as long as he or she is prepared to answer. If other students on the team—those who are not the current spokesperson—hear a conclusion based on hidden reasoning, they can signal to the spokesperson to hit the buzzer.

When a buzzer goes off, pause wherever you are in the paragraph. The team that buzzed in can have a few seconds to confer about its answer before the spokesperson answers. This time for discussion is important in order to keep the entire team engaged because it allows students other than the current spokesperson to come up with an answer. We suggest, however, that the time for discussion be kept brief (perhaps ten seconds) to maintain the pace of the game and prevent students from buzzing in before they actually have an answer ready. Give students enough time to relay their responses to the spokesperson, and then prompt the team for its answer.

When giving the team's answer, the spokesperson should begin with, "Are you saying . . ." and finish with the hidden reason or unstated assumption that underlies the paragraph's conclusions. For example, a teacher might read the following paragraph:

> MICHAEL MANDELBAUM: The world's governments . . . could, if they chose, circumscribe or abolish altogether, by banding together to oppose it, the American role as the world's policeman. But they have done and shown no signs of doing any such thing. (Intelligence Squared U.S., 2008a, p. 19)

A spokesperson could buzz in and answer, "Are you saying that if other countries didn't want America to be the world's police force, then they would do something about it?" This is an example of a hidden foundational premise. It sets up the following standardized argument:

> If other countries did not want America to be the world's police force, then they would try to change things.

> They have not tried to change things.

> Therefore, other countries *do* want America to be the world's police force.

Students may also answer with a more general interpretation of a hidden premise—one that could be used in other arguments, such as, "Are you saying that a lack of direct opposition is the same as agreement?" This premise still creates an interesting standardized argument:

A lack of direct opposition is the same as agreement.

The rest of the world has not directly opposed America's role as the world's police force.

Therefore, the rest of the world agrees with America's role as the world's police force.

This hidden foundational premise is more general; it can be extrapolated onto other similar arguments in which people assume that an absence of explicit contradiction means tacit agreement.

In this particular example, the argument's conclusion actually goes unstated as well—the speaker leads the audience to draw a specific conclusion without directly stating it. Students can also answer by making that conclusion explicit: "Are you saying that the rest of the world *wants* the United States to be its police force?" Any of these answers would be correct for this example, and there are others that would also be legitimate. Note, however, that this game does not ask students to form a complete syllogism or argument before answering—they need only state one hidden reason or unstated assumption.

If a team buzzes in and either doesn't have an answer ready within a few seconds or answers with a statement that does not make sense for the claim (for example, for the preceding paragraph, "Are you saying that police officers always carry guns?" would not be a correct answer), another team can take the opportunity to "steal" the point. If there is only one other team, the chance goes to them automatically; if there are multiple other teams, the first one to buzz in gets the opportunity to steal first.

 If you are using the paragraphs provided at the end of this chapter, it is possible that students could come up with an answer that is not listed as an example response or one you have not thought of (if you are using paragraphs you found or created). This is a good thing! It shows that they are using their reasoning skills. If a student presents an answer that is not immediately clear to you, feel free to ask him or her to further explain the answer or to generate a standardized argument based on the answer.

If you read an entire paragraph without any of the teams buzzing in, we recommend that you read the paragraph again, pausing after each sentence to give students the opportunity for deeper reflection. If students still do not buzz in, we recommend presenting an answer (for example, a hidden premise) and offering a point to the first team to create a syllogism based on the given answer that leads to a conclusion found in the paragraph.

Wrap-Up

If students come up with a correct answer, that team gets a point. If a team tries to steal and does so successfully, it gets the point. If the second team also answers incorrectly, you may want to talk through that example with the class. After an answer has been submitted and the point awarded, pick up where you left off in the paragraph if there are more conclusions to be examined or begin again with a new paragraph.

Variation

For older students, this game can be expanded for a further challenge. Instead of using the paragraphs provided in this book or those you have found or written, have students write their own paragraphs with poor reasoning or unstated assumptions. They can work in small groups to create a paragraph that mimics a political or persuasive speech. In that paragraph, they hide at least one instance of a conclusion or assumption that needs its reasoning exposed. When it is time to play the game, each team could read its paragraph to the other teams and judge whether the ensuing answers are legitimate. Alternatively, you could read the student-generated paragraphs, but you would have to clarify to students that they should not play during the round their paragraph is used (since they already know the answers).

Paragraphs for Are You Saying . . . ?

Here we provide paragraphs for you to read aloud or display during a game of Are You Saying . . . ? Each paragraph is titled to give context and also includes several examples of answers students might give based on the text. These examples are not exhaustive. For reproducible versions of these items, visit **marzanoresearch .com/activitiesandgames**.

From a Fox News panel on the causes of Islamic radicalism

WILLIAM COHEN, FORMER SECRETARY OF DEFENSE: What we have to do is to go after the hard core, to root out the hard core terrorists who are inflicting these terrible, terrible crimes against humanity . . . [and] then look to how can we help elevate the people in various parts of the world so that the jihadists aren't able to really manipulate and exploit them. So I think we have to have a two-pronged attack. Go after the terrorists and root them out as best we can and then try to raise the level of civil support and social support for those groups so they aren't vulnerable to the jihadist (Fox News Channel, 2008b).

Are you saying . . . that it is the United States' responsibility to fight terrorism?

. . . that people in the Middle East are lowly and need to be elevated?

. . . that terrorism exists because of a lack of civil support?

From a Fox News panel on the causes of Islamic radicalism

WILLIAM COHEN, FORMER SECRETARY OF DEFENSE: British Prime Minister Tony Blair, for example, indicated that this is not a clash of civilizations. It's a clash within a civilization. Namely you've got elements in the Muslim community that are waging war against those Muslims who want to stay in the 21st century and embrace modernity. And it's going to take not just the United States. . . . Other countries have to come to the bar now and . . . we've got to approach this on a global basis because the terrorism is not regional, it's global (Fox News Channel, 2008b).

Are you saying . . . that the majority of Muslim people are not extremists?

. . . that Islamic extremists have old-fashioned, outdated values?

. . . that global issues must be addressed by all countries together?

From Chrysler's report to the federal government, requesting bailout funds following the economic crash of 2008

Chrysler anticipates that the Federal loan will function as an additional adequate assurance to our suppliers, customers and employees that the Company will make it through this extraordinary time in our nation's economy, assuming, among other things, that Chrysler Financial has financing capacity at the wholesale and retail level sufficient to support Chrysler's production volumes. At Chrysler, 75 percent of our dealers rely on Chrysler Financial to finance their business, and 50 percent of all customers finance their vehicle purchases through Chrysler Financial. With credit markets frozen, our customers—average working Americans—do not have access to competitive financing to purchase or lease vehicles . . . our dealers do not have access to market competitive funding to place wholesale orders for new vehicles . . . resulting in the constriction of cash inflows to Chrysler. Chrysler Financial is in need of immediate liquidity support (Nardelli, 2008, p. 5).

Are you saying . . . that people trust the government to make good investments?

. . . that Chrysler should receive a loan because it helps average working Americans?

From Chrysler's report to the federal government, requesting bailout funds following the economic crash of 2008

Mr. Nardelli [CEO of Chrysler] receives an annual salary of $1 from Chrysler. In addition, Mr. Nardelli receives no health care, insurance or similar benefits from the Company. On average, Chrysler's executive salaries are in the 2nd quartile when compared to similarly situated companies, which in general, is below competitive market levels. Furthermore, the Company did not pay salaried merit increases or performance bonuses in 2008, and has not planned salaried merit increases or performance bonuses for 2009. Management has no options or restricted stock units. Top management will continue to share in the sacrifices of the salaried workforce and bear 100% of their healthcare premium costs (Nardelli, 2008, p. 6).

Are you saying . . . that Chrysler is fiscally responsible?

. . . that Chrysler deserves a loan because its executives make less money than executives at other companies?

From Chrysler's report to the federal government, requesting bailout funds following the economic crash of 2008

Providing Cars and Trucks People Want to Buy: Chrysler has made substantial progress in its product line to improve fuel efficiency, quality, technology and consumer appeal. . . . Chrysler's viability plan includes 24 major product launches through 2012, including a wide portfolio of hybrid electric-drive vehicles within several categories: Neighborhood Electric Vehicles (NEV), City Electric Vehicles (CEV), Range-extended Electric Vehicles (ReEV), and full-function battery electric vehicles (BEV) (Nardelli, 2008, p. 6).

Are you saying . . . that people want to buy hybrid cars?

From an episode of *Larry King Live* on the subject of the economic crash in 2008

JEAN CHATZKY, MONEY EXPERT, AUTHOR, *PAY IT DOWN*: Even if you don't feel as if your job is potentially at risk, it is. And that means you have to take a good, hard look at your finances at home. And if you don't have a six month emergency cushion or even a nine or 12-month emergency cushion, now—before you lose that job—is the time to stop spending and start putting away as much money as you can, because not only are we losing more jobs, it's taking more time to get the next one. So people really have to learn how to pull back, scale it in like our grandparents did, so that we can weather this storm (Hirzel, 2008).

Are you saying . . . that everyone should have enough money saved up to last up to a year?

. . . that people generally spend too much money?

. . . that the current economic crisis is similar to the Great Depression, World War II, or other historical periods of economic concern?

From an episode of *Larry King Live* on the subject of the economic crash in 2008

DAVID THEALL, PRODUCER, *LARRY KING LIVE*: [Reading comments from viewers] Eric thinks it is the unemployed . . . who should be helped first. He said they suffer the most, so they should be the first priority. Matthew, on the other hand, thinks homeowners need the help first because—his logic—people need a place to live before they need an overpriced American car. Now, the majority of the comments support the auto industry. Amber says—she asked this question: "Doesn't anyone realize what will happen if the big three go under?" And Hillary also thinks that the auto industry should be helped first with government funds. She says: "Only for the employees' sake, let's keep what little we have left in America" (Hirzel, 2008).

Are you saying . . . that people should be helped in order of level of suffering?

. . . that having a house is more important than having a car?

. . . that car manufacturers are very important to the American economy?

. . . that giving loans to car companies will help their employees?

. . . that it is important to keep manufacturing jobs in America?

From an episode of *Larry King Live* on the subject of the economic crash in 2008

LARRY KING, HOST: Jean, with a lame duck president, are we kind of in a vacuum at the worst possible time?

JEAN CHATZKY, MONEY EXPERT, AUTHOR, *PAY IT DOWN*: Washington may be in a vacuum, but I don't think that means that individuals sitting at home need to be in that vacuum. There are very many things, as Ali [Velshi, CNN Correspondent] has been pointing out, that are really within our control. If you still have a job, then you save. If you still have a 401(k) that is matching your contributions . . . get in there and grab every last one of those matching dollars, before they start taking them away (Hirzel, 2008).

Are you saying . . . that President Bush can't do anything about the economic crisis because he is about to leave office?

. . . that people can help themselves and do not need to rely on the government to fix the economic crisis?

. . . that when companies are in trouble they usually take away employee benefits?

From an episode of *Larry King Live* on the subject of the economic crash in 2008

BEN STEIN, ECONOMIST, AUTHOR: It's . . . unthinkable—in the midst of a jobs deterioration, such as we're having now, to kick another two or three million people out of work right away—you can be an ideological purist about the auto industry and their failings. You can be as ideologically pure as you want when we get back to full employment. But right now, we cannot lose any more jobs. We've got to keep the auto industry going. . . . I completely agree the auto companies have made big mistakes. I completely agree they've got to streamline themselves. You do not yell at a patient who's had a heart attack on his way to the coronary care unit. You get him fixed, then deal with his moral problems later (Hirzel, 2008).

Are you saying . . . that compromises have to be made in times of difficulty?

. . . that values should be sacrificed to serve the greater good?

. . . that giving loans to car companies will help their employees and people in general?

. . . you should help people or entities who are in trouble, even if their problems are their own fault?

From an episode of *Larry King Live* on the subject of the economic crash in 2008

ROBERT LUTZ, VICE CHAIRMAN OF DEVELOPMENT, GENERAL MOTORS: We are on the brink. And what everybody has to understand is that this is not a question of everybody in Detroit suddenly becoming stupid. We have excellent executives in Detroit. Alan Mulally is the gentleman who saved . . . the Boeing commercial airline business. Bob Nardelli has a terrific background as CEO of Home Depot. Before that, he was a senior executive at General Electric. . . . This industry in Detroit does basically a terrific job. We matched the Japanese on productivity. We match them on quality. We have highly fuel efficient vehicles. General Motors has more vehicles that get over 30 miles per gallon on the highway than any other car. We have the most efficient trucks and so forth (Hirzel, 2008).

    Are you saying . . . that people can be judged on what they have done in the past?

        . . . that Japanese car companies are very productive and make high-quality cars?

        . . . that American car companies' being on the brink of bankruptcy is not their fault?

From Larry King's interview with Paula Deen

LARRY KING, HOST: Paula Deen. By the way, Michelle Obama was a guest on your show, "Paula's Party," back in September. . . . What was that like? Did you feed her?

PAULA DEEN, CHEF: Honey, she can eat. I was so thrilled. I fried her shrimp, Larry. And she ate even all through the commercial break. And you know I said, I like this girl. I believe she's real (Hirzel, 2008).

    Are you saying . . . that women who eat a lot are more authentic ("real") than women who don't eat as much?

From Larry King's interview with Paula Deen

LARRY KING, HOST: What makes southern cooking different?

PAULA DEEN, CHEF: Well, we—we're not afraid to season our pots. We love the use of ham hock. We love the use of butter and bacon. And my grandmother, Larry, cooked that way until she was 91 years old and then it finally got her but you know at 91, I'll take that, honey. I will take 91 (Hirzel, 2008).

    Are you saying . . . that fat makes food taste better?

        . . . that food that has less fat does not taste as good?

        . . . that you will live a long time because your grandmother did?

        . . . that eating unhealthy food is not bad for you because you might still live to be very old?

From CNN news anchor Fareed Zakaria's remarks on U.S. involvement in the Middle East

FAREED ZAKARIA, NEWS ANCHOR: By every account, the situation there and in Pakistan's tribal areas is deteriorating fast. The Taliban are getting stronger, taking more territory, becoming more powerful politically. Obama's solution to the problem—which is also John McCain's solution, and has also been proposed by Secretary of Defense Robert Gates—is to send in more troops—20,000, 30,000. But will that work? The Soviet Union, after all, sent in 150,000 troops into the country, and it couldn't end the rebellions against it. More likely, we will have to try to make deals with local warlords, some of whom will be Taliban figures—if they will agree to turn on al Qaeda and make peace with us. But that means slowing down on the nation-building and modernization of the Afghan state, which tends to take power away from traditional tribal leaders (CNN, 2008).

> *Are you saying* . . . that the United States cannot win the war in Afghanistan because the Soviet Union did not win their war there?
>
> . . . that we should first try to win with our military, and then try diplomacy if strength does not work?
>
> . . . that sometimes you have to make deals with some of your enemies to beat some of your other enemies?
>
> . . . that a modern state and tribal leaders tend to be mutually exclusive?

From Fareed Zakaria's interview with Al Gore on the future of the American auto industry, following the economic crash in 2008

AL GORE, FORMER U.S. VICE PRESIDENT, NOBEL PEACE PRIZE WINNER: Well, I think the whole industry should be transformed. It's really tragic that General Motors, for example, allowed Toyota to get a seven-year head start on the hybrid drive train in the Prius that is now positioned to really be a dominant feature of the industry in this century. I personally believe that the U.S. auto fleet should make a transition as quickly as possible toward plug-in hybrid electric vehicles. I think that the twin problems of the climate crisis and the economic crisis can both be addressed by investing in a transformation of our energy and transportation infrastructure to focus on renewable sources of energy. And at the same time, our security vulnerability to a potential cutoff of the world's access to Persian Gulf, Middle East oil should be addressed, at long last, without delay. And shifting to electric vehicles instead of petroleum vehicles is the best way to do that.

FAREED ZAKARIA, NEWS ANCHOR: If you look at the situation right now with oil prices down to $50 a barrel—the lowest in two or three years—are we back to a familiar cycle where once the price of oil gets back down, the impetus for these alternate energies will dissipate (CNN, 2008)?

> *Are you saying* . . . that energy is both an economic issue and an environmental issue?
>
> . . . that hybrid electric vehicles will be the norm in the future?
>
> . . . that we should not count on the Middle East as a reliable source of oil?
>
> . . . that people only care about renewable energy for economic reasons?

From Fareed Zakaria's interview with Al Gore on the future of the American auto industry, following the economic crash in 2008

AL GORE, FORMER U.S. VICE PRESIDENT, NOBEL PEACE PRIZE WINNER: China and India, and other developing countries, all have exactly the same excuse for not moving on the climate crisis. Their common excuse is, "Wait a minute. The United States hasn't done anything. It's the wealthiest country in the world, the natural leader of the world. Why doesn't the U.S. act?" And I think that when the U.S. acts, it will be by far the most effective way to improve the odds that China and India, and other smaller developing economies, will also act. They know that it's in their own interest to tackle this problem (CNN, 2008).

> *Are you saying* . . . that the United States should set an example for other countries?
>
> . . . that other countries depend on the U.S. to act first?

From Fareed Zakaria's interview with Tom Friedman on the future of the American auto industry, following the economic crash in 2008

TOM FRIEDMAN, FOREIGN AFFAIRS COLUMNIST, *NEW YORK TIMES*: [U.S. car companies] didn't come to Washington and say, "We have a plan. We have a plan to make General Motors, Chrysler and Ford the best auto companies in the world. We're going to make the cleanest, greenest, most competitive, high design cars. We're going to make the Apple iPod of cars. This is so exciting." No, they came and said, "Give me some money, or I'll die on your doorstep, and bring down three million more Americans with me" (CNN, 2008).

  Are you saying . . . that the iPod is a high-quality, high-design product?

     . . . that car companies have an enormous impact on the economy?

     . . . that we should hold car companies to a higher standard if the government gives them loans?

From Fareed Zakaria's interview with Tom Friedman on the future of the American auto industry, following the economic crash in 2008

TOM FRIEDMAN, FOREIGN AFFAIRS COLUMNIST, *NEW YORK TIMES*: The fatal thing is for us to think, "Wow. This $700 billion sounds like a big number. We should be able to help everybody in trouble." But everybody's in trouble, because the banking system has broken down. Until we fix the banking system, we're going to be running around treating the symptoms (CNN, 2008).

  Are you saying . . . that the banking system affects everyone?

     . . . that the banking system is the main source of the economic crisis?

     . . . that treating the symptoms of a problem does not fix the cause?

From Fareed Zakaria's interview with Tom Friedman on the future of the American auto industry, following the economic crash in 2008

TOM FRIEDMAN, FOREIGN AFFAIRS COLUMNIST, *NEW YORK TIMES*: The first [key aspect of the financial crisis] is the degree of leverage that's out there. Second is the globalization of it. The third is the complexity of it—the fact that . . . people didn't understand how [the financial markets] worked on the upside, let alone the downside. And it started in America. When one of these crises starts in Thailand, when it starts in Mexico, we can insulate ourselves from it. When it starts in America, no one can insulate themselves (CNN, 2008).

  Are you saying . . . that the United States' economy affects the entire world?

     . . . that the economies of countries like Thailand and Mexico do not affect the entire world?

From the General Motors report to the federal government, requesting bailout funds following the economic crash in 2008

GM is woven into the very fabric of America. It has been the backbone of U.S. manufacturing, is a significant investor in research and development, and has a long history of philanthropic support of communities across the country. The auto industry today remains a driving engine of the U.S. economy, employing 1 in 10 American workers, and is one of the largest purchasers of U.S. steel, aluminum, iron, copper, plastics, rubber, and electronic and computer chips. Indeed, GM's "Keep America Rolling" sales campaign, following the September 11 attacks, is credited by many as having prevented an extended recession in 2001 (General Motors Corporation, 2008, p. 7).

> *Are you saying* . . . that GM should get money from the government because it has done good things for the U.S. economy in the past?
>
> . . . that when people buy cars, it helps the U.S. economy?

From the General Motors report to the federal government, requesting bailout funds following the economic crash in 2008

Therefore, GM must reluctantly, but necessarily, turn to the U.S. Government for assistance. Absent such assistance, the company will default in the near term, very likely precipitating a total collapse of the domestic industry and its extensive supply chain, with a ripple effect that will have severe, long-term consequences to the U.S. economy (General Motors Corporation, 2008, p. 8).

> *Are you saying* . . . that there is no other entity that could help GM stay out of bankruptcy?
>
> . . . that it is in the best interest of the government and the people for the government to give GM a loan?

From the General Motors report to the federal government, requesting bailout funds following the economic crash in 2008

The company also sees significant potential to engage in broader industry collaboration on a number of important fronts. For example, we see benefits accruing to the economy and the environment with U.S. automakers and suppliers teaming with the U.S. Government to create shared production joint ventures for first- and second-generation technology commercialization. The U.S. Government could also play a key role in providing the needed "venture capital" and become a major customer for these early generation vehicles, paving the way for the commercially high sales volumes necessary for new technology to deliver cost-effective, societal benefits. The U.S. taxpayers would also benefit from the "spin-off" value of the United States-based technology production ventures that would result. Strategic partnerships among Government, industry and academia to develop appropriate green mobility products in response to shifting energy resources, consumer demand for greener transportation, promising advanced technology and new community design will be key to meeting the Nation's energy and environmental objectives (General Motors Corporation, 2008, p. 27).

> *Are you saying* . . . that the government should invest in businesses?
>
> . . . that collaboration is required for progress?

From a speech by Barack Obama announcing his economic recovery plan

We won't do it [economic recovery] the old Washington way. We won't just throw money at the problem. We'll measure progress by the reforms we make and the results we achieve—by the jobs we create, by the energy we save, by whether America is more competitive in the world. . . . We need to act with the urgency this moment demands to save or create at least two and a half million jobs so that the nearly two million Americans who've lost them know that they have a future (Obama, 2008b).

> *Are you saying* . . . that the government usually tries to fix problems by spending a lot of money on them?
>
> . . . that it is the government's responsibility to protect the citizens from economic crisis?

From a speech by Barack Obama announcing his economic recovery plan

Third, my economic recovery plan will launch the most sweeping effort to modernize and upgrade school buildings that this country has ever seen. We will repair broken schools, make them energy-efficient, and put new computers in our classrooms. Because to help our children compete in a 21st century economy, we need to send them to 21st century schools (Obama, 2008b).

Are you saying . . . that spending money on education will help the economy recover?

. . . that the aim of education is that students will become productive members of the economy?

From a speech by Barack Obama announcing his economic recovery plan

As we renew our schools and highways, we'll also renew our information superhighway. It is unacceptable that the United States ranks 15th in the world in broadband adoption. Here, in the country that invented the internet, every child should have the chance to get online (Obama, 2008b).

Are you saying . . . that if you invented something, you should stay the best at it forever?

From Barack Obama's speech to the National Governors Association

As President, I will not simply ask our nation's governors to help implement our economic recovery plan. I will ask you to help design that plan. Because if we're listening to our governors, we'll not only be doing what's right for our states, we'll be doing what's right for our country. That's how we'll grow our economy—from the bottom up. And that's how we'll put America on the path to long-term prosperity (Obama, 2008a).

Are you saying . . . that what is good for individual states is also good for the whole country?

. . . that improving the economy from the bottom up will create longer-lasting change than other options for recovery?

From Barack Obama's speech to the National Governors Association

I won't stand here and tell you that you'll like all the decisions I make. You probably won't. But I promise you this—as President, I will seek your counsel. I will listen to you, especially when we disagree. And we will once again be true partners in the work of rebuilding our economy, strengthening our states, and lifting up our entire country (Obama, 2008a).

Are you saying . . . that people are guaranteed to disagree sometimes?

. . . that people can disagree and still work together?

From Barack Obama's speech to the National Governors Association

To solve this crisis and to ease the burden on our states, we need action—and action now. That means passing an economic recovery plan for both Wall Street and Main Street that jumpstarts our economy, helps save or create two and a half million jobs, puts tax cuts into the pockets of hard-pressed middle class families, and makes a down payment on the investments we need to build a strong economy for years to come (Obama, 2008a).

Are you saying . . . that a problem will only get better with action, and won't get better if you ignore it?

. . . that helping citizens is just as important as helping banks and corporations?

From a Fox News panel discussing terrorist attacks in India

YOUSAF RAZA GILLANI, PAKISTANI PRIME MINISTER: Pakistan has nothing to do with this incident. Pakistan has no link with this act. We condemn it, and we condemned it. The whole nation condemns it. We are already the victim of terrorism and extremism (Fox News Channel, 2008a).

> *Are you saying* . . . that if you have something bad done to you, you will not do it to others?

From a Fox News panel discussing terrorist attacks in India

CHARLES KRAUTHAMMER, SYNDICATED COLUMNIST: [This is] an American issue as well, because part of our objective in the region is to get India and Pakistan to stop facing off against each other as they have for 60 years. They have had three wars, a lot of terror activity coming out of Pakistan over the Kashmir issue—and to try to get India and Pakistan, who are each our allies, to face the real issue, which is Islamic radicalism, especially in Afghanistan and in the wilder territories of Pakistan (Fox News Channel, 2008a).

> *Are you saying* . . . that it is the United States' responsibility to solve problems in other countries?
>
> > . . . that people should put aside their differences and work together if there is a bigger problem?

From a Fox News panel discussing terrorist attacks in India

CHARLES KRAUTHAMMER, SYNDICATED COLUMNIST: There obviously are Pakistanis involved here. I'm sure something as sophisticated as this attack is not home grown in India. Only the terrorists trained in Pakistan and elsewhere would have the wherewithal to pull it off. However, by sending their official head of ISI [Pakistan's intelligence service], and by the statement that we saw of the elected officials of Pakistan, it's a way of saying that it perhaps is a wrong element, but it's not [their] government (Fox News Channel, 2008a).

> *Are you saying* . . . that Pakistan has more numerous and sophisticated terrorists than India?
>
> > . . . that there can be entities within a country that act without the approval of the government?
> >
> > . . . that if the government had something to do with the attack, they would not help investigate it?

From a Fox News panel discussing terrorist attacks in India

JEFF BIRNBAUM, MANAGING EDITOR DIGITAL, *THE WASHINGTON TIMES*: I think there is actually the chance here that once the smoke clears initially, that India and Pakistan will work together along with the West to understand that the enemy here is al Qaeda or its elaborated cells around the world. That's clearly where this came from. Even if we learn that the actual terrorists were based in Pakistan, which is perfectly possible here, it's clear that they were inspired not by the Pakistan government or the Pakistanis so much as a worldwide system of terror that is come next through the Internet and directed against western countries (Fox News Channel, 2008a).

> *Are you saying* . . . that there can be entities within a country that act without the approval of the government?
>
> > . . . that the primary aim of terrorist organizations is to hurt western countries?

From a Fox News panel discussing terrorist attacks in India

FRED BARNES, EXECUTIVE EDITOR, *THE WEEKLY STANDARD*: In the short run—and I don't know what the short run is, but probably several years—Indian and Pakistani relations will get worse. You notice the Indian prime minister wasn't accusing the Pakistani government [of supporting terrorists], but he was saying you have these safe havens. And you haven't wiped them out. That's where these people probably came from, and maybe they did. Look, it is bound to get worse. . . . Worsening relations between India and Pakistan means that the terrorists achieve one of their aims. Another one was to stir more hatred between Muslims in India, 140 million of them . . . and Hindus in India. What will probably happen next year as a result will be there will be a Hindu nationalist government elected there that will be less likely to have good relations with Pakistan (Fox News Channel, 2008a).

> *Are you saying* . . . that if a country fails to eliminate terrorist groups within its borders, that country is somewhat complicit in the actions of those terrorists?
>
> . . . that Pakistan is turning a blind eye to terrorist activity within its borders?
>
> . . . that different religious groups cannot get along with each other?

From a Fox News panel discussing terrorist attacks in India

FRED BARNES, EXECUTIVE EDITOR, *THE WEEKLY STANDARD*: As far as the U.S. is concerned, our aim has been to ease relations between the two countries [India and Pakistan] so the new Pakistani government can focus on these safe havens in northern Pakistan and rout the terrorists from out of there. And they were beginning to do a little of that, but I don't think we're going to see much more of that now. . . . I think this means that Obama will have to devote more money not just to Afghanistan, as we know, but also towards Pakistan to rout out these terrorists (Fox News Channel, 2008a).

> *Are you saying* . . . that it is the United States' responsibility to solve problems in other countries?
>
> . . . that a government cannot focus on solving two different problems at the same time?

From Barack Obama's 2012 campaign speech in Newton, Iowa

Newton knows something about . . . the trends that we had seen even before the financial crisis hit. . . . When you hear somebody say we should cut more taxes, especially for the wealthiest Americans . . . we did that—2000, 2001, 2003. When you hear people say that we should cut back more on the rules we put in place for banks and financial institutions to avoid another taxpayer bailout—well, we tried that. When people say that we should just wait until the housing market hits bottom and hope that it comes back . . . that's not an answer for people. . . . We've tried . . . these ideas for nearly a decade. It did not work. We saw manufacturing moving offshore. We saw a few people do very well, but too many families struggling just to get by (Obama, 2012).

> *Are you saying* . . . that things that failed in the past will fail in the present as well?
>
> . . . that problems do not solve themselves, they require direct action?
>
> . . . that if companies hire people in other countries instead of the U.S., that's bad?
>
> . . . that it's better to have moderate success for a lot of people than great success for only a few?

From Barack Obama's 2012 campaign speech in Newton, Iowa

We have done a whole lot to make sure that those men and women who have served us in Iraq and Afghanistan, that we are serving them as well as they've served us—treating them with the honor and respect that they have earned when they come home. So we put together the Post-9/11 GI Bill so they're able to go back and get some training and skills. . . . Congress should create what we're calling a Veterans Jobs Corps, so that we can help communities across America put our returning heroes back to work as police officers and firefighters and park rangers (Obama, 2012).

Are you saying . . . that people who fight in wars deserve benefits when they get home?

. . . that people who fight in wars need help readjusting to civilian life?

. . . that all war veterans are heroes?

. . . that veterans are better suited to some jobs (such as police officers and firefighters) than others?

From a speech by Barack Obama regarding oil and gas subsidies

Today, members of Congress have a simple choice to make: They can stand with the big oil companies, or they can stand with the American people (Obama, 2013).

Are you saying . . . that things that are good for oil companies are bad for Americans, and vice versa?

From a speech by Barack Obama regarding oil and gas subsidies

We all know that drilling for oil has to be a key part of our overall energy strategy. We want U.S. oil companies to be doing well. We want them to succeed. . . . The fact is, we're producing more oil right now than we have in eight years, and we're importing less of it as well. For two years in a row, America has bought less oil from other countries than we produce here at home. . . . American oil is booming (Obama, 2013).

Are you saying . . . that American oil companies are beneficial to the U.S. economy?

. . . that it's better to produce oil in our own country than to buy it from other countries?

. . . that we can't produce enough energy to power the whole country without oil?

From a speech by Barack Obama regarding oil and gas subsidies

I don't want folks . . . to have to pay more at the pump every time that there's some unrest in the Middle East and oil speculators get nervous about whether there's going to be enough supply. I don't want our kids to be held hostage to events on the other side of the world (Obama, 2013).

Are you saying . . . that the price of oil is affected by geopolitics and speculation, not just supply and demand?

From Mitt Romney's 2011 campaign speech in Bedford, New Hampshire

We are Americans. And we will not surrender our dreams to the failures of this President. We are bigger than the misguided policies and weak leadership of one man (Romney, 2011).

Are you saying . . . that Americans are persistent and never give up?

. . . that the effects of a president are temporary and don't affect the average American very much?

. . . that President Obama is doing a bad job and trying to take our dreams away?

From Mitt Romney's 2011 campaign speech in Bedford, New Hampshire

Just a couple of weeks ago in Kansas, President Obama lectured us about Teddy Roosevelt's philosophy of government. But he failed to mention the important difference between Teddy Roosevelt and Barack Obama. Roosevelt believed that government should level the playing field to create equal opportunities. President Obama believes that government should create equal outcomes (Romney, 2011).

Are you saying . . . that equal opportunity is not the same as equal outcome?

From Mitt Romney's 2011 campaign speech in Bedford, New Hampshire

And tonight, I ask each of you to remember how special it is to be an American. I want you to remember what it was like to be hopeful and excited about the future, not to dread each new headline. When you spent more time looking for a house to buy than searching for a new job; when you spent more time thinking about a vacation with your family than how to make it to the next paycheck. That America is still out there. An America when you weren't afraid to look at your retirement savings or the price at the pump. An America when you never had to wake up to hear a President apologizing for America. I say let's fight for that America. The America that brings out the best in each of us, that challenges us to be better and bigger than ourselves. This election, let's fight for the America we love (Romney, 2011).

Are you saying . . . that people should not apologize for their mistakes?

. . . that if everyone is not successful and happy, there is something wrong with America?

. . . that the current president is to blame for the economic downturn?

From Mitt Romney's 2012 campaign speech at the Virginia Military Institute

Last month our nation was attacked again. A U.S. Ambassador and three of our fellow Americans are dead, murdered in Benghazi, Libya. Among the dead were three veterans. All of them were fine men on a mission of peace and friendship to a nation that clearly longs for both (Romney, 2012).

Are you saying . . . that embassies are considered part of the country they represent, rather than the country they are actually in?

. . . that attacking United States citizens is the same as attacking the United States?

. . . that Libya wants peace and friendship with the United States?

. . . that ambassadors and other people who work at embassies are there for peaceful, nonviolent, or diplomatic reasons?

From Mitt Romney's 2012 campaign speech at the Virginia Military Institute

We've seen this struggle before. It would be familiar to General George Marshall. In his time, the ashes of [World War II], another critical part of the world was torn between democracy and despotism. Fortunately, we had leaders of courage and vision, both Republicans and Democrats, who knew that America had to support friends who shared our values and prevent today's crises from becoming tomorrow's conflicts (Romney, 2012).

Are you saying . . . that the Middle East today is like Europe after World War II?

      . . . that if you fix a problem today, it will not become a bigger problem tomorrow?

      . . . that you should stand behind your friends in times of crisis?

      . . . that good leadership qualities can exist in anyone, regardless of political affiliation?

From Mitt Romney's 2012 campaign speech at the Virginia Military Institute

The relationship between the president of the United States and the prime minister of Israel, for example, our closest ally in the region, has suffered great strains. The president explicitly stated that his goal was to put daylight between the United States and Israel, and he's succeeded. This is a dangerous situation that has set back the hope of peace in the Middle East and emboldened our mutual adversaries, especially Iran. Iran today has never been closer to a nuclear weapons capability. It has never posed a greater danger to our friends, our allies and to us. And it has never acted less deterred by America, as was made clear last year, when Iranian agents plotted to assassinate the Saudi ambassador in our nation's capital. And yet when millions of Iranians took to the streets in June of 2009; when they demanded freedom from a cruel regime that threatens the world; when they cried out, are you with us or are you with them, the American president was silent (Romney, 2012).

Are you saying . . . that the only thing stopping Iran from attacking Israel is that the United States backs Israel?

      . . . that the Iranian government and its people are at odds and do not have the same values?

      . . . that if you are not with someone, you are against them and with their enemies?

      . . . that doing nothing is the same as helping an enemy?

From Mitt Romney's 2012 campaign speech at the Virginia Military Institute

I will put the leaders of Iran on notice that the United States and our friends and allies will prevent them from acquiring nuclear weapons capability. I will not hesitate to impose new sanctions on Iran and . . . will tighten the sanctions we currently have. I will restore the permanent presence of aircraft carrier task forces in both the Eastern Mediterranean and the [Persian] Gulf. And I'll work with Israel to increase our military assistance and coordination. For the sake of peace, we must make clear to Iran through actions, not just words, that their nuclear pursuit will not be tolerated (Romney, 2012).

Are you saying . . . that force is the best way to deal with threats and maintain peace?

      . . . that actions speak louder than words?

      . . . that it is the United States' responsibility to solve problems in other countries?

From a debate on the topic "America should police the world"

MAX BOOT: I think the answer's pretty obvious. It's the country with the most vibrant economy, the most fervent devotion to liberty, and the most powerful military. In the 19th century, Great Britain battled enemies of all mankind such as slave traders and pirates, preserved the balance of power on the continent, and kept the world's seas open to commerce. Today the only nation that can play an equivalent role is the United States of America (Intelligence Squared U.S., 2008a, p. 6).

Are you saying . . . that economic and military power give a country international authority?

. . . that international power is always used for good?

. . . that whichever country is most powerful should police the world?

From a debate on the topic "America should police the world"

MAX BOOT: The US is obligated to defend civilization, and that is precisely what we are doing. That is why American troops have fought in places like Bosnia, Kosovo, Afghanistan and Iraq to . . . restore the rule of law and uphold human rights. That is why American troops are still stationed from South Korea to Germany, to prevent aggression and a return of dangerous rivalries (Intelligence Squared U.S., 2008a, p. 7).

Are you saying . . . that military presence or action is the best way to keep the peace?

From a debate on the topic "America should police the world"

MAX BOOT: America has been the greatest force for good in the world in the past century. Just think of what happened when we did *not* act as globo-cop. Think of what happened in 1914, in 1939. By contrast, think of what happened when we *did* act as globo-cop. Think of what happened in 1945, and 1989. American intervention made possible the defeat of Nazism, and Communism. American isolationism made possible the outbreak of two world wars (Intelligence Squared U.S., 2008a, p. 8).

Are you saying . . . that World Wars I and II would not have happened if the United States had intervened earlier?

. . . that the Axis Powers would have won World War II and the Communist Bloc would not have broken up if the United States had stayed out of those conflicts?

. . . that our allies deserve little credit for their roles in those conflicts?

From a debate on the topic "America should police the world"

MAX BOOT: During the 1990s we ignored our policing responsibilities in Afghanistan. As the civil war raged between the Taliban and the Northern Alliance, our leaders said in essence what Britain's leaders said in the 1930s—that there is no reason to be concerned about a quarrel in a faraway country between people of whom we know nothing. Well on 9-11 we found out why we should care (Intelligence Squared U.S., 2008a, p. 9).

Are you saying . . . that the United States has a duty to solve problems in other countries?

. . . that it is in the United States' best interest to solve problems in other countries?

. . . that the September 11th terrorist attacks on the World Trade Center would not have happened if we had intervened earlier?

. . . that all conflicts in the world are our business because they could affect us in the future?

From a debate on the topic "America should police the world"

ELLEN LAIPSON: Can we be the beat cop that Max talked about? Do we know the neighborhood? Do we speak the language? Do we know the culture so that we can diffuse [sic] conflict before it breaks into violence (Intelligence Squared U.S., 2008a, p. 13)?

Are you saying . . . that a good police officer knows well the area and people that he or she is
policing?

. . . that cultural awareness is necessary for mediation and diplomacy?

From a debate on the topic "America should police the world"

MICHAEL MANDELBAUM: The world's governments . . . could, if they chose, circumscribe or abolish altogether, by banding together to oppose it, the American role as the world's policeman. But they have done and shown no signs of doing any such thing (Intelligence Squared U.S., 2008a, p. 19).

Are you saying . . . that the rest of the world wants the United States to be its police force?

. . . that a lack of direct opposition is the same as agreement?

From a debate on the topic "America should police the world"

DOUGLAS MURRAY: America has the right to be and should continue to be . . . the world's policeman. It's not your force as a nation which I think allows you that right, it's America's virtues that allow it that right (Intelligence Squared U.S., 2008a, p. 28).

Are you saying . . . that the United States is a virtuous country and has good values?

From a debate on the topic "America should police the world"

IAN BREMMER: [Americans don't necessarily] like the idea of giving billions of dollars of aid after a tsunami in Indonesia when we can't build our own homes in New Orleans (Intelligence Squared U.S., 2008a, p. 35).

Are you saying . . . that the U.S. government spends too much money on other countries and not enough on helping its own people?

. . . that Americans want the U.S. government to focus on domestic problems?

From a debate on the topic "America should police the world"

MICHAEL MANDELBAUM: The United States as the global policeman is not as legitimate as the New York City police force is. And it cannot be because there is no global government, no global state to give it legitimacy. But it has enough legitimacy, because nobody opposes it, as they would if they didn't like it and felt threatened by it. . . . I think there is a threat . . . to the American role as the world's governments, but it doesn't come from other countries. It comes from the mounting costs of social welfare, of our entitlement programs, the great threat to the American role as the world's policeman and to global order comes not from China . . . it comes from Medicare (Intelligence Squared U.S., 2008a, pp. 49–50).

Are you saying . . . that police forces get their legitimacy from the government?

. . . that a lack of direct opposition is the same as agreement?

. . . that an entity is legitimate if no one challenges it?

. . . that people always challenge things they don't like or things by which they feel threatened?

. . . that the U.S. spends too much money on its own people?

. . . that the U.S. needs to remain the most powerful country?

From a debate on the topic "America should police the world"

MATTHEW PARRIS: America has two great weapons. One is force and the other is persuasion, the power of moral persuasion. They are not complementary. The more force is used the more the power of moral persuasion will be undermined (Intelligence Squared U.S., 2008a, p. 68).

> *Are you saying . . .* that the use of force is immoral?
>
> . . . that people respond negatively to the use of force?
>
> . . . that force and moral persuasion are mutually exclusive?

From a debate on the topic "Ban genetically engineered babies"

NITA FARAHANY: The public can and should decide what limits if any there should be on the uses of genetic engineering. But a complete ban would just drive the practice into back alleys or overseas. Criminalizing genetic engineering will make the practice hidden from public view so that we will have no idea whether Sharon and women like her are using unsafe and unsavory practitioners to carry out genetic engineering (Intelligence Squared U.S., 2013, p. 10).

> *Are you saying . . .* that *ban* and *criminalize* are the same thing?
>
> . . . that bans are never effective and just create black markets?
>
> . . . that the desire for genetic engineering is so great that people would take the risk of doing it illegally?
>
> . . . that banning it now means banning it forever?

From a debate on the topic "Ban genetically engineered babies"

NITA FARAHANY: Recently new research shows the powerful effect of taking folate during pregnancy and how it reduces the incidence of autism in children. And yet no one thinks that we should ban folate (Intelligence Squared U.S., 2013, p. 9).

> *Are you saying . . .* that genetic engineering is just the same as anything else we do to make sure our babies are born healthy?
>
> . . . that things with good effects should never be banned?

From a debate on the topic "Ban genetically engineered babies"

NITA FARAHANY: The United Kingdom, notoriously conservative about reproductive technologies, has given the green light in the use of these technologies (Intelligence Squared U.S., 2013, p. 10).

> *Are you saying . . .* that genetic engineering must be safe if a cautious country has accepted it?

From a debate on the topic "Ban genetically engineered babies"

NITA FARAHANY: Now imagine just for a moment how we would enforce the outright ban that the resolution calls for. Would we forcibly genetically test all babies? . . . Would the government appear in Sharon's hospital room or at airports with handcuffs to arrest her or her child? Would we forcibly sterilize Sharon and her baby? Is this the kind of society that you want to live in (Intelligence Squared U.S., 2013, p. 10)?

Are you saying . . . that genetic engineering would be available even if banned?

. . . that enforcing a ban means putting people in jail if they violate it?

. . . that bans are a function of totalitarian governments?

From a debate on the topic "Ban genetically engineered babies"

LORD ROBERT WINSTON: And, of course, what we have to understand is that we now know that the environmental influence on the embryo, the environmental influence on the fetus has a massive [effect on] . . . how it grows up. And, in fact, really, what we should be trying to do—rather than trying to risk making abnormal babies . . . is to improve the environment so that the DNA functions in the best possible way (Intelligence Squared U.S., 2013, p. 13).

Are you saying . . . that genetic engineering is likely to create abnormal babies?

. . . that nature and nurture are both important to raising a child?

. . . that nurture is easier and safer to change than a child's nature?

From a debate on the topic "Ban genetically engineered babies"

LEE SILVER: You throw the dice, you hold your breath, you hope your child is healthy. It won't have to be that way in the future when we learn how to take the genetic dice, place them on the table in the way that is going to promote health . . . for the [unborn] child (Intelligence Squared U.S., 2013, p. 17).

Are you saying . . . that having a child is a gamble in regard to its health?

. . . that risk is bad, at least in this situation?

. . . that genetic engineering eliminates risk?

From a debate on the topic "Ban genetically engineered babies"

NITA FARAHANY: The most ethical thing to do in circumstances where the only way to prevent a particular type of disease where we readily have a technology available that people will avail themselves of either in this country or another one is to give the green light to proceed (Intelligence Squared U.S., 2013, p. 19).

Are you saying . . . that people are going to use genetic engineering one way or another, so we should just make it legal?

. . . that genetic engineering prevents disease?

From a debate on the topic "Ban genetically engineered babies"

SHELDON KRIMSKY: Sharon was mentioned. I don't know her personally. And I'm so happy that she had a successful pregnancy. But she had choices. One of her choices was to adopt someone else's egg and have a baby. . . . It wouldn't be her DNA but it would be somebody else's DNA. Another choice would be for her to adopt a child, which, you know, is certainly a desirable thing to do in a world where there are children who need adoption. What is the urgency of people to have their DNA in their child (Intelligence Squared U.S., 2013, pp. 19–20)?

Are you saying . . . that the relationship between parent and child is not only biological?

. . . that it's better and less risky to adopt than to use genetic engineering?

From a debate on the topic "Ban genetically engineered babies"

SHELDON KRIMSKY: Over millions of years, mistakes have been bred out to a great extent. And it's remarkable how many children are born normally with the billions and billions of biochemical actions that take place from the fertilized egg until the child is born. So a lot of mistakes were bred out of the system, and it's taken millions of years before the human genome has evolved. Now we're saying, okay, we can get a few technologists to tinker with that and do a better job at the balancing the homeostasis of what I consider an ecosystem, a genetic ecosystem. And my colleague here has pointed out how many abnormalities occur when these genetic mice are manipulated (Intelligence Squared U.S., 2013, p. 34).

> *Are you saying . . .* that the development of a baby is too complicated for us to reliably understand and engineer?
>
> . . . that these things are best left to nature?
>
> . . . that mice are far less complicated than babies and we can't even get *that* right, so we shouldn't even try with humans?

From a debate on the topic "Ban genetically engineered babies"

NITA FARAHANY: There are still uncertainties with IVF [in vitro fertilization] and yet he's in favor of going ahead with IVF. And why is that? Because we have to act in the face of uncertainty in life. I agree, there has not been a strong showing of any link between autism, maybe it has something [to do with the] age of mothers who are undergoing IVF, we don't know. But I think the much more important question to ask is, we've been using technologies that have some uncertain risks, are the lives worth living that have resulted from those technologies (Intelligence Squared U.S., 2013, p. 36)?

> *Are you saying . . .* that if a technology has positive effects it should be utilized, regardless of risk or negative effects?
>
> . . . that some risk is the same as a lot of risk?

From a debate on the topic "Ban genetically engineered babies"

LEE SILVER: We don't stop people who are both carriers for the same mutation at reproducing, even though they have 25 percent risk of having a child with a serious disease. We shouldn't discriminate against people just because they're infertile (Intelligence Squared U.S., 2013, p. 36).

> *Are you saying . . .* that banning genetic engineering prevents people from reproducing?
>
> . . . that preventing people from reproducing is a form of discrimination?
>
> . . . that all risk is equal?

From a debate on the topic "Ban genetically engineered babies"

LORD ROBERT WINSTON: I've got no problem with genetically modified plants. I think actually it would be an important technology for the world, given the problems with water supply. I think we have to differentiate very substantially from what happens in genetically modified crops from what happens actually in human beings (Intelligence Squared U.S., 2013, p. 44).

> *Are you saying . . .* that more complicated organisms create more risk with respect to genetic engineering, so we should be more cautious with them?
>
> . . . that all risk is not equal?

From a debate on the topic "Google violates its 'Don't Be Evil' motto"

RANDAL PICKER: Google says, we're gonna live by a motto, and that model is . . . we're not gonna be evil. Seemingly asking us to hold Google to a higher standard, they're very clear. There'll be times when they will sacrifice the short-run interests of Google for the public good. I don't think what's legal is the standard to evaluate for Google, Google asks us for something much more (Intelligence Squared U.S., 2008b, p. 6).

Are you saying . . . that not being evil means serving the public good?

. . . that what is legal does not always serve the public good?

From a debate on the topic "Google violates its 'Don't be evil' motto"

RANDAL PICKER: I'm a Google Ad Words advertiser. . . . You bid on keyword terms, if you win the auction your ads are supposed to show up. . . . I know my ad is out there. It didn't show up, indeed no ads showed up, and indeed if you look at the statistics, 50 percent of the time when you run a search on Google, and they produce results, the organic search results, there are no ads next to it. . . . Why, because if very few people are bidding [on a term] then I ought to be able to buy it for a very low price and Google's interest is not served by that (Intelligence Squared U.S., 2008b, pp. 7–8).

Are you saying . . . that Google's main concern is making money?

. . . that Google only shows advertisements if it is making money from them?

From a debate on the topic "Google violates its 'Don't be evil' motto"

JIM HARPER: Perhaps that phrase ["don't be evil"] was intended in a sort of, "Let's not be a greasy corporation" sense. Even by that standard, Google is not evil, Google is great. Google brings information and empowerment to the masses in ways we couldn't have imagined just a few years ago (Intelligence Squared U.S., 2008b, p. 11).

Are you saying . . . that giving information to people is a great thing or a noble cause?

. . . that most corporations are evil?

. . . that Google is better than most corporations?

From a debate on the topic "Google violates its 'Don't be evil' motto"

JIM HARPER: If my colleagues at the far end of the table wish to characterize Google as evil, they should foreswear the use of Google products, and find the other products, which there are, and use those instead (Intelligence Squared U.S., 2008b, p. 13).

Are you saying . . . that if you believe a company is doing bad things, you should never use their products?

From a debate on the topic "Google violates its 'Don't be evil' motto"

HARRY LEWIS: [Google] wanted to be the number-one search engine in the world, it started to do business in China. And the Chinese said, we don't want you to show our citizens the world as it really is . . . and, Google said, okay. . . . Google didn't choose the lesser of two evils when faced with the Chinese ultimatum; it chose the more profitable of the two evils. . . . Google had a choice between morality and money, and it chose money (Intelligence Squared U.S., 2008b, pp. 15–16).

Are you saying . . . that morality and money are mutually exclusive?

. . . that more profit and greater evil are the same?

From a debate on the topic "Google violates its 'Don't be evil' motto"

HARRY LEWIS: Suppose Google were not a search engine company, but a pharmaceutical company. And it was told by the Chinese government that it could sell aspirin in China, only if it also made certain forms of brainwashing drugs and thought control medications. And that was the condition on which it could sell aspirin in China. No responsible American company would make that deal with the Chinese authorities, and that is exactly what Google is doing in the digital realm (Intelligence Squared U.S., 2008b, pp. 17–18).

Are you saying . . . that censoring the Internet is tantamount to brainwashing people?

. . . that Google's presence in China is irresponsible and hurts Chinese citizens?

From a debate on the topic "Google violates its 'Don't be evil' motto"

JEFF JARVIS: The real purpose of the "Don't Be Evil" pledge is to give employees the license to remind their bosses of this in meetings. So, a geek can stand there and say, is that evil? . . . It's useful. Imagine, ladies and gentleman, if we had that phrase, "don't be evil," chiseled over every door on Wall Street. Would we not have a better world today? . . . So, I think it's important to just recognize that the rule itself is good. The fact that Google asks it is good (Intelligence Squared U.S., 2008b, p. 29).

Are you saying . . . that it's the thought that counts?

. . . that Wall Street is evil?

. . . that bosses and executives prioritize money over morality?

. . . that questioning authority is good?

From a debate on the topic "Google violates its 'Don't be evil' motto"

KEVIN WILLIAMSON [audience member]: For those who are arguing for the motion, aren't you arguing that Google is in fact violating a different motto, which would say "don't do evil," versus a motto that says "don't be evil." Every business makes some sort of compromise, every business makes a mistake. Everybody who's ever paid a dollar in taxes has made a compromise with evil at some point (Intelligence Squared U.S., 2008b, p. 57).

Are you saying . . . that *doing* evil and *being* evil are different?

. . . that everyone does evil sometimes?

. . . that the government is evil?

From a debate on the topic "Google violates its "Don't be evil' motto"

JIM HARPER: You should oppose the motion . . . because Google is, at its heart, a good company that provides extraordinary services to the public, and makes extraordinary amounts of information available to the public, and is working around the world to make information available (Intelligence Squared U.S., 2008b, pp. 66–67).

Are you saying . . . that intentions matter in determining if someone or something is evil?

. . . that making information available is good?

. . . that good effects can outweigh evil effects?

From a debate on the topic "Good riddance to mainstream media"

JIM VANDEHEI: Mainstream media, for the longest time, I don't think it was always as good as portrayed or always as great as we sort of mythicize. And, for the longest time it was basically run by old white men who are [politically] left of center who are deciding how all of us view the news (Intelligence Squared U.S., 2009, p. 15).

Are you saying . . . that the people who control media outlets influence how we receive information?

. . . that the mainstream media is more liberal than conservative?

From a debate on the topic "Good riddance to mainstream media"

JIM VANDEHEI: And I can tell you there's probably a lot of businessmen and women in the audience because this is New York (Intelligence Squared U.S., 2009, p. 16).

Are you saying . . . that a large portion of the New York population consists of business people?

From a debate on the topic "Good riddance to mainstream media"

JIM VANDEHEI: What new media's done is it's ripped down that wall, between the institution and the reader, and it's opened up, I think it's made it more transparent and it's allowed you the reader to participate more in what we're doing and even some of you to participate in the journalism that we're doing (Intelligence Squared U.S., 2009, p. 17).

Are you saying . . . that there is a separation between traditional media producers and consumers?

. . . that the general population's participation in the journalism process is a good thing?

From a debate on the topic "Good riddance to mainstream media"

KATRINA VANDEN HEUVEL: The fact is that nobody but [mainstream media] institutions like the *New York Times*, the *Washington Post*, the *Wall Street Journal* . . . and a small group of regional papers do most of the reporting in this country that the rest of us depend on to try to hold power accountable (Intelligence Squared U.S., 2009, p. 23).

Are you saying . . . that the point of journalism is to provide checks and balances for powerful people and institutions?

. . . that only a few media institutions do most of the reporting in the U.S.?

From a debate on the topic "Good riddance to mainstream media"

JOHN HOCKENBERRY: Those in the corporate for-profit media in the music business that said somehow the means of distribution being freed from the record companies to people who actually play and use music was going to destroy music in some sense: that if the record business went away somehow music would be affected, that somehow the art form of music and the quality of music would be affected. . . . The technology enabled people suddenly to be a part of something that they were not permitted to be a part of. Why? Because the for-profit structure of mainstream media prevented them. It's an old story in America. When the means of distribution goes out of the hands of the small set of individuals and individual institutions that control it, change is afoot. This is a moment we should embrace (Intelligence Squared U.S., 2009, p. 27).

Are you saying . . . that mainstream media outlets see themselves as gatekeepers of quality?

. . . that traditional media outlets are inherently exclusive?

. . . that new media gives a larger group of people access to and control of the information stream?

. . . that the trend toward crowd-sourced media is a positive change?

From a debate on the topic "Good riddance to mainstream media"

JOHN HOCKENBERRY: At the height of the war in Iraq . . . the number one news broadcast reporting on that war was owned by a defense contractor (Intelligence Squared U.S., 2009, p. 28).

Are you saying . . . that traditional media outlets are influenced by their owners?

. . . that money and power conflict with impartiality?

From a debate on the topic "Good riddance to mainstream media"

JOHN HOCKENBERRY: The best journalists are people who don't do it for the money. We want to create institutions that are all about doing it for the money and then we expect that the values of journalism and reporting are going to be maintained in that structure (Intelligence Squared U.S., 2009, p. 29)?

Are you saying . . . that money corrupts values?

. . . that being motivated by money makes you less good at your job?

From a debate on the topic "Good riddance to mainstream media"

DAVID CARR: Balloon Boy [a falsified news story] was a trending topic on Twitter for four days straight. It's all Twitter could talk about. They weren't talking about the elections in Iraq, the elections in Afghanistan that have gone wrong. They weren't talking about the bombings in Iraq. They were talking about John and Kate [reality television stars] (Intelligence Squared U.S., 2009, p. 31).

Are you saying . . . that the general population is easily distracted by sensational events and reality television?

. . . that international political events are more important than entertainment?

From a debate on the topic "Good riddance to mainstream media"

KATRINA VANDEN HEUVEL: We do need large, powerful institutions, barnacles attached, to take on powerful forces, whether corporate or government. . . . Not to demean the new media, but we need to find ways of working together to salvage quality journalism, which I believe is a public good in a society where there are too many voiceless and powerless (Intelligence Squared U.S., 2009, p. 87).

Are you saying . . . that crowd-sourced reporting does not create quality journalism?

. . . that large institutions can only be kept in check by other large institutions?

. . . that traditional journalism provides a voice for people who are unable to speak out for themselves?

From a debate on the topic "Good riddance to mainstream media"

JIM VANDEHEI: You can't do public service journalism, investigative reporting or foreign policy unless you make money or unless you have government subsidy or unless you have a not-for-profit status. You have to make money to be able to support doing the foreign coverage, to support doing the investigative coverage (Intelligence Squared U.S., 2009, p. 89).

> *Are you saying* . . . that journalism is expensive?
>
> > . . . that money enables rather than corrupts?

From a debate on the topic "Snowden was justified" (National Security Agency system administrator Edward Snowden released thousands of classified documents to media outlets)

BEN WIZNER: Edward Snowden is justified because he provided to journalists and through them to us information that we had a right to know and that we had a need to know. The government had not just concealed this information, it had lied to us about it (Intelligence Squared U.S., 2014, p. 8).

> *Are you saying* . . . that citizens have a right to know what their government is doing?
>
> > . . . that governments should not lie to their citizens?

From a debate on the topic "Snowden was justified" (National Security Agency system administrator Edward Snowden released thousands of classified documents to media outlets)

R. JAMES WOOLSEY: Mr. Snowden pledged to protect the Constitution against enemies foreign and domestic, but he didn't do that. What he did was release—steal and release—material that went to, among others, Hezbollah, al-Qaeda, Hamas, Pyongyang, Tehran and so on. In the real world, you can't have a principle that it is really important to release material, but you're only going to release it to nice people; you're not going to let terrorists and dictators peruse it and use it (Intelligence Squared U.S., 2014, p. 11).

> *Are you saying* . . . that real-world practicality is more important than principles?
>
> > . . . that you should never break a promise, even if it goes against your morals?

From a debate on the topic "Snowden was justified" (National Security Agency system administrator Edward Snowden released thousands of classified documents to media outlets)

ANDREW MCCARTHY: We actually set up this system with exactly the checks and balances that were at issue . . . when too much power was reposed in one person. And now where are we with Edward Snowden? We are right back to one person who's judge, jury, lawgiver, one person who decides what American secrets get kept and what gets exposed to our enemies (Intelligence Squared U.S., 2014, p. 17).

> *Are you saying* . . . that it's bad for one person to have too much power?

From a debate on the topic "Snowden was justified" (National Security Agency system administrator Edward Snowden released thousands of classified documents to media outlets)

BEN WIZNER: [The court that approved NSA surveillance] is a court that quite properly was set up to hear warrant applications in secret. When you're seeking a warrant, you don't need an adversarial process. We don't want the person who we're conducting surveillance on to know that we've sought a warrant. What this court started to do over the last decade was to write long opinions—30, 50, 80 pages long—ruling on whether whole programs of surveillance were consistent with federal statutes and consistent with the Constitution. They did that without the benefit of any adversary. They did that without anybody arguing the other side in front of these courts. Many of these judges who have left the court have said they would have benefited from an adversary (Intelligence Squared U.S., 2014, p. 26).

Are you saying . . . that hearing an opposing opinion is helpful in making important decisions?

From a debate on the topic "Snowden was justified" (National Security Agency system administrator Edward Snowden released thousands of classified documents to media outlets)

BEN WIZNER: [Edward Snowden] certainly has told Barton Gellman of the Washington Post that he did complain regularly internally. . . . He did report his concerns to superiors. . . . One time when he reported concerns to superiors in a posting in Geneva, he was reprimanded and punished for it. This is the experience of people who complained in the intelligence community is that they either get ignored or they get crushed (Intelligence Squared U.S., 2014, pp. 31–32).

Are you saying . . . that Edward Snowden only released NSA information as a last resort?

From a debate on the topic "Snowden was justified" (National Security Agency system administrator Edward Snowden released thousands of classified documents to media outlets)

ANDREW MCCARTHY: If we were going to have effective counterterrorism, we needed the cooperation of our allies because there were many, many places in the world where they had good sources, and we didn't. And we couldn't protect the country without that. When you reveal not only our secrets, but their secrets, and you convince them that they might as well not tell us anything because we can't keep a secret, then we lose that cooperation (Intelligence Squared U.S., 2014, p. 44).

Are you saying . . . that secrets are necessary for international security and relations?

From a debate on the topic "Too many kids go to college"

CHARLES MURRAY: Knowing what major a person had doesn't tell you very much. Yeah, if it's math, if it's hard sciences, if it's engineering, okay. But what does it mean if you have a political science degree . . . if you're going to an employer and saying you ought to hire me. It doesn't really mean anything (Intelligence Squared U.S., 2011b, p. 12).

Are you saying . . . that variety in college curriculums makes degrees meaningless?

. . . that science, technology, engineering, and math (STEM) programs are more standardized than other majors?

. . . that degrees in STEM fields are more valuable than others?

From a debate on the topic "Too many kids go to college"

VIVEK WADHWA: Peter, you didn't know what you wanted to be when you were young. Most children don't know. They're muddling through it. . . . They learn by interacting with other people and getting ideas from other students who have diverse backgrounds. That's how they decide what they're going to be (Intelligence Squared U.S., 2011b, p. 33).

Are you saying . . . that college is not just about academic education?

. . . that interacting with new people and ideas is crucial to becoming an adult?

From a debate on the topic "The two-party system is making America ungovernable"

ARIANNA HUFFINGTON: There is huge mistrust of our national institutions, politicians, business people, the media. And the rise of social media, the rise of the Internet has made it possible for young people especially to connect with each other, to reject the existing system, to opt out of politics and try to find solutions in their own communities, bypassing the political system. That's not ultimately healthy because democracy is not a spectator sport (Intelligence Squared U.S., 2011a, p. 5).

Are you saying . . . that people need to work within the existing system to effect change?

From a debate on the topic "The two-party system is making America ungovernable"

ZEV CHAFETS: Compared to [a] utopia, [the American system is] a replaceable system. If you compare it to the rest of the systems of the world, it's a pretty good system (Intelligence Squared U.S., 2011a, p. 15).

Are you saying . . . that we should judge things based on comparisons to what already exists, rather than to an ideal?

From a debate on the topic "The two-party system is making America ungovernable"

ZEV CHAFETS: There was a time when there was slavery. And there was a time when women couldn't vote. And there was a time . . . when African-Americans couldn't vote. And all those things no longer are the case. They all changed. And they all changed under the two-party system (Intelligence Squared U.S., 2011a, p. 18).

Are you saying . . . that if something has been useful or good in the past, it continues to be useful and good in the present and future?

From a debate on the topic "The two-party system is making America ungovernable"

ARIANNA HUFFINGTON: Well, the primary way [to "shake up a dysfunctional and stagnant two-party system"] is to allow more competition. All of us believe in competition, right? It's the essence of a private enterprise, freedom-based system. We believe in competition in everything except politics. When it comes to politics, you've got to pick your party and run with your party, and actually espouse whatever the party stands for at that particular moment (Intelligence Squared U.S., 2011a, p. 25).

Are you saying . . . that competition creates better outcomes?

. . . that politicians are not free to express their own opinions?

12 Rule Breakers
For high school students

This game is based on a classic cognitive psychology and reasoning experiment designed by Peter C. Wason in 1966. In the experiment, a participant is shown four cards with a letter or a number on each (as shown in figure 12.1) and given a rule such as, "If a card has a vowel on one side, then it has an even number on the other side."

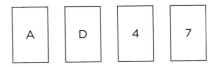

Figure 12.1: Classic Wason task.

The participant is then asked to decide which cards he or she *needs* to flip over to determine whether the rule is untrue. Less than 10 percent of participants managed to choose the correct cards; most fell victim to confirmation bias and only selected cards that would confirm the rule (A and 4), rather than examples that could disprove it (A and 7).

Other versions of selection task experiments expanded on Wason's original findings. Given more concrete descriptive situations and rules, like "If a person goes to Boston, then he takes the subway," performance generally improved, but the rate of success still remained below 50 percent of subjects (Cosmides & Tooby, 1992). Further experiments by Leda Cosmides (1985, 1989) and others focused on social contract rules, like "If a person is drinking beer, then he is over 18," and found a substantial increase in the rate of correct selections. These social contract problems cued participants

Reasoning Skills

- Applying rules and patterns
- Asking questions to challenge assumptions
- Hypothetical reasoning

Materials

- Sets of Rule Breakers cards (see pages 265–282 and online reproducibles)

to detect "cheaters"—instances of breaking a social contract rule in which a benefit is received (drinking beer) without having paid the requisite cost (being over 18). Interestingly, people's intuitive reasoning led them to the correct answers most often when they were asked to detect "cheaters."

When confronted with reasoning tasks such as these, people tend to use intuitive reasoning or shortcuts and then seek to confirm what they have quickly decided is the right answer. In some cases (such as social contract problems), this may lead to the correct response, but more abstract scenarios require more precise, analytical thinking. This game uses variations on the classic Wason selection task to give students practice with hypothetical reasoning and avoiding confirmation bias.

Setup

The only materials required for this game are sets of Rule Breakers cards (see pages 265–282 and online reproducibles). Although students can play individually, we recommend smaller groups of two to four students. You will need a set of cards for each group and will need to decide whether all groups will all have the same set of cards or different sets. If all the sets are the same, it allows for more whole-class discussion; if sets are different, you can simply redistribute them for subsequent rounds. It is crucial that the cards be set out with the correct sides facing up, so if scheduling and space allow, you might consider laying out the sets of cards beforehand.

 To help you and your students identify which side of the card should be face up when set out to play Rule Breakers, we have shaded gray the face-up side of each card in the sets on pages 265–282, as well as in the online reproducible versions. If you choose to create your own cards, we recommend using shading, a symbol, or another method to indicate which side of each card should be face up.

If each group has a different set of cards, the group will also need a slip of paper that states the conditional rule to go along with the set. If each group has a copy of the same set, you may choose to write or display the conditional rule on the board and read it aloud to the whole class. Make sure to choose sets of cards that are appropriate to students' age, ability, and level of experience with these selection tasks. If it is their first time playing this game, we strongly recommend that you use only sets with rules that express social contracts (for example, "If you are drinking alcohol, then you are over 21," "If you have a new watch, then you have paid $20," and so on). Concrete, real-world descriptive rules (for example, "If a person goes to Boston, then he takes the subway," "If a person eats at a restaurant, then she orders salmon," and so on) and causal rules (for example, "If a vase falls on the floor, then it breaks," "If you drink spoiled milk, then you will get sick," and so on) are slightly more challenging, while abstract or unfamiliar rules (for example, "If a card has a vowel on one side, then it has an even number on the other side," "If there is a farm animal on one side, there is a piece of silverware on the other side," and so on) are the most difficult.

This book includes sets of premade selection task cards (see pages 265–282), but you may also design your own. If you decide to make your own, follow the steps in tables 12.1 and 12.2 (page 262) to ensure that your sets work properly. Table 12.1 shows the steps for creating Rule Breakers cards for abstract rules.

Table 12.1: How to Create Rule Breakers Cards for Abstract Rules

Step	Abstract Example
1. Identify two categories. Each card will have an item from one category on one side and an item from the other category on the other side.	animals and kitchenware
2. Come up with a conditional statement that relates two subcategories of your original categories.	If there is a farm animal on one side, there is a piece of silverware on the other side.
3. Identify the antecedent (subcategory in the "if" clause) and the consequent (subcategory in the "then" clause) of the statement.	Antecedent: farm animal Consequent: piece of silverware
4. Create the face-up sides of four cards as follows: • one example of the antecedent • one counterexample of the antecedent (still fits in the larger category, but not the subcategory) • one example of the consequent • one counterexample of the consequent (still fits in the larger category, but not the subcategory)	• pig • lion • spoon • plate
5. The example of the antecedent and the counterexample of the consequent are the correct cards that students should choose to flip over, so at least one of them must have a counterexample to the rule on the back.	• pig/phone AND/OR • plate/chicken
6. Fill in the back side of the other two cards. It is not important whether these are examples or counterexamples (although they should be in the opposite category from the item on the front of the card), as these cards are irrelevant to disproving the rule.	• lion/knife • spoon/monkey

Table 12.2 shows the steps for creating Rule Breakers cards for social contract rules.

Table 12.2: How to Create Rule Breakers Cards for Social Contract Rules

Step	Social Contract Example
1. Compose a conditional statement that expresses a social contract.	If you have a new watch, then you paid $20.
2. Identify the benefit and the cost in the statement.	Benefit: new watch Cost: paid $20
3. Create the face-up sides of four cards as follows: • one example of benefit received • one example of benefit not received • one example of cost paid • one example of cost not paid	• new watch • earrings • paid $20 • paid $0
4. The example of benefit received and the example of cost not paid are the correct cards that students should choose to flip over, so at least one of them must have a counterexample to the rule (a cheater) on the back.	• new watch/paid less than $20 AND/OR • paid $0/new watch
5. Fill in the back side of the other two cards; it is not important whether these are examples or counterexamples (although they should be the opposite of the item on the front of the card in terms of costs and benefits), as these cards are irrelevant to disproving the rule.	• earrings/paid $15 • paid $20/new pants

Figure 12.2 depicts a set of cards correctly laid out (for the abstract rule "If there is a farm animal on one side, then there is a piece of silverware on the other side").

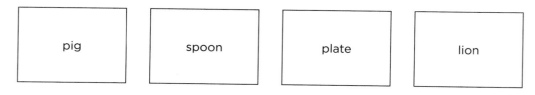

Figure 12.2: Array of Rule Breakers cards for an abstract rule.

The order of the cards in the row does not matter, but there must be one face-up instance each of the antecedent ("if" clause), not-antecedent, consequent ("then" clause), and not-consequent.

Figure 12.3 shows a set of cards correctly laid out for a social contract rule (for the rule "If you have a new watch, then you paid $20").

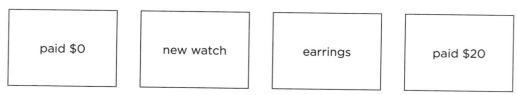

Figure 12.3: Array of Rule Breakers cards for a social contract rule.

In this case, there must be one face-up instance each of benefit received, benefit not received, cost paid, and cost not paid.

Before students play this game, we recommend you discuss with them the types of conditional rules (social contract, concrete descriptive, and abstract), the associated terminology (cost, benefit, cheater, example, counterexample, antecedent, and consequent), and what constitutes breaking or disproving the conditional rule. Also, alert students to the two categories (for example, animals and kitchenware) involved in their tasks. Tell students that they will always need to flip over exactly two cards and there will always be at least one card (and sometimes two cards) to disprove the rule. In other words, the rule will always be wrong; students must select the two cards that can prove it is wrong.

Play

Once the students have their sets of cards, they should lay them out, shaded sides up, without looking at the face-down sides. Then, they look at what information they already have (what is face-up on the cards) and think about what information they still need to determine the truth of the conditional rule. Emphasize to students that they need to think, discuss, and plan with their groups before taking any action on the cards.

 With social contract rules, the answer is often intuitive; however, you should encourage students to examine their snap judgments and be systematic in their thinking before turning over the cards. If they are conscious of the process, the transition to more challenging variations will go more smoothly.

The system for detecting cheaters in social contract problems is fairly simple, and you might choose to teach these steps to your students or allow them to figure them out on their own. The steps are as follows:

1. Identify the cost and the benefit in the rule.

2. Because cheating is defined as receiving a benefit without paying the cost, students should find the cards that represent "received benefit" and "did not pay cost."

3. Flip over those cards to detect potential cheaters.

A similar process works for systematically solving the descriptive and abstract versions of the selection task:

1. Identify the antecedent ("if" clause) and the consequent ("then" clause) in the rule. You can also refer to these as cause and effect, precondition and result, what comes first and what happens later, or any other terms that will help students conceptualize the relationship between the items.

2. Because breaking the rule is defined as the existence of the antecedent without the consequent following it, students should find the cards that represent the example of the antecedent and the counterexample of the consequent.

3. Flip over those cards to find out if the conditional rule is false.

Depending on the content of the rule (social contract, concrete descriptive, or abstract), these tasks can be challenging. They require a significant level of hypothetical reasoning—imagining what will happen if various choices are made about which cards to turn over. If students become confused or frustrated, you might ask leading questions like the following to help put them on the right track:

◆ What constitutes breaking the rule in this situation?

◆ (For social contract rules) What is the cost that must be paid? What is the benefit?

♦   What information do you need to prove the rule false?

♦   What information will you get if you turn over that card?

Students may also find it useful to write down what they know, what they need to know, and possible outcomes based on various decisions.

Once they have talked about the information and come up with a plan, each group gets one chance to turn over only the two cards they *need* to flip over to show that the conditional statement is untrue. After turning over the cards, students must then reassess their information. Can they conclusively disprove the rule? Are they still lacking information that they need to make a determination? Ask students to decide if they have the right information and explain the reasoning behind which cards they flipped over.

Wrap-Up

If the class plays multiple rounds of the game (either in the short or long term), you can assign points as follows. If the group has flipped the correct cards and can explain their reasoning, they receive two points. If the group flipped the wrong cards but has recognized the error and can explain why their choices are inconclusive or which cards they should have flipped, they receive one point. If the group has chosen cards at random or can't explain their reasoning, they receive zero points.

Rules and Card Sets for Rule Breakers

These sets of cards and accompanying rules are organized into three categories:

1. Social contract rules—These sets are the most intuitive to solve, and we recommend that students play with them before moving on to the more abstract sets. Social contract rules involve cost-benefit interactions between people.

2. Concrete descriptive rules—These sets also describe situations that could exist in real life, but do not have the cost-benefit distinctions of social contract rules, making them slightly more difficult to solve.

3. Abstract rules—The rules in these sets describe only the relationship between the items on the front and back of the cards, which have no connection to real life. They require abstract reasoning and are very challenging for most people.

Teachers can use the sets listed here to create cards for Rule Breakers—simply copy the corresponding fronts (shaded gray) and backs (white) onto the fronts and backs of index cards. These sets also serve as answer keys—the cards that students should turn over are marked on both sides with a bolder outline. When copying the sets, do not indicate the answers on the cards themselves. For reproducible sets of the fronts and backs of each set of cards listed here (without the bold outline), visit **marzanoresearch.com/activitiesandgames**. The online sets can be printed double sided and cut apart to create aligned sets of cards without needing to copy them by hand.

Social Contract Rules

If you are drinking alcohol, then you are over 21.

drinking beer	drinking soda	twenty-seven years old	fifteen years old
twenty-two years old	nineteen years old	drinking beer	drinking beer

If you have a new watch, then you paid $20.

new watch	new earrings	paid twenty dollars	paid zero dollars
paid zero dollars	paid twenty-five dollars	new watch	no items

If you are old, then you can demand that people respect you.

demands respect	does not demand respect	old	young
young	young	demands respect	does not demand respect

If someone is serving you, then they deserve your courtesy.

she is serving you	she is not serving you	you are nice to her	you are mean to her
you are mean to her	you are nice to her	she is not serving you	she is serving you

If you use the last of something, then you should replace it.

used up the toilet paper	there is still half a roll of toilet paper	replaced the toilet paper	left an empty toilet paper roll on the dispenser
replaced the toilet paper	did not replace the toilet paper	used up the toilet paper	used up the toilet paper

If an item does not belong to you, then ask before you use it.

she wore my clothes	she wore her own clothes	asked first	didn't ask first
asked first	didn't ask	she wore her own clothes	she wore my clothes

If you buy a ticket, then you waited in line.

has a ticket	does not have a ticket	waited in line	cut in the line
cut in the line	waiting in line	has a ticket	does not have a ticket

If you receive a gift, then you must write a thank-you note.

received a gift	did not receive a gift	wrote a thank-you note	did not write a thank-you note
did not write a thank-you note	did not write a thank-you note	received a gift	received a gift

If someone makes dinner for you, then you should wash the dishes.

Sara's mom made dinner for her	Sara made her own dinner	Sara washed the dishes	Sara left her dirty dishes in the sink
Sara left her dirty dishes in the sink	Sara washed the dishes	Sara made her own dinner	Sara made her own dinner

If you are driving on the toll road, then you paid two dollars and fifty cents.

driving on the toll road	driving on the freeway	paid two dollars and fifty cents	paid zero dollars
paid zero dollars	paid zero dollars	driving on the freeway	driving on the toll road

If you are sick, then you stay home from school.

Tara stayed home from school	Tara went to school	Tara is sick	Tara is not sick

Tara is not sick	Tara is not sick	Tara stayed home from school	Tara went to school

If you are reading a book, then you've finished your test.

Veronica is reading a book	Veronica is staring into space	Veronica finished her test	Veronica did not finish her test

Veronica did not finish her test	Veronica did not finish her test	Veronica is reading a book	Veronica is not reading a book

If you want me to do you a favor, then you should ask nicely.

I will do you a favor	I will not help you	you asked nicely	you asked rudely

you asked rudely	you asked rudely	I will do you a favor	I will not help you

If you got extra credit, then you must have stayed after class.

you got extra credit	you did not get extra credit	you stayed after class	you did not stay after class

you did not stay after class	you did not stay after class	you got extra credit	you did not get extra credit

If you are riding in an elevator, then you face the door.

you are riding the elevator	you are taking the stairs	you are facing the door	you are facing the wall

you are facing the wall	you are looking at the floor	you are riding the elevator	you are in a time-out

If you get to cut the cake, then you let me choose which piece I want first.

you get to cut the cake	you did not cut the cake	you let me choose first	you did not let me choose first
you let me choose first	I chose first	you cut the cake	you cut the cake

If you work overtime, then you get paid extra.

Robert got paid extra	Erika worked overtime	Lily did not get paid extra	Hanna went home
Robert worked overtime	Erika did not get paid extra	Lily worked overtime	Hanna got paid extra

If you receive recognition, then you must have worked hard.

Delilah got an award	Kadeisha did not receive an award	Mariah worked hard	Sam is lazy
Delilah worked hard	Kadeisha worked hard	Mariah got an award	Sam got an award

If you want to be taken seriously, then you dress nicely.

Debbie is taken seriously	Chris is not taken seriously	Uma wears a suit	Neville dresses poorly
Debbie dresses poorly	Chris dresses poorly	Uma is taken seriously	Neville is taken seriously

If you are having dessert, then you must have eaten your vegetables.

having dessert	eating fruit	finished vegetables	spread vegetables around on the plate
did not eat vegetables	did not eat vegetables	eating dessert	not eating dessert

If you have written a book, then you may call yourself an author.

calls herself an author	wrote a book	does not call herself an author	did not write a book
did not write a book	calls herself an author	wrote a book	calls herself an author

If you have paid for the room, then you may stay in the hotel.

staying in the hotel	paid for the room	not staying in the hotel	did not pay for the room
did not pay for the room	not staying in the hotel	paid for the room	staying in the hotel

If you have given us your email address, then you may receive the discount.

received discount	gave email address	did not receive discount	did not give email address
gave email address	received discount	gave email address	received discount

If you read my diary, then I can rightly be mad at you.

you read my diary	you did not read my diary	I am mad at you	I am not mad at you
I am mad at you	I am mad at you	you read my diary	you read my diary

If you ride a bicycle, then you must obey the rules of the road.

I ride a bicycle	I walk	I obey the rules of the road	I ignore the rules of the road
I ignore the rules of the road	I ignore the rules of the road	I drive a car	I walk

If you shake on a deal, then you must follow through.

we shook on it	we did not shake on it	you followed through	you did not follow through
you followed through	you did not follow through	we shook on it	we shook on it

If you drive your friend to the park, then she will buy you ice cream.

she bought you ice cream	you drove her to the park	she did not buy you ice cream	you did not drive her to the park
you drove her to the park	she bought you ice cream	you drove her to the park	she bought you ice cream

If you are seeing a movie at the theater, then you must not bring your own food.

Declan is seeing a movie at the theater	Kirstie is watching a movie at home	Gerald did not bring his own food	Tess brought her own food
he did not bring his own food	she brought her own food	he is watching a movie at home	she is seeing a movie at the theater

If you say "trick or treat," then you get a piece of candy.

got a piece of candy	said "trick or treat"	did not get a piece of candy	did not say "trick or treat"
did not say "trick or treat"	got a piece of candy	did not say "trick or treat"	did not get a piece of candy

If you ride in a taxi, then you tip the driver.

riding in a taxi	taking the subway	tipped the driver	did not tip the driver
did not tip the driver	did not tip the driver	riding in a limo	taking the subway

Concrete Descriptive Rules

If Meegan goes to a restaurant, then she orders pasta.

Meegan is at a restaurant	Meegan is eating at home	Meegan is eating pasta	Meegan is eating a salad

Meegan is eating pasta	Meegan is eating pasta	Meegan is at a friend's house	Meegan is at a restaurant

If you go to Boston, then you take the subway.

you are in Boston	you are in Manchester	you take the subway	you drive from place to place

you drive from place to place	you drive from place to place	you are in Boston	you are in Denver

If you live in New Hampshire, then you can find trees everywhere.

you live in New Hampshire	you live in Arizona	you can find trees everywhere	you cannot see a single tree

you can find trees everywhere	there are only cacti	you live in the woods	you live in New Hampshire

If you go to Denver, then you will see mountains.

you are in Denver	you are in Kansas	you see mountains	you do not see mountains

you do not see mountains	you do not see mountains	you are in Alaska	you are not in Denver

If you go to the electronics store, then you will buy a new television.

you are at the electronics store	you are at a restaurant	you are buying a new television	you are buying a massage chair

you are buying a radio	you are eating salmon	you are at the dump	you are at the electronics store

If you are in St. Louis, then you are in Missouri.

you are in St. Louis	you are in Jefferson City	you are in Missouri	you are in Michigan
you are in Missouri	you are in Missouri	you are in Kansas City	you are in St. Louis

If you eat all the cookies, then the plate is empty.

you ate all the cookies	Brian ate all the cookies	the plate is empty	there are still cookies left
there are still cookies left	the plate is empty	the dog ate the cookies	you only ate one cookie

If there is a horse, then it is in a barn.

horse	dog	in a barn	in the house
in a barn	in the car	cow	horse

If you are at the FIFA World Cup in 2014, then you are in Brazil.

you are at the World Cup	you are at home	you are in Brazil	you are not in Brazil
you are not in Brazil	you are in Brazil	you are exploring the Amazon	you are at the World Cup

If you are in the office, then there is a phone.

in the office	in the parking lot	phone	no phone
no phone	car	at the bank	in the office

If I have paper, then I also have a pen.

I have paper	I do not have paper	I have a pen	I do not have a pen
I do not have a pen	I do not have a pen	I have a pencil	I have paper

If there is a power outage, then we will play board games.

there is a power outage	the lights are still on	we are playing board games	we are drinking tea
we are playing outside	we are playing board games	the lights are still on	there is a power outage

If you are in Iraq, then you are in the Middle East.

you are in Iraq	you are in Lebanon	you are in the Middle East	you are in Europe
you are not in the Middle East	you are in the Middle East	you are in Afghanistan	you are in Iraq

If you are deep under water, then your ears hurt.

you are deep under water	you are high in the air	your ears hurt	your ears feel fine
your ears hurt	your ears hurt	you are high in the air	you are deep under water

If there is a lead brick, then it is heavy.

lead brick	regular brick	heavy	light
light	five pounds	an elephant	a balloon

If you are in Chile, then you are south of the Equator.

you are in Chile	you are in Colombia	you are south of the Equator	you are north of the Equator
you are north of the Equator	you are north of the Equator	you are in Argentina	you are in Mexico

If you have pale skin, then you are at a high risk for skin cancer.

you have pale skin	you have dark skin	you are at a high risk for skin cancer	you are at a low risk for skin cancer
you are at a high risk for skin cancer	you are at a high risk for skin cancer	you have had many sunburns	you have pale skin

If you are at the camping store, then you will be surrounded by outdoorsy people.

you are at the camping store	you are in the mall	you are surrounded by outdoorsy people	the people around you prefer the city
the people around you prefer the city	the people around you prefer the city	you are in the woods	you are at the theater

If you are cleaning, then I am playing video games.

you are cleaning	you are sleeping	I am playing video games	I am not playing video games
I am playing video games	I am playing video games	you are sleeping	you are cleaning

If the air conditioning is on, then the window is closed.

the air conditioning is on	the air conditioning is off	the window is closed	the window is open
the window is open	the window is open	the air conditioning is on	the air conditioning is off

If you have a broken arm, then you get an x-ray.

broken arm	broken nose	got an x-ray	got an MRI
did not get an x-ray	got an x-ray	broken leg	no broken bones

If you drink coffee, then you have energy.

drinking coffee	drinking water	lots of energy	tired
lots of energy	lots of energy	drinking soda	drinking coffee

If you go to another country, then you cross a border.

in another country	not in another country	crossed a border	did not cross a border
crossed a border	did not cross a border	in another country	in another country

If you eat pizza, then you eat cheese.

eating pizza	eating cereal	eating cheese	not eating cheese
not eating cheese	not eating cheese	eating pizza	eating pizza

If there is a keyboard, then there is a monitor.

keyboard	no keyboard	monitor	no monitor
monitor	no monitor	no keyboard	keyboard

If you are alone, then you are happy.

you are alone	you are with people	you are happy	you are unhappy
you are unhappy	you are lonely	you are alone	you are alone

If you are in a city, then there are lots of people.

in a city	in the country	lots of people	very few people
very few people	very few people	in the city	in the country

If it lives in the sea, then it is a fish.

lives in the sea	lives on land	is a fish	is not a fish
is a whale	is a cow	lives in the sea	lives in the sea

If it flies in the air, then it is a bird.

flies in the air	does not fly	is a bird	is a fish
is a flying fish	is a penguin	flies in the air	lives in the lake

If you read lots of books, then you are smart.

reads lots of books	never reads	is smart	is not smart
is not smart	is not smart	reads lots of books	never reads

Abstract Rules

If there is a vowel on one side, then there is an even number on the other side.

U	B	4	7
6	O	T	E

If there is a farm animal on one side, then there is a piece of silverware on the other side.

pig	lion	spoon	plate
phone	cutting board	okapi	chicken

If there is a primary color on one side, then there is a children's book on the other side.

red	purple	*Goodnight Moon*	*Atlas Shrugged*
Where the Wild Things Are	*Crime and Punishment*	pink	yellow

If there is a human bone on one side, then there is a U.S. president on the other side.

ulna	skin	Harry S. Truman	Winston Churchill
Vladimir Putin	José Mujica	foot	hair

If there is a nocturnal animal on one side, then there is a flowering plant on the other side.

owl	squirrel	rose	pine tree
grass	maple	cougar	robin

If there is a historical event on one side, then there is a phase of the moon on the other side.

the Civil War	Julie ate breakfast	full moon	two moons
waxing gibbous	sunset	Apollo 11 moon landing	1849 Gold Rush

If there is a word beginning with T on one side, then there is a number less than one on the other side.

tragic	youthful	.8	four
.025	six	terrible	timeless

If there is a four-legged, hooved animal on one side, then there is a sea mammal on the other side.

horse	chipmunk	whale	sea urchin
dolphin	rainbow trout	elk	zebra

If there is an insect on one side, then there is a hawk on the other side.

ant	lobster	eagle	chickadee
egret	lobster	caterpillar	termite

If there is a portable phone on one side, then there is a portable computer on the other side.

cell phone	rotary phone	laptop	desktop computer
tablet	the Internet	payphone	car phone

If there is an odd number on one side, then there is a consonant on the other side.

five	eight	M	O
V	E	four	nine

If there is a poet on one side, then there is a physicist on the other side.

Walt Whitman	J. K. Rowling	Isaac Newton	Jacques Cousteau
Neil deGrasse Tyson	Charles Darwin	Emily Dickinson	William Carlos Williams

If there is a tree on one side, then there is a crab on the other side.

oak tree	violet	hermit crab	oyster
horseshoe crab	codfish	iris	maple tree

If there is a marker on one side, then there is a whiteboard on the other side.

permanent marker	pencil	whiteboard	paper
paper	paper	crayon	marker

If Frank is on one side, then his sister is on the other side.

Frank	Jim	Frank's sister	Frank's brother
Frank's sister	Ruth	Jim	Frank

If there is a word that starts with B on one side, then there is a number starting with five on the other side.

brain	nebula	five hundred seventy-nine	thirty-two
sixty-four	ninety	bell	tube

If there is a hammer on one side, then there is an airport on the other side.

hammer	screwdriver	airport	train station
airport	marina	awl	hammer

If there is a crocodile on one side, then there is a blue jay on the other side.

crocodile	alligator	blue jay	chickadee
chickadee	finch	alligator	crocodile

If there is a velociraptor on one side, then there is a ladybug on the other side.

velociraptor	triceratops	ladybug	beetle
ladybug	beetle	apatosaurus	velociraptor

If there are two of the same letter on one side, then there are two of the same number on the other side.

QQ	TH	33	78
11	62	MM	YY

If there is a triangle on one side, then there is a coyote on the other side.

triangle	rhombus	coyote	wolf

coyote	bear	circle	triangle

If there is a country on one side, then there is an ocean on the other side.

Canada	California	Indian Ocean	Mississippi River

Arctic Ocean	Atlantic Ocean	Florida	Ukraine

If there is a fruit that grows on trees on one side, then there is a vegetable that grows in the ground on the other side.

orange	strawberry	carrot	green bean

radish	potato	blackberry	apple

If there is a name on one side, then there is an age on the other side.

Erma	xylophone	thirty-five	five feet eight inches

sixty-three	eight	Jocinda	Patty

If there is a circle on one side, then there is nothing on the other side.

circle	square		something

	cube	circle	circle

If seventeen is on one side, then the letter N is on the other side.

seventeen	four hundred eighty-six	N	B
T	W	seventeen	seventeen

If there is a dog on one side, then there is a leash on the other side.

dog	ferret	leash	electric fence
electric fence	leash	cat	dog

If there is a dessert on one side, then there is a vegetable on the other side.

cake	bread	peas	pear
broccoli	pudding	yam	pie

If there is a globe on one side, then there is a library on the other side.

globe	map	library	school
city hall	road	globe	globe

If there is an earthquake on one side, then there is a frog on the other side.

earthquake	tsunami	frog	salamander
frog	newt	volcanic eruption	earthquake

References and Resources

Achieve. (2013). *Appendix H – Understanding the scientific enterprise: The nature of science in the Next Generation Science Standards*. Accessed at www.nextgenscience.org/sites/ngss/files/Appendix%20H%20-%20The%20Nature%20of %20Science%20in%20the%20Next%20Generation%20Science%20Standards%204.15.13.pdf on July 2, 2014.

Adamovic, J. (2012). *Logic puzzles*. Accessed at http://brainden.com/forum/index.php/topic/127-humans-and-monkeys/ on June 13, 2014.

Adjovi, L. (2014, June 16). Why some people want facial scars. *BBC News Magazine*. Accessed at www.bbc.com/news /magazine-27412311 on June 19, 2014.

American Federation of Teachers. (1985). Critical thinking: It's a basic. *American Teacher*, 21.

Anderson, R. C., Chinn, C., Chang, J., Waggoner, M., & Yi, H. (1997). On the logical integrity of children's arguments. *Cognition and Instruction, 15*(2), 135–167.

Anderson, R. C., Chinn, C., Waggoner, M., & Nguyen, K. (1998). Intellectually stimulating story discussions. In J. Osborn & F. Lehr (Eds.), *Literacy for all* (pp. 170–196). New York: Guilford Press.

Angelou, M. (1969). *I know why the caged bird sings*. New York: Ballantine Books.

Aubrey, A. (2014, June 6). Doughnut day downer: Palm oil in pastries drives deforestation. *NPR*. Accessed at www.npr .org/blogs/thesalt/2014/06/06/319231081/doughnut-day-downer-palm-oil-in-pastries-drives-deforestation on June 18, 2014.

Austen, I. (2014, June 17). Despite protests, Canada approves Northern Gateway oil pipeline. *The New York Times*. Accessed at www.nytimes.com/2014/06/18/business/energy-environment/canada-approves-northern-gateway -pipeline.html?ref=science on June 18, 2014.

Austen, J. (1813). *Pride and prejudice*. London: Penguin Books.

Bakhtin, M. (1981). *The dialogic imagination: Four essays* (C. Emerson & M. Holquist, Trans.). Austin: University of Texas Press.

Best Brain Teasers. (2013). *Logical reasoning puzzles with answers*. Accessed at http://dailybrainteaser.blogspot.com/2013/04 /logical-reasoning-puzzles-with-answers.html on June 16, 2014.

Beyer, B. K. (1988). *Developing a thinking skills program*. Boston: Allyn & Bacon.

Big Riddles. (2009). *Reasoning riddles*. Accessed at www.bigriddles.com/reasoning-riddles on June 13, 2014.

Blumenthal, R. (2014, June 18). Protection sought for vast and ancient Inca road. *The New York Times.* Accessed at www.nytimes.com/2014/06/19/arts/design/protection-sought-for-vast-and-ancient-incan-road.html?action=click &contentCollection=U.S.&module=MostEmailed&version=Full&region=Marginalia&src=me&pgtype=article on June 19, 2014.

Braw, E. (2014, June 15). What should teenagers read at school? *Newsweek.* Accessed at www.newsweek.com/what -should-teenagers-read-school-254547 on June 18, 2014.

Brickell, G., Ferry, B., & Harper, B. (2002, December). *Developing informal reasoning skills in ill-structured environments. A case study into problem-solving strategies.* Paper presented at the annual conference of the Australasian Society for Computers in Learning in Tertiary Education, Auckland, New Zealand.

Cahill, L., Gorski, L., & Le, K. (2003). Enhanced human memory consolidation with post-learning stress: Interactions with the degree of arousal at encoding. *Learning and Memory, 10*(4), 270–274.

Cavallo, A. M. L. (1996). Meaningful learning, reasoning ability, and students' understanding and problem solving of topics in genetics. *Journal of Research in Science Teaching, 33*, 625–656.

Charles, D. (2014, June 16). Hunting for alien bug and seed invaders at Baltimore's port. *NPR.* Accessed at www.npr.org /blogs/thesalt/2014/06/16/319499925/hunting-for-alien-bug-and-seed-invaders-at-baltimores-port on June 20, 2014.

CNN. (2008, November 23). Interview with Al Gore; interview with Thomas Friedman [Transcript]. In *Fareed Zakaria GPS* [Television series]. Accessed at http://transcripts.cnn.com/TRANSCRIPTS/0811/23/fzgps.01.html on April 8, 2014.

College Board. (1983). *Academic preparation for college: What students need to know and be able to do.* New York: College Entrance Examination Board.

Commission on the Humanities. (1980). *The humanities in American life.* Berkeley: University of California Press.

Cosmides, L. (1985). *Deduction or Darwinian algorithms? An explanation of the "elusive" content effect on the Wason selection task.* Unpublished doctoral dissertation, Harvard University, Cambridge, MA.

Cosmides, L. (1989). The logic of social exchange: Has natural selection shaped how humans reason? Studies with the Wason selection task. *Cognition, 31*, 187–276.

Cosmides, L., & Tooby, J. (1992). Cognitive adaptations for social exchange. In J. Barkow, L. Cosmides, & J. Tooby (Eds.), *The adapted mind: Evolutionary psychology and the generation of culture* (pp. 163–228). New York: Oxford University Press.

de Bono, E. (1985). The CoRT thinking program. In J. W. Segal, S. F. Chipman, & R. Glaser (Eds.), *Thinking and learning skills: Vol. 1. Relating instruction to research* (pp. 363–388). Hillsdale, NJ: Erlbaum.

Doyle, A. C. (1891). *The five orange pips.* Accessed at www.eastoftheweb.com/short-stories/UBooks/FiveOran.shtml on June 19, 2014.

Dr. Seuss. (1960). *Green eggs and ham.* New York: Random House.

Eilperin, J. (2014, June 17). Obama proposes vast expansion of Pacific Ocean sanctuaries for marine life. *The Washington Post.* Accessed at www.washingtonpost.com/politics/obama-will-propose-vast-expansion-of-pacific-ocean-marine -sanctuary/2014/06/16/f8689972-f0c6-11e3-bf76-447a5df6411f_story.html on June 20, 2014.

Epstein, J. A., & Harackiewicz, J. (1992). Winning is not enough: The effects of competition and achievement orientation on intrinsic interest. *Personality and Social Psychology Bulletin, 18*(2), 128–138.

Evans, J. S. B. T. (2002). Logic and human reasoning: An assessment of the deduction paradigm. *Psychological Bulletin, 128*(6), 978–996.

Evans, J. S. B. T. (2003). In two minds: Dual-process accounts of reasoning. *Trends in Cognitive Science, 7*(10), 454–459.

Evans, J. S. B. T., & Over, D. E. (1996). *Rationality and reasoning.* New York: Psychology Press.

Expand Your Mind. (n.d.). *Logic problems.* Accessed at www.expandyourmind.com/logicproblems/logic_problems.shtml on June 16, 2014.

Faulkner, W. (1930). *A rose for Emily.* Accessed at www.eng.fju.edu.tw/English_Literature/Rose/el-text-E-Rose.htm on June 18, 2014.

Feuerstein, R., Rand, Y., Hoffman, M. B., & Miller, R. (1980). *Instrumental enrichment.* Baltimore: University Park Press.

Flemming, L. (2014). *Drawing inferences.* Accessed at www.laflemm.com/reso/inference.html on June 17, 2014.

Foroohar, R. (2014, June 19). 2030: The year retirement ends. *TIME Magazine.* Accessed at http://time.com/2899504/2030 -the-year-retirement-ends on June 19, 2014.

Fox News Channel. (2008a, November 28). Panel discusses terror attacks in India [Transcript]. In *Special Report with Brit Hume* [Television series]. Accessed at www.realclearpolitics.com/articles/2008/11/panel_discusses_terror_attacks .html on April 8, 2014.

Fox News Channel. (2008b, December 1). Cohen & Chopra on causes of Islamic radicalism [Transcript]. In *Hannity & Colmes* [Television series]. Accessed at www.realclearpolitics.com/articles/2008/12/cohen_chopra_on_causes .html on April 8, 2014.

Fulton, A. (2014, June 12). Has the FDA brought on a cheese apocalypse? Probably not. *NPR.* Accessed at www.npr.org /blogs/thesalt/2014/06/12/321239442/has-the-fda-brought-on-a-cheese-apocalypse-probably-not on June 18, 2014.

Futrell, M. H. (1987). A message long overdue. *Education Week, 7*(14), 9.

General Motors Corporation. (2008). *Restructuring plan for long-term viability: Submitted to Senate Banking Committee and House of Representatives Financial Services Committee.* Accessed at www.freep.com/assets/PDF/1202gmplan .pdf on April 8, 2014.

Gillies, R. M., & Haynes, M. (2011). Increasing explanatory behaviour, problem-solving, and reasoning within classes using cooperative group work. *Instructional Science, 39,* 349–366.

Gilovich, T. (1991). *How we know what isn't so.* New York: Free Press.

Good, T. L., & Brophy, J. E. (2003). *Looking in classrooms* (9th ed.). Boston: Allyn & Bacon.

Guthrie, C. (2010, June 16). Heads and tails [Web log post]. Accessed at http://theweeklyriddle.blogspot.com/2010/06 /heads-and-tails.html on June 16, 2014.

Hall, J. (n.d.). *Inferences worksheets.* Accessed at www.havefunteaching.com/worksheets/reading-worksheets/inferences -worksheets on June 17, 2014.

Haystead, M. W., & Marzano, R. J. (2009). *Meta-analytic synthesis of studies conducted at Marzano Research on instructional strategies.* Englewood, CO: Marzano Research.

Hellman, M. (2014, June 19). Washington street outside Chinese embassy may be renamed "Liu Xiaobo." *TIME Magazine.* Accessed at http://time.com/2899146/street-outside-chinese-embassy-renamed-liu-xiaobo-dc on June 20, 2014.

Heneman, K., & Zidenberg-Cherr, S. (2007). *Nutrition and health info-sheet for health professionals: Some facts about energy drinks.* Accessed at http://nutrition.ucdavis.edu/content/infosheets/fact-pro-energydrinks.pdf on July 2, 2014.

Hirzel, C. (Director). (2008, December 5). Unemployment soars! [Transcript]. In *Larry King Live* [Television series]. Atlanta, GA: Cable News Network. Accessed at http://transcripts.cnn.com/TRANSCRIPTS/0812/05/lkl.01.html on April 8, 2014.

Khan Academy. (n.d.). *Online tutorial on logical reasoning.* Accessed at www.khanacademy.org/math/geometry/logical-reasoning on July 12, 2014.

Intelligence Squared U.S. (Producer). (2008a, February 12). *America should be the world's policeman* [Transcript]. Accessed at http://intelligencesquaredus.org/images/debates/past/transcripts/AmericaWorldPoliceman-021208.pdf on April 8, 2014.

Intelligence Squared U.S. (Producer). (2008b, November 18). *Google violates its "don't be evil" motto* [Transcript]. Accessed at http://intelligencesquaredus.org/images/debates/past/transcripts/Google-111808.pdf on April 8, 2014.

Intelligence Squared U.S. (Producer). (2009, October 27). *Good riddance to mainstream media* [Transcript]. Accessed at http://intelligencesquaredus.org/images/debates/past/transcripts/mainstream-media.pdf on April 8, 2014.

Intelligence Squared U.S. (Producer). (2011a, February 15). *The two-party system is making America ungovernable* [Transcript]. Accessed at http://intelligencesquaredus.org/images/debates/past/transcripts/two-party.pdf on April 8, 2014.

Intelligence Squared U.S. (Producer). (2011b, October 12). *Too many kids go to college* [Transcript]. Accessed at http://intelligencesquaredus.org/images/debates/past/transcripts/college.pdf on April 8, 2014.

Intelligence Squared U.S. (Producer). (2013, February 13). *Prohibit genetically engineered babies* [Transcript]. Accessed at http://intelligencesquaredus.org/images/debates/past/transcripts/021313%20genetic%20engineering.pdf on April 8, 2014.

Intelligence Squared U.S. (Producer). (2014, February 13). *Snowden was justified* [Transcript]. Accessed at http://intelligencesquaredus.org/images/debates/past/transcripts/021214%20Snowden.pdf on April 8, 2014.

Ito, T. A., Larsen, J. T., Smith, N. K., & Cacioppo, J. T. (2002). Negative information weighs more heavily on the brain: The negativity bias in evaluative categorizations. In J. T. Cacioppo (Ed.), *Foundations in social neuroscience* (pp. 575–597). Cambridge, MA: MIT Press.

Johnson-Laird, P. N. (2008). *How we reason.* New York: Oxford University Press.

Joyce, C. (2014, June 12). Maybe dinosaurs were a coldblooded, warmblooded mix. *NPR.* Accessed at www.npr.org/2014/06/12/320803925/maybe-dinosaurs-were-a-cold-blooded-warm-blooded-mix on June 19, 2014.

Kahneman, D. (2011). *Thinking, fast and slow.* New York: Farrar, Straus & Giroux.

Kendall, J. S., & Marzano, R. J. (2000). *Content knowledge: A compendium of standards and benchmarks for K–12 education* (3rd ed.). Aurora, CO: McREL.

Kennedy, D. O., & Scholey, A. B. (2004). A glucose-caffeine "energy drink" ameliorates subjective and performance deficits during prolonged cognitive demand. *Appetite, 42,* 331–333.

Klenk, V. (2008). *Understanding symbolic logic* (5th ed.). Upper Saddle River, NJ: Prentice Hall.

Krug, N. (2014, June 10). Running with dogs: 5Ks and canines. *The Washington Post.* Accessed at www.washingtonpost.com/lifestyle/wellness/running-with-dogs-5ks-and-canines/2014/06/10/0e673264-ea65-11e3-9f5c-9075d5508f0a_story.html on June 17, 2014.

Krulwich, R. (2014, June 8). Big moments get less weighty: Whatever happened to stiff paper? *NPR.* Accessed at www.npr.org/blogs/krulwich/2014/06/08/318601983/big-moments-get-less-weighty-whatever-happened-to-stiff-paper on June 17, 2014.

Kryjevskaia, M., & Stetzer, M. R. (2013). Examining inconsistencies in student reasoning approaches. *American Institute of Physics Conference Proceedings, 1513,* 226–230.

Lawson, A. E. (2001). Using the learning cycle to teach biology concepts and reasoning patterns. *Journal of Biological Education, 35*(4), 165–169.

Lawson, A. E., Alkhoury, S., Benford, R., Clark, B., & Falconer, K. A. (2000). What kinds of scientific concepts exist? Concept construction and intellectual development in college biology. *Journal of Research in Science Teaching, 37*, 996–1018.

Lin, T. J., & Anderson, R. C. (2008). Reflections on collaborative discourse, argumentation, and learning. *Contemporary Educational Psychology, 33*(3), 443–448.

Lipman, M., Sharp, A. M., & Oscanyan, F. S. (1979). *Philosophical inquiry: An instructional manual to accompany* Harry Stottlemeier's Discovery. Upper Montclair, NJ: Institute for the Advancement of Philosophy for Children.

Lipman, M., Sharp, A. M., & Oscanyan, F. S. (1980). *Philosophy in the classroom* (2nd ed.). Philadelphia: Temple University.

Lowry, N., & Johnson, D. W. (1981). Effects of controversy on epistemic curiosity, achievement, and attitudes. *The Journal of Social Psychology, 115*(1), 31–43.

Machado, A. (2014, June 18). How millennials are changing travel. *The Atlantic.* Accessed at www.theatlantic.com /international/archive/2014/06/how-millennials-are-changing-international-travel/373007 on June 19, 2014.

Macur, J. (2014, June 16). Quiet about adversary, U.S. posts a victory that speaks volumes. *The New York Times.* Accessed at www.nytimes.com/2014/06/17/sports/worldcup/in-world-cup-opener-the-united-states-defense-rises-to-the -occasion.html?hp on June 20, 2014.

Marzano, R. J. (1992). *A different kind of classroom: Teaching with Dimensions of Learning.* Alexandria, VA: Association for Supervision and Curriculum Development.

Marzano, R. J. (2007). *The art and science of teaching: A comprehensive framework for effective instruction.* Alexandria, VA: Association for Supervision and Curriculum Development.

Marzano, R. J., & Arredondo, D. E. (1986). *Tactics for thinking: Teacher's manual.* Aurora, CO: McREL.

Marzano, R. J., Brandt, R. S., Hughes, C. S., Jones, B. F., Presseisen, B. Z., Rankin, S. C., et al. (1988). *Dimensions of thinking: A framework for curriculum and instruction.* Alexandria, VA: Association for Supervision and Curriculum Development.

Marzano, R. J., & Dole, J. A. (1985). Teaching the basic relationships between sentences. *Reading, 19*(1), 24–34.

Marzano, R. J., & Heflebower, T. (2012). *Teaching & assessing 21st century skills.* Bloomington, IN: Marzano Research.

Marzano, R. J., Paynter, D. E., & Doty, J. K. (2003). *The pathfinder project: Exploring the power of one—Teacher's manual.* Conifer, CO: Pathfinder Education.

Marzano, R. J., & Pickering, D. J. (with Arredondo, D. E., Blackburn, G. J., Brandt, R. S., Moffett, C. A., Paynter, D. E., Pollock, J. E., & Whisler, J. S.). (1997). *Dimensions of learning: Teacher's manual* (2nd ed.). Alexandria, VA: Association for Supervision and Curriculum Development.

Mercer, N., Dawes, L., Wegerif, R., & Sams, C. (2004). Reasoning as a scientist: Ways of helping children to use language to learn science. *British Educational Research Journal, 30*, 359–377.

Mercier, H. (2011). Reasoning serves argumentation in children. *Cognitive Development, 26*(3), 177–191.

Merriam-Webster's collegiate dictionary (11th ed.). (2012). Springfield, MA: Merriam-Webster.

Moriarty, B., Douglas, G., Punch, K., & Hattie, J. (1995). The importance of self-efficacy as a mediating variable between learning environments and achievement. *British Journal of Educational Psychology, 65*(1), 73–84.

Morton, D. (n.d.a). *Inferences worksheets.* Accessed at www.ereadingworksheets.com/free-reading-worksheets/reading -comprehension-worksheets/inferences-worksheets on June 17, 2014.

Morton, D. (n.d.b). *Making inferences 3.* Accessed at www.ereadingworksheets.com/reading-worksheets/making -inferences-3.pdf on October 20, 2014.

Murphy, P. K., Wilkinson, I. A. G., Soter, A. O., & Hennessey, M. N. (2009). Examining the effects of classroom discussion on students' comprehension of text: A meta-analysis. *Journal of Educational Psychology, 101*(3), 740–764.

Nardelli, R. (2008). *United States House Committee on Financial Services: Chrysler's plan for short-term and long-term viability.* Accessed at www.freep.com/assets/PDF/1202chryslerplan.pdf on April 8, 2014.

National Education Goals Panel. (1991). *The National Education Goals report: Building a nation of learners.* Washington, DC: Author.

National Governors Association Center for Best Practices & Council of Chief State School Officers. (2010a). *Common Core State Standards for English language arts & literacy in history/social studies, science, and technical subjects.* Washington, DC: Authors.

National Governors Association Center for Best Practices & Council of Chief State School Officers. (2010b). *Common Core State Standards for mathematics.* Washington, DC: Authors.

National Research Council. (2012). *A framework for K–12 science education: Practices, crosscutting concepts, and core ideas.* Washington, DC: National Academies Press.

National Science Board Commission on Precollege Education in Mathematics, Science and Technology. (1983). *Educating Americans for the 21st century.* Washington, DC: Author.

Nawrot, P., Jordan, S., Eastwood, J., Rotstein, J., Hugenholtz, A., & Feeley, M. (2003). Effects of caffeine on human health. *Food Additives and Contaminants, 20*, 1–30.

Neuhaus Education Center. (n.d.). *Stories for making inferences.* Accessed at http://neuhaus.org/stories-for-making-inferences/ on June 17, 2014.

Nisbett, R. E., Fong, G. T., Lehman, D. R., & Cheng, P. W. (1987). Teaching reasoning. *Science, 238*(4827), 625–631.

NGSS Lead States. (2013). *Next Generation Science Standards: For states, by states.* Washington, DC: National Academies Press.

Obama, B. (2008a, December 2). *Obama's remarks to the National Governors Association* [Transcript]. Accessed at www.realclearpolitics.com/articles/2008/12/obamas_remarks_to_the_national.html on April 8, 2014.

Obama, B. (2008b, December 6). *Obama announces parts of his economic recovery plan* [Transcript]. Accessed at www.realclearpolitics.com/articles/2008/12/obama_announces_parts_of_his_e.html on April 8, 2014.

Obama, B. (2012, May 24). *Remarks by the President on energy in Newton, Iowa* [Transcript]. Accessed at www.whitehouse.gov/the-press-office/2012/05/24/remarks-president-energy-newton-iowa on April 8, 2014.

Obama, B. (2013, March 29). *Remarks by the President on oil and gas subsidies* [Transcript]. Accessed at www.whitehouse.gov/the-press-office/2012/03/29/remarks-president-oil-and-gas-subsidies on April 8, 2014.

Oswego City School District. (2011). *Lesson: Making inferences.* Accessed at www.studyzone.org/testprep/ela4/o/makinginferencel.cfm on June 17, 2014.

Panel on the General Professional Education of the Physician and College Preparation for Medicine. (1984). *Physicians for the 21st century: The GPEP report.* Washington, DC: Association for American Colleges.

Park, A. (2014, June 19). Here's how kids can get better grades. *TIME Magazine.* Accessed at http://time.com/2897377/heres-how-kids-can-get-better-grades on June 18, 2014.

Paul, R. W. (1984). Critical thinking: Fundamental to education for a free society. *Educational Leadership, 42*(1), 4–14.

Pearson Education. (2011). *Making inferences.* Accessed at https://perspective.pearsonaccess.com/content/resources/learningresources/rd/pdf/prd1361SK.pdf on June 17, 2014.

Piaget, J. (1928). *The child's conception of the world.* London: Routledge.

Quellmalz, E. S. (1987). Developing reasoning skills. In J. B. Baron & R. J. Sternberg (Eds.), *Teaching thinking skills: Theory and practice*. New York: W. H. Freeman.

Reder, L. M. (1980). The role of elaboration in comprehension and retention of prose: A critical review. *Review of Educational Research, 50*(1), 5–53.

Reeve, J., & Deci, E. L. (1996). Elements of the competitive situation that affect intrinsic motivation. *Personality and Social Psychology Bulletin, 22*(1), 24–33.

Reyner, L. A., & Horne, J. A. (2002). Efficacy of a "functional energy drink" in counteracting driver sleepiness. *Physiology and Behavior, 75*, 331–335.

Ricketts, J. A., & Brooks, L. (1983). The high school chemistry laboratory can strengthen abstract reasoning skills. *Proceedings of the Indiana Academy of Science, 93*, 385–390.

Roberge, J. J. (1970). A study of children's abilities to reason with basic principles of deductive reasoning. *American Educational Research Journal, 7*(4), 583–596.

Rogers, K., & Simms, J. A. (2015). *Teaching argumentation: Activities and games for the classroom*. Bloomington, IN: Marzano Research.

Romney, W. M. (2011, December 20). Remarks in Bedford, New Hampshire [Transcript]. Accessed at www.presidency .ucsb.edu/ws/index.php?pid=98263#axzz1kJexgGxl on April 8, 2014.

Romney, W. M. (2012, October 8). Remarks at Virginia Military Institute [Transcript]. Accessed at www.nytimes.com /2012/10/09/us/politics/mitt-romney-remarks-at-virginia-military-institute.html?pagewanted=all on April 8, 2014.

Roozendaal, B. (2003). Systems mediating acute glucocorticoid effects on memory consolidation and retrieval. *Progress in Neuro-Psychopharmacology and Biological Psychiatry, 27*(8), 1213–1223.

Royal, M. (n.d.). *Some deductive reasoning logic problems*. Accessed at www.public.asu.edu/~royal/Deductive_Logic _Challenges.htm on June 16, 2014.

Sadler, T. D. (2004). Informal reasoning regarding socioscientific issues: A critical review of research. *Journal of Research in Science Teaching, 41*(5), 513–536.

Sanchez, J. (2014, June 10). MRE pizza may be a slice of home. *CNN*. Accessed at http://eatocracy.cnn.com/2014/06/10/mre -pizza/?hpt=li_mid on June 18, 2014.

Savoca, M. R., Evans, C. D., Wilson, M. E., Harshfield, G. A., & Ludwig, D. A. (2004). The association of caffeinated beverages with blood pressure in adolescents. *Archives of Pediatrics and Adolescent Medicine, 158*, 473–477.

Schneider, W., & Shiffrin, R. M. (1977). Controlled and automatic human information processing: I. Detection, search, and attention. *Psychological Review, 84*(1), 1–66.

Scholey, A. B., & Kennedy, D. O. (2004). Cognitive and physiological effects of an "energy drink": An evaluation of the whole drink and of glucose, caffeine, and herbal flavouring fractions. *Psychopharmacology, 176*, 320–330.

Severson, K. (2014, June 16). Gluten-free eating appears to be here to stay. *The New York Times*. Accessed at www.nytimes .com/2014/06/18/dining/gluten-free-eating-appears-to-be-here-to-stay.html?hp&_r=0 on June 19, 2014.

Shayer, M., & Adey, P. S. (1993). Accelerating the development of formal thinking in middle and high school students IV: Three years after a two-year intervention. *Journal of Research in Science Teaching, 30*, 351–366.

Shors, T. J., Weiss, C., & Thompson, R. F. (1992). Stress-induced facilitation of classical conditioning. *Science, 257*(5069), 537–539.

Specter, M. (2014, May 19). Partial recall. *The New Yorker*. Accessed at www.newyorker.com/reporting/2014/05/19/140519fa _fact_specter on June 19, 2014.

Sperber, D. (2001). An evolutionary perspective on testimony and argumentation. *Philosophical Topics, 29*, 401–413.

Stanovich, K. E., & West, R. F. (1999). Individual differences in reasoning and the heuristics and biases debate. In P. L. Ackerman, P. C. Kyllonen, & R. D. Roberts (Eds.), *Learning and individual differences: Process, trait, and content determinants* (pp. 389–407). Washington, DC: American Psychological Association.

Stanovich, K. E., West, R. F., & Toplak, M. E. (2011). The complexity of developmental predictions from dual process models. *Developmental Review, 31*, 103–118.

Townsend, L. (2013, December 2). Why are we more scared of raw egg than reheated rice? *BBC News Magazine.* Accessed at www.bbc.com/news/magazine-25154046 on June 18, 2014.

Truesdell, J. (2014, June 13). Miss USA Nia Sanchez denies she faked a move to Nevada to win pageant. *PEOPLE Magazine.* Accessed at www.people.com/article/miss-usa-nia-sanchez-accused-of-faking-move-nevada on June 19, 2014.

Twain, M. (1875). *Mark Twain's sketches: New and old.* Hartford, CT: American Publishing Company.

Uruguay squad's caramel spread confiscated in Brazil. (2014, June 17). *BBC News.* Accessed at www.bbc.com/news/world-latin-america-27889343 on June 17, 2014.

U.S. Department of Agriculture. (2010). *Dietary guidelines for Americans.* Accessed at www.cnpp.usda.gov/Publications/DietaryGuidelines/2010/PolicyDoc/PolicyDoc.pdf on July 2, 2014.

Van Honk, J., Kessels, R. P. C., Putnam, P., Jager, G., Koppeschaar, H. P. F., & Postma, A. (2003). Attentionally modulated effects of cortisol and mood on memory for emotional faces in healthy young males. *Psychoneuroendocrinology, 28*(7), 941–948.

Wallace, K. (2014, June 13). Do modern dads get enough credit? *CNN Parents.* Accessed at www.cnn.com/2014/06/13/living/fathers-day-dads-changing-parents/index.html?hpt=li_t3 on June 18, 2014.

Wason, P. C. (1966). Reasoning. In B. M. Foss (Ed.), *New horizons in psychology* (pp. 135–151). Harmondsworth, England: Penguin Books.

Webb, N. M., Franke, M. L., De, T., Chan, A. G., Freund, D., Shein, P., et al. (2009). "Explain to your partner": Teachers' instructional practices and students' dialogue in small groups. *Cambridge Journal of Education, 39*(1), 49–70.

Webb, N. M., Franke, M. L., Ing, M., Chan, A., De, T., Freund, D., et al. (2008). The role of teacher instructional practices in student collaboration. *Contemporary Educational Psychology, 33*(3), 360–381.

Weinstein, C. E., & Mayer, R. E. (1986). The teaching of learning strategies. In M. C. Wittrock (Ed.), *Handbook of research on teaching* (pp. 315–327). New York: Macmillan.

Zablocki, J. (n.d.). *Logic riddles.* Accessed at http://goodriddlesnow.com/logic-riddles on August 13, 2014.

Index

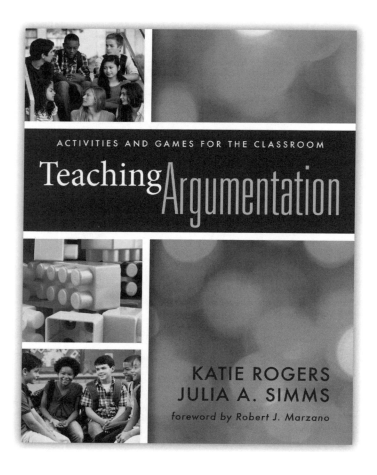